Alberta
Road Atlas
DELUXE EDITION

TABLE OF CONTENTS

How to Use this Atlas

come see us @ www.mapart.com

MapArt. DIRECTION + DESIGN

PRODUCTION TEAM   Malcolm Buchan   Brent Carey   Michael Foell
Karen Gillingham   Mike Grasby   Oksana Kutna   Werner Mantei
Salina Morrow   Carl Nanders   Dave Scott   Kyu Shim
Samiha Sleiman   Shaun Smith   Sam Tung-Ding Ho
Matthew Wadley   Craig White   Jessie Zhang   Marlene Ziobrowski

© mapmobility corp.

Published by Peter Heiler Ltd.
Distribution by **MapArt Publishing Corp.**
70 Bloor St. E., Oshawa, Ontario L1H 3M2
☎ 905-436-2525   FAX 905-723-6677
Printed in Canada   ✦   Imprimé au Canada

DESTINATIONS - indicate the town or city the road or highway leads to.

NORTH ARROWS - indicate general direction pointing north.

GRID REFERENCES - are used to locate places, streets or roads in the index. See page 120 or 122 for further explanation.

PAGE ARROWS - indicate continued coverage of the map and page.

PAGE NUMBER

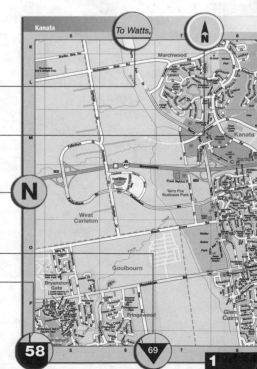

1

Scale 1:5 500 000 *Échelle*

N

100   0   100   200 kilometres
kilomètres

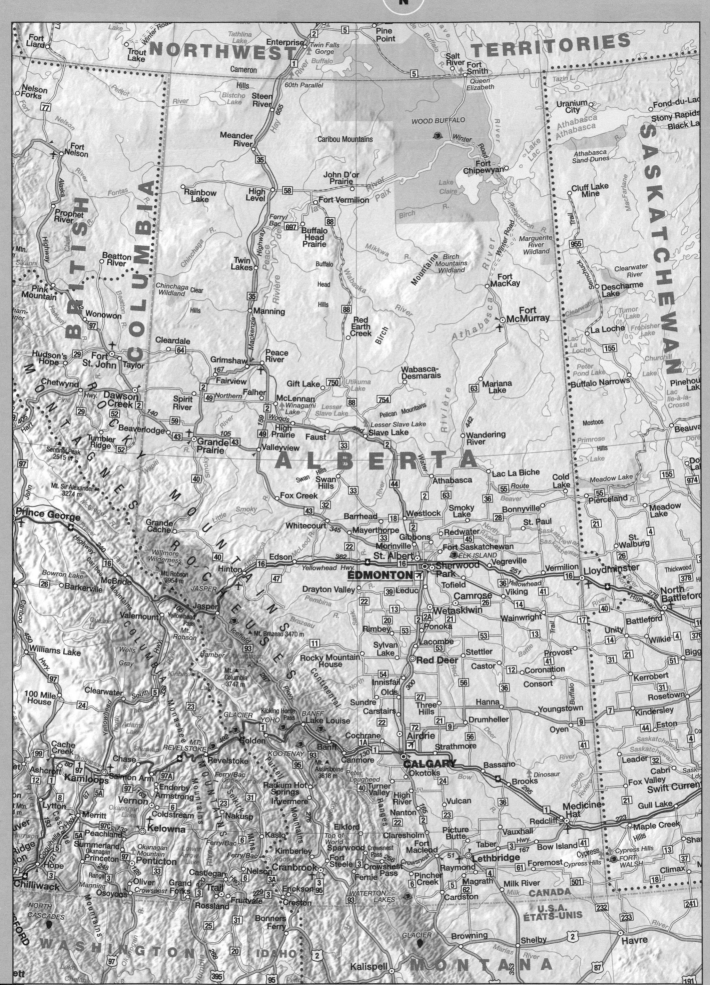

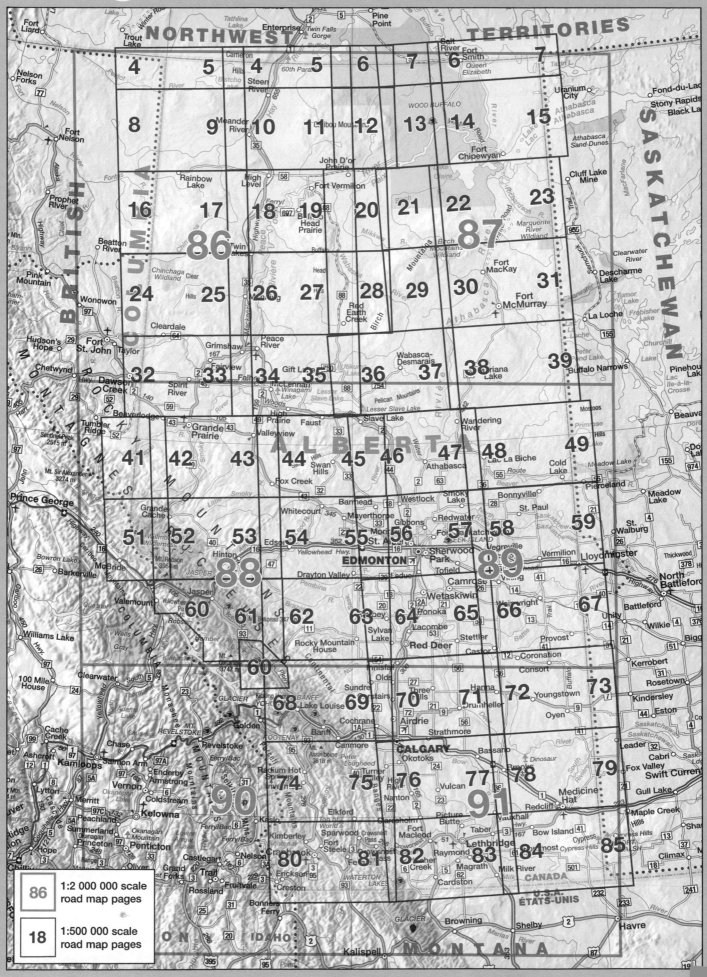

Key Map legend:

86	1:2 000 000 scale road map pages
18	1:500 000 scale road map pages

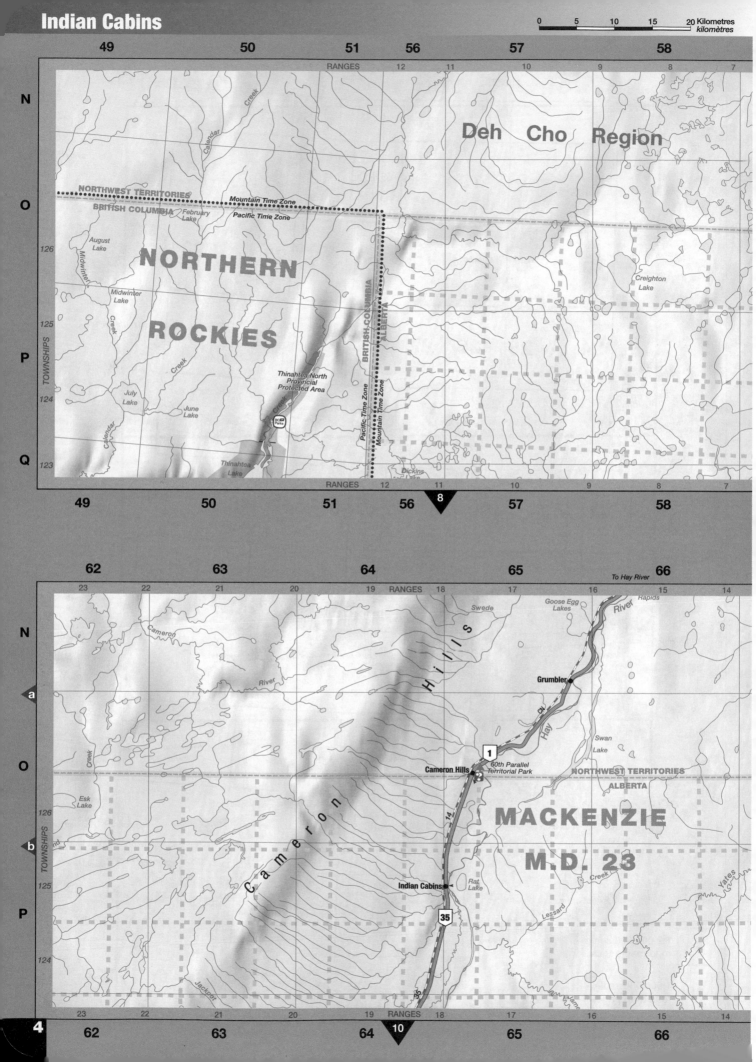

Indian Cabins

Scale: 0 5 10 15 20 Kilometres / kilomètres

Top map:

RANGES 12 11 10 9 8 7

49 50 51 56 57 58

Deh Cho Region

N
O
P
Q

NORTHWEST TERRITORIES — Mountain Time Zone
BRITISH COLUMBIA — Pacific Time Zone

NORTHERN ROCKIES

February Lake

August Lake
Midwinter
Midwinter Lake
Creek
July Lake
June Lake
Calendar
Thinahtea Lake

Calendar Creek
Creek
Creek

Thinahtea North Provincial Protected Area
BC Parks

Creighton Lake

BRITISH COLUMBIA / ALBERTA

Pacific Time Zone / Mountain Time Zone

Dickins Lake

TOWNSHIPS 126 125 124 123

RANGES 12 11 10 9 8 7

49 50 51 56 57 58

▼ 8

Bottom map:

23 22 21 20 19 RANGES 18 17 16 15 14

62 63 64 65 66

To Hay River

N
a
O
b
P

Cameron
River
Creek

Swede
Hills
Goose Egg Lakes
River Rapids

Grumbler

CN
Hay

Swan Lake

Cameron Hills
1
60th Parallel Territorial Park
NORTHWEST TERRITORIES
ALBERTA

Esk Lake

MACKENZIE
M.D. 23

Cameron

14

Indian Cabins
Rat Lake
Lessard Creek
Yates

35

Jackpot

35

TOWNSHIPS 126 125 124

23 22 21 20 19 RANGES 18 17 16 15 14

62 63 64 65 66

4

▼ 10

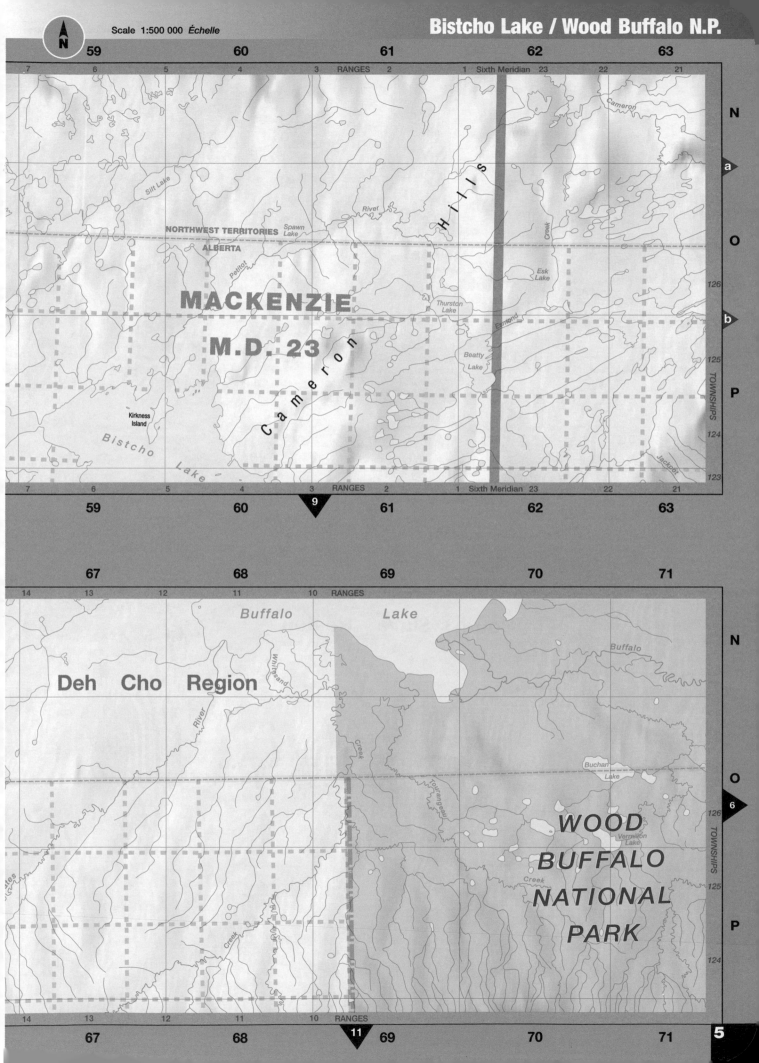

Scale 1:500 000 *Échelle*

N

59 **60** **61** **62** **63**

7 6 5 4 3 RANGES 2 1 Sixth Meridian 23 22 21

N

a

O

126

b

125

P

124

123

NORTHWEST TERRITORIES

ALBERTA

Spawn Lake

Silt Lake

Petitot

River

Hills

Cameron

Creek

Esmond

Esk Lake

Thurston Lake

Beatty Lake

Jackpot

MACKENZIE

M.D. 23

Cameron

Kirkness Island

Bistcho Lake

TOWNSHIPS

7 6 5 4 3 RANGES 2 1 Sixth Meridian 23 22 21

59 **60** ▼9 **61** **62** **63**

67 **68** **69** **70** **71**

14 13 12 11 10 RANGES

Buffalo *Lake*

N

O

126

◄6

125

P

124

Buffalo

Buchan Lake

Whitesand

River

Creek

Tourangeau

Vermilion Lake

Creek

Creek

Deh Cho Region

WOOD

BUFFALO

NATIONAL

PARK

TOWNSHIPS

14 13 12 11 10 RANGES

67 **68** ▼11 **69** **70** **71**

5

0   5   10   15   20 Kilometres
kilomètres

70   **71**   **72**   **73**   **78**   **79**

N   Fifth Meridian   N

Buffalo

Skillet
Lake

Copp

O   O

River

NORTHWEST TERRITORIES
ALBERTA

5   Buchan
Lake   River   7

WOOD

Vermilion
Lake   Kilome
Lake

BUFFALO

Creek

NATIONAL

O   O

PARK

P   Fifth Meridian   P

70   **71**   **12**   **72**   **73**   **78**   **79**

---

82   **83**   **84**   **85**   **86**

13   12   RANGES   11   10   9   8   7

N   Little Bent Tree
Lake   Nautawa
Lake   N

South   Slave   Region

River   Blackman
Lake

a   River   a

Salt River

Schaefer

Little Buffalo River
Falls Territorial Park   Sawmill
I.   Cunningham
Landing   Queen Elizabeth
Territorial
Park   Wood Buffalo National Park
Fort Smith Visitor Reception Centre/   Lakes

Salt
Mountain   16   Bell Rock   Fort Smith
McDougal   Fort Smith Mission Territorial Historic Park   Telklini
Lake

O   5   23   Rd.   Donovan Lake   O

Fort Smith

Northern
Life Museum   Fort Smith
Settlement   NORTHWEST TERRITORIES
ALBERTA

126   Mountain
Rapids

Fitzgerald
Portage
Rd.   Pelican
Rapids   Tulip
Lake

b   Salt Plains
Overview   b

Brine   Slave

TOWNSHIPS   WOOD   BUFFALO

125   River   Cassette
Rapids

Parsons
Lake
Rd.   NATIONAL   Smith
Landing
Settlement   Fitzgerald

P   PARK   Creek   P

Salt River

124   Rainbow
Lakes   Ryan
Island

Pine
Lake
Rd.   Grass
Lake

McLelland
Lake

6   **82**   **83**   **84**   **14**   **85**   **86**

13   12   RANGES   11   10   9   8   7

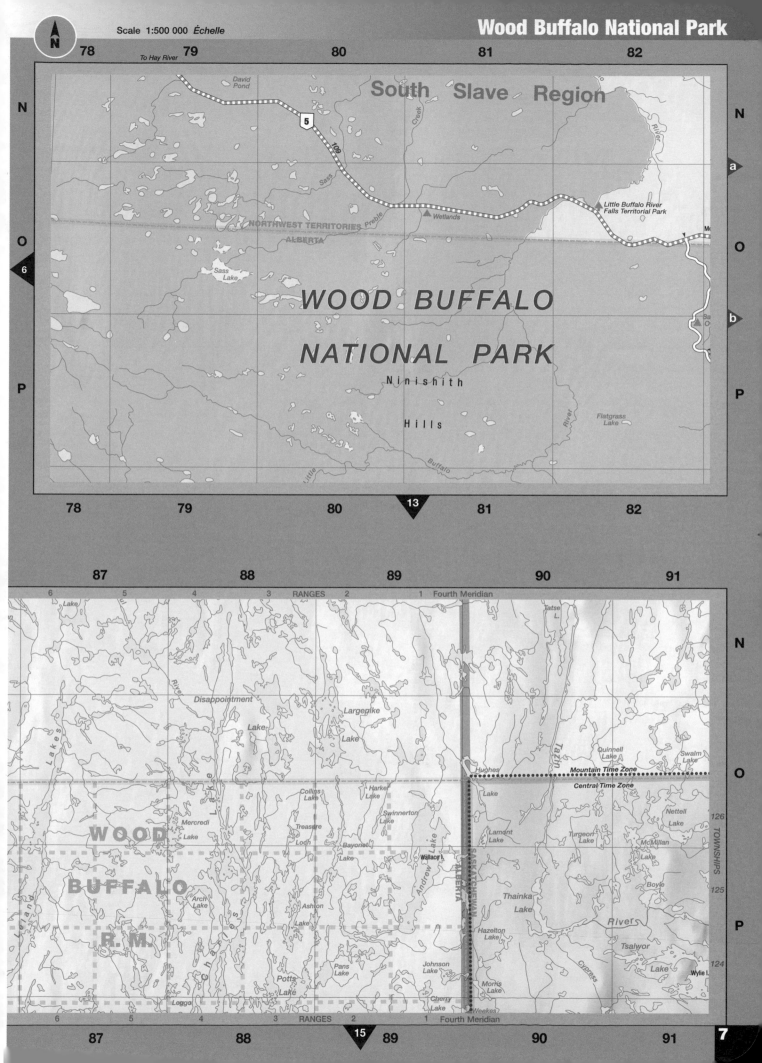

Scale 1:500 000 *Échelle*

N

78   79   80   81   82

To Hay River

David Pond

South Slave Region

5

109

Sass

Creek

River

N

O

6

Sass Lake

NORTHWEST TERRITORIES

ALBERTA

Preble

Wetlands

Little Buffalo River
Falls Territorial Park

Mc

a

O

b

Sa
O

P

WOOD BUFFALO

NATIONAL PARK

Ninishith

Hills

River

Flatgrass Lake

P

Little

Buffalo

78   79   80   13   81   82

87   88   89   RANGES   90   91

6   5   4   3   RANGES   2   1   Fourth Meridian

Lake

Tatse L.

N

River

Disappointment

Largepike

Lake

Lake

Lake

Tazin

Quinnell Lake

Swalm Lake

Lakes

Hughes   **Mountain Time Zone**

Central Time Zone

O

Collins Lake

Harker Lake

Lake

Nettell Lake

126

WOOD

Mercredi Lake

Swinnerton Lake

Treasure Loch

Lamont Lake

Turgeon Lake

McMillan Lake

TOWNSHIPS

Bayonet

SASKATCHEWAN

ALBERTA

Andrew   Lake

Lake

Wallace L.

Boyle

125

BUFFALO

Arch Lake

Thainka Lake

River

Cypress

Leland

Chelles

Ashton

Lake

Hazelton Lake

Tsalwor Lake

124

R.M.

Pans Lake

Johnson Lake

Wylie L.

Potts Lake

Morris Lake

Leggo

Cherry Lake

Weekes

6   5   4   3   RANGES   2   1   Fourth Meridian

87   88   15   89   90   91

P

7

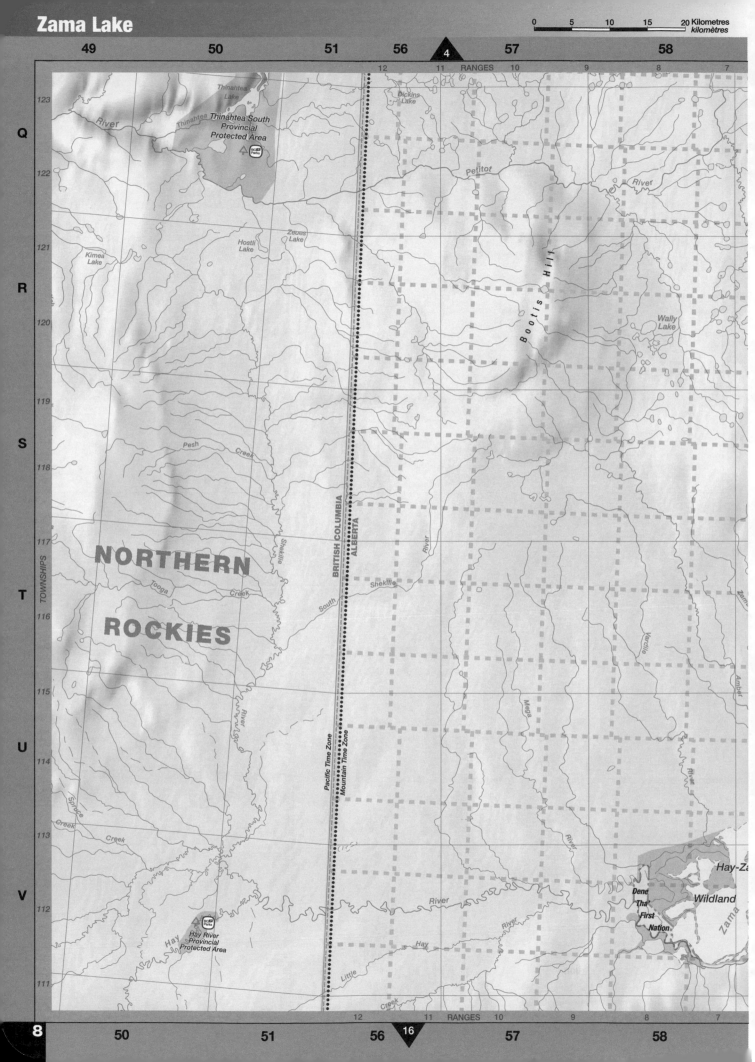

Kilometres
kilomètres

0 5 10 15 20

49   50   51   56   4   57   58

RANGES
12   11   10   9   8   7

Q

123

Thinahtea
Lake

River

Thinahtea   Thinahtea South
Provincial
Protected
Area

BC Parks

Dickins
Lake

Petitot

Rivet

122

R

121

Kimea
Lake

Hostli
Lake

Zeues
Lake

Bootis Hill

120

Wally
Lake

119

S

Pesh

Creek

118

Shekilie

River

Shekilie

117

NORTHERN

BRITISH COLUMBIA
ALBERTA

T

Tooga

Creek

South

116

ROCKIES

Mega

Varilie

U

River

115

Pacific Time Zone
Mountain Time Zone

114

River

Spruce

113

Creek

Creek

River

112

V

Hay River
Provincial
Protected Area

BC Parks

Hay

River

River

River

River

Zama

Hay-Za

Dene
Tha'
First
Nation

Wildland

Ambar

111

Hay

Little

Creek

RANGES
12   11   10   9   8   7

50   51   56   16   57   58

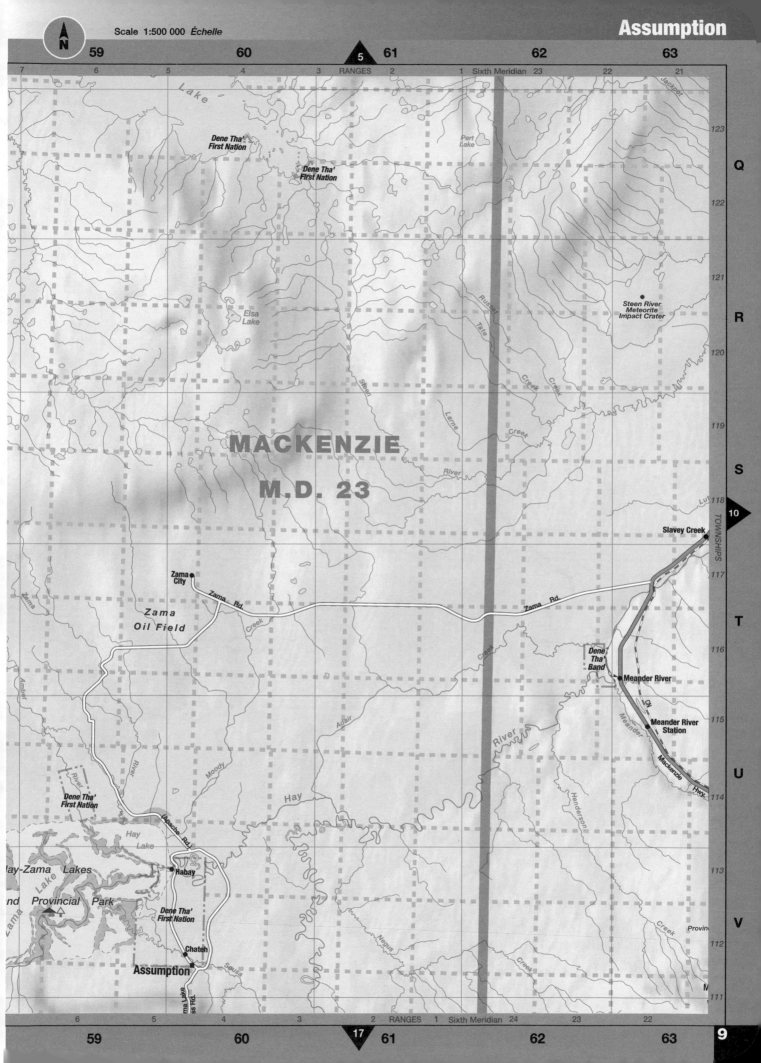

Scale 1:500 000 *Échelle*

MACKENZIE

M.D. 23

Zama Oil Field

Dene Tha' First Nation

Dene Tha' First Nation

Elsa Lake

Steen River Meteorite Impact Crater

Pert Lake

Slavey Creek

Zama City

Zama Rd.

Zama Rd.

Dene Tha' Band

Meander River

Meander River Station

Dene Tha' First Nation

Hay Lake

Hay-Zama Lakes

Provincial Park

Habay

Dene Tha' First Nation

Chateh

Assumption

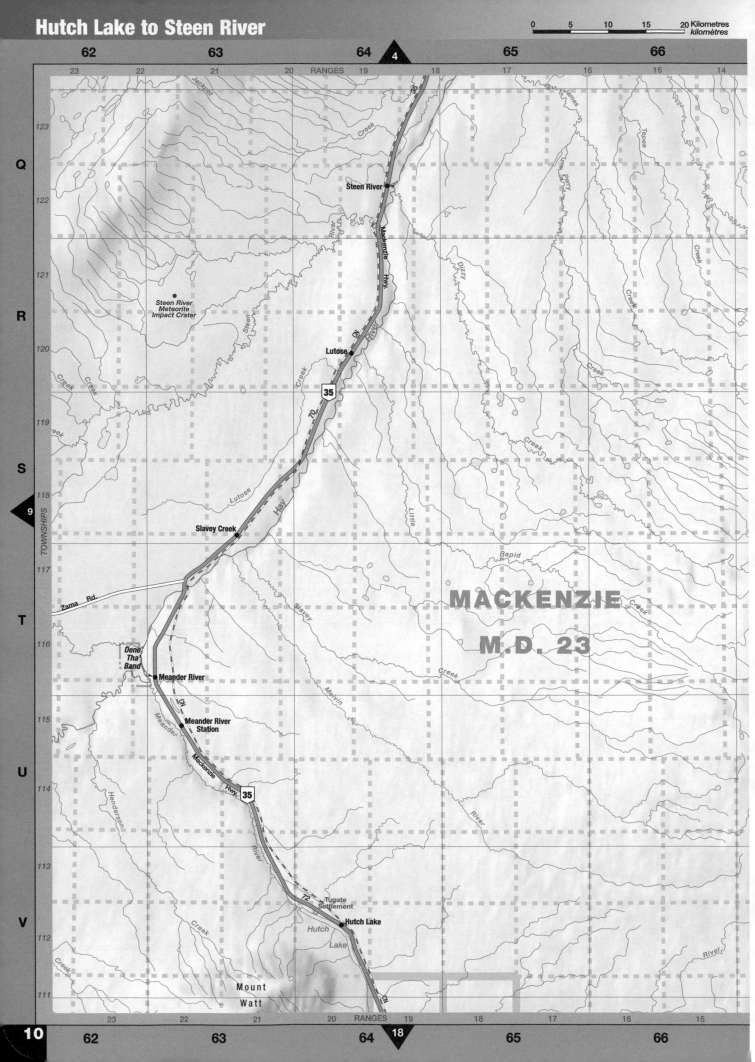

0   5   10   15   20 Kilometres
kilomètres

62   63   64 ▼4   65   66

23   22   21   20   RANGES   19   18   17   16   15   14

Q
123

122
Steen River ●

R
121

Steen River
Meteorite
Impact Crater ●

120
Lutose ●

119
35
70

S
118

9
Lutose Creek

Slavey Creek ●
117

T
116
Zama Rd.

Dene
Tha'
Band

Meander River ●
115
CN

Meander River
Station ●

MACKENZIE

M.D. 23

U
114
Mackenzie   Hwy.   **35**
113

112
Tugate
Settlement
Hutch Lake ●
Hutch
Lake

111
Mount
Watt

CN

23   22   21   20   RANGES   19   18   17   16   15

62   63   64 ▼18   65   66

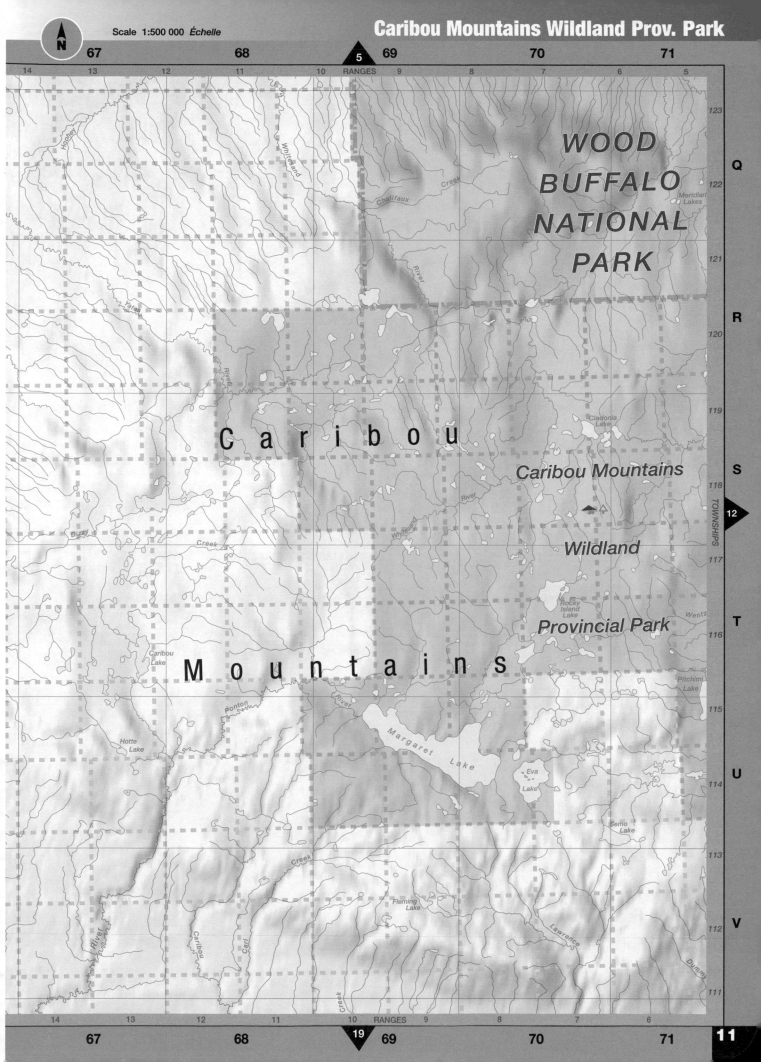

Scale 1:500 000 *Échelle*

N

WOOD
BUFFALO
NATIONAL
PARK

C a r i b o u

Caribou Mountains

Wildland

Provincial Park

M o u n t a i n s

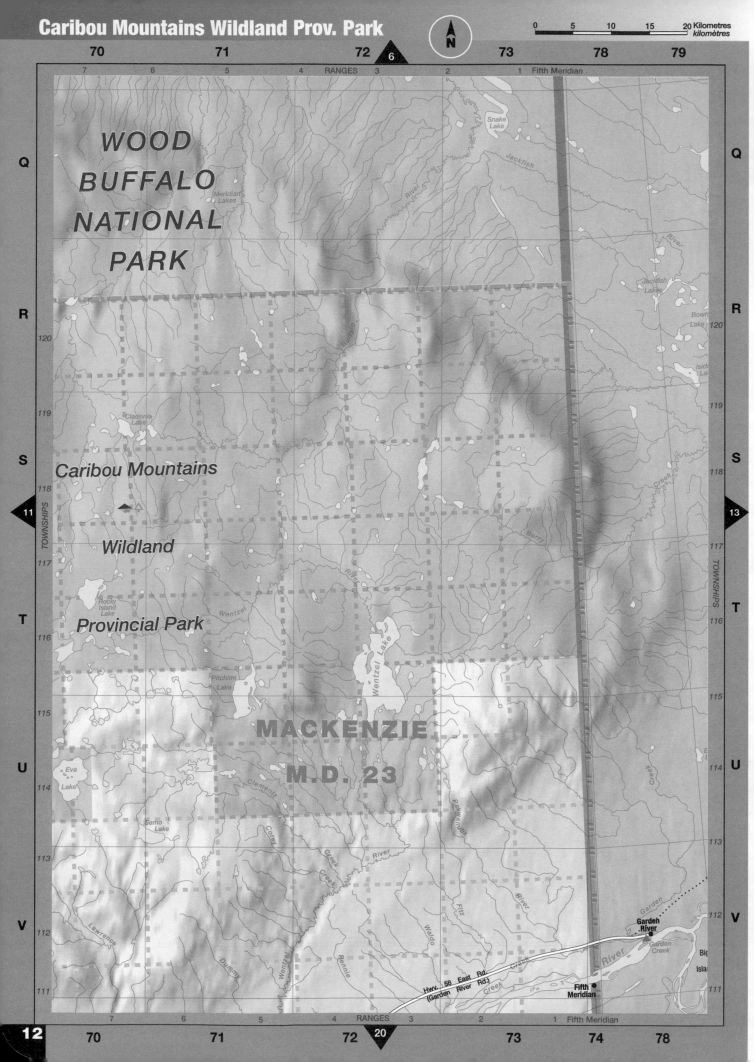

0   5   10   15   20 Kilometres
kilomètres

N

70   71   72   **6**   73   78   79

7   6   5   4   RANGES   3   2   1   Fifth Meridian

Q

WOOD

BUFFALO

Snake Lake

NATIONAL

Jackfish River

PARK

Meridian Lakes

Jackfish Lakes

R   120   119

Bowm Lake

Cladonia Lake

Isidc La

S   118

Caribou Mountains   Creek

117   Berry

Wildland

Wentzel River

Rocky Island Lake

Wentzel

T   116

Provincial Park

Pitchimi Lake   Wentzel Lake

115

MACKENZIE

Eva Lake

U   114   **M.D. 23**

Clements

Pakwanuik

Semo Lake

113

Corey Creek   River

Creek   Creek

V   112

Lawrence   Fitz   River   Garden

Waldo   **Gardeh River**   Garden Creek

Dummx   Rennie   River   Big Isla

Wentzel   Creek

111   Hwy. 58 East Rd. (Garden River Rd.)   **Fifth Meridian**

7   6   5   4   RANGES   3   2   1   Fifth Meridian

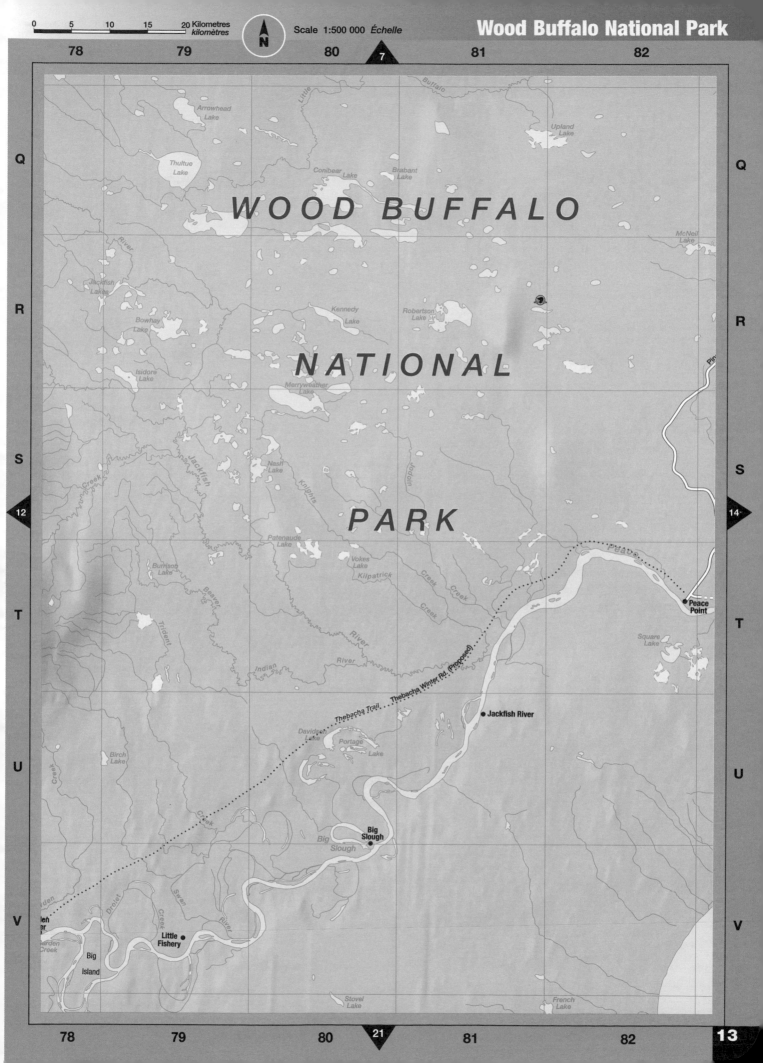

0   5   10   15   20 Kilometres
kilomètres

Scale 1:500 000 *Échelle*

N

78   79   7   80   81   82

Q   Q

Arrowhead
Lake

Little

Buffalo

Upland
Lake

Thultue
Lake

Conibear
Lake

Brabant
Lake

McNeil
Lake

WOOD BUFFALO

R   R

River

Jackfish
Lakes

Kennedy
Lake

Robertson
Lake

Pin

Bowhay
Lake

NATIONAL

Isidore
Lake

Merryweather
Lake

S   S

12   Jackfish   14

PARK

Nash
Lake

Peace

Knights

Joddin

Patenaude
Lake

Vokes
Lake

Creek

T   Creek   T

Burntso
Lake

Kilpatrick

Creek

Square
Lake

Beaver

Creek

Peace
Point

Trident

River

Indian

River

Thebacha Winter Rd. (Proposed)

Thebacha Trail

● Jackfish River

U   U

Birch
Lake

Creek

Davidson
Lake

Portage
Lake

Creek

Swan

Big
Slough

**Big
Slough**

Droïet

Creek

den
r

V   Creek   V

arden
Creek

River

**Little
Fishery** ●

Big
Island

Stovel
Lake

French
Lake

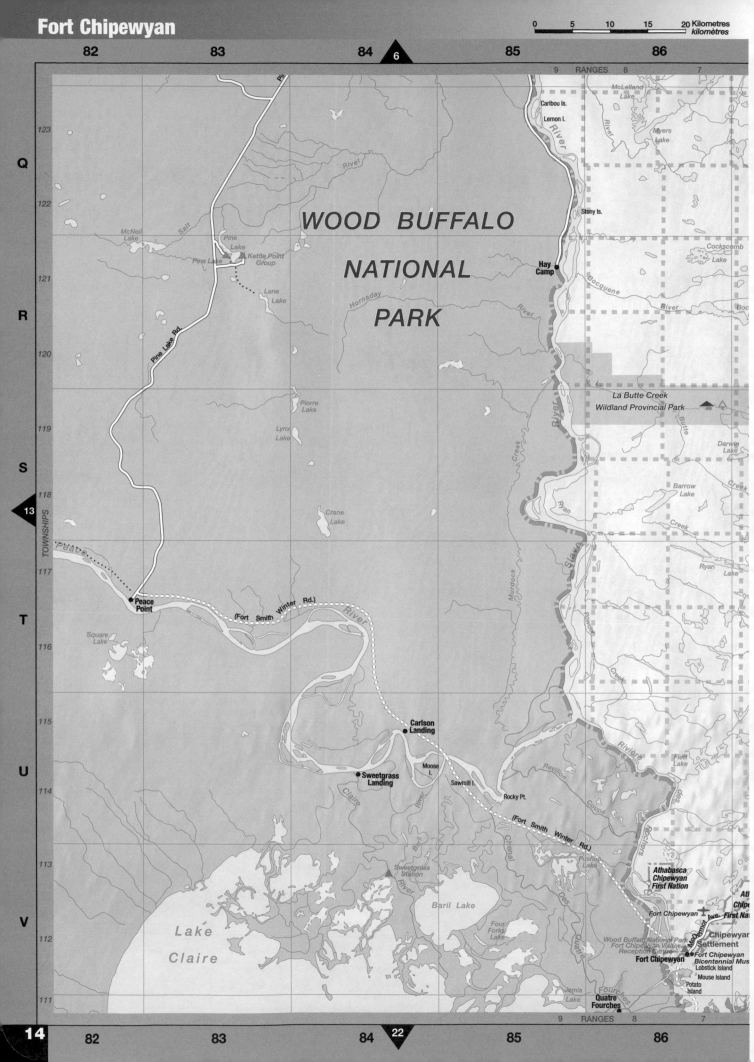

0   5   10   15   20 **Kilometres**
kilomètres

82   83   84   **6**   85   86

9   RANGES   8   7

Q

123

Caribou Is.

Lemon I.

122

Stony Is.

McNeil
Lake

Pine
Lake

Kettle Point
Group

Pine Lake

River

Hay
Camp

WOOD BUFFALO

NATIONAL

PARK

Salt

Lane
Lake

R

121

120

119

Pierre
Lake

Lynx
Lake

Myers
Lake

McLelland
Lake

Cockscomb
Lake

River

Bocquene   *River*

Boc

La Butte Creek
Wildland Provincial Park

Darwin
Lake

S

118

13

Crane
Lake

Barrow
Lake

Butte

Creek

TOWNSHIPS

Peace

Peace
Point

(Fort Smith Winter Rd.)

River

Creek

Ryan

Creek

Powder   *Creek*

Slavey

Ryan
Lake

T

117

116

Square
Lake

Murdock

U

115

114

Carlson
Landing

Sweetgrass
Landing

Moose
I.

Sawmill I.

Rocky Pt.

Claire

River

Baril

River

Revillon

Coupé

Chenal

Flett
Lake

Rivière

Rochers

V

113

112

111

Sweetgrass
Station

Baril Lake

Four Forks
Lake

Lake
Claire

(Fort Smith Winter Rd.)

Pushup
Lake

Des

Quatre

Jemis
Lake

**Quatre
Fourches**

**Athabasca
Chipewyan
First Nation**

Fort Chipewyan

Wood Buffalo National Park
Fort Chipewyan Visitor
Reception Centre

Fort Chipewyan

**Chipewyan
Settlement**

**Fort Chipewyan
Bicentennial Mus**

Lobstick Island

Mouse Island

Potato
Island

Atl
Chip
First Na

Max Cannot Ave.

14

82   83   84   **22**   85   86

9   RANGES   8   7

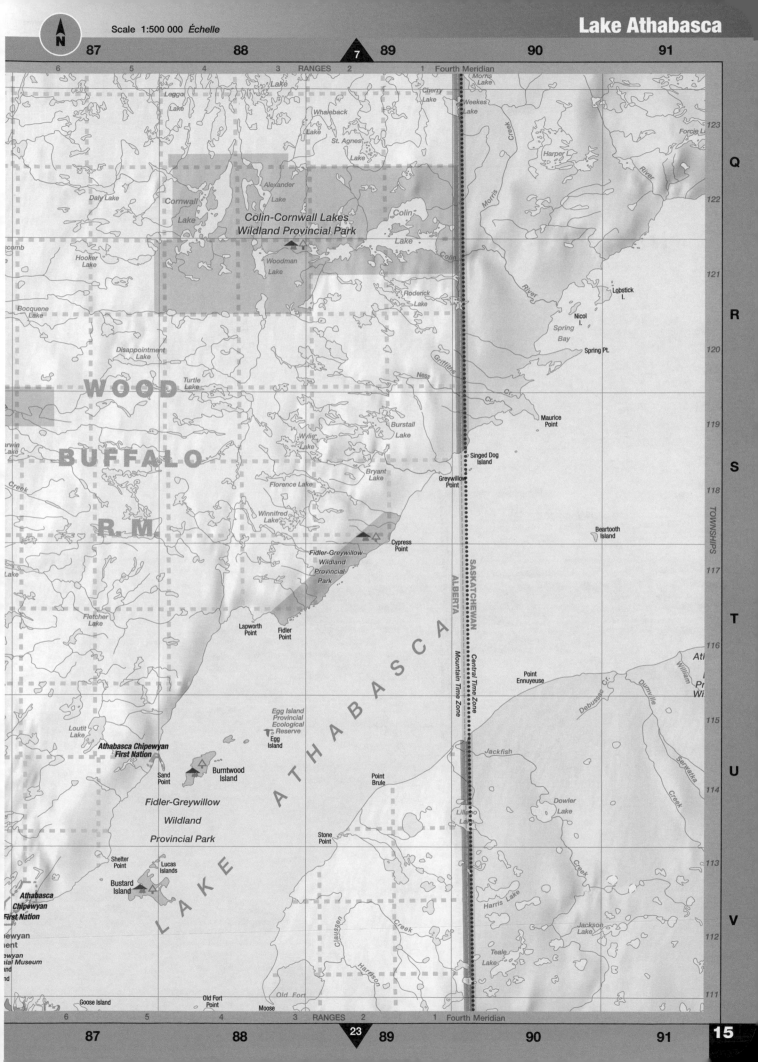

Scale 1:500 000 *Échelle*

N

87 88 7 89 90 91

6 5 4 3 RANGES 2 1 Fourth Meridian

Morris Lake
Weekes Lake
Cherry Lake
Leggo Lake
Lake
Whaleback Lake
Forcie L.

123

Q

St. Agnes Lake
Daly Lake
Cornwall Lake
Colin
Colin Lake
Harper L.
Morris Creek
River

122

Colin-Cornwall Lakes Wildland Provincial Park

Alexander Lake

Hooker Lake
Woodman Lake
Roderick Lake
Lobstick I.
Nicol I.

121

R

Bocquene Lake
Colin
Spring Bay
Spring Pt.

120

W O O D
Disappointment Lake
Turtle Lake
Ness
Griffiths
River

Maurice Point

119

B U F F A L O
Wylie Lake
Burstall Lake

Cr.

Singed Dog Island

S

R . M .
Florence Lake
Bryant Lake
Greywillow Point

Beartooth Island

118

Winnifred Lake
Fidler-Greywillow Wildland Provincial Park
Cypress Point

TOWNSHIPS

117

Fletcher Lake
Lapworth Point
Fidler Point

ALBERTA SASKATCHEWAN

T

Mountain Time Zone Central Time Zone

116

Atl
Wi
Pr

Point Ennuyeuse

Debussac Cr.
Dumville
Servatka Creek
William

115

Egg Island Provincial Ecological Reserve
Egg Island
Jackfish

Loutit Lake
Athabasca Chipewyan First Nation
Sand Point
Burntwood Island
Point Brule
Dowler Lake

U

L A K E   A T H A B A S C A

Lilippo La.
Harris Lake
Creek

114

Fidler-Greywillow
Stone Point

Wildland

Shelter Point
Lucas Islands

113

Provincial Park

Bustard Island

Athabasca Chipewyan First Nation
ewyan
nt
Clausen Creek
Teale Lakes
Jackson Lake

112

V

ewyan
ial Museum
nd

Harrison

Goose Island
Old Fort Point
Moose
Old Fort

111

6 5 4 3 RANGES 2 1 Fourth Meridian

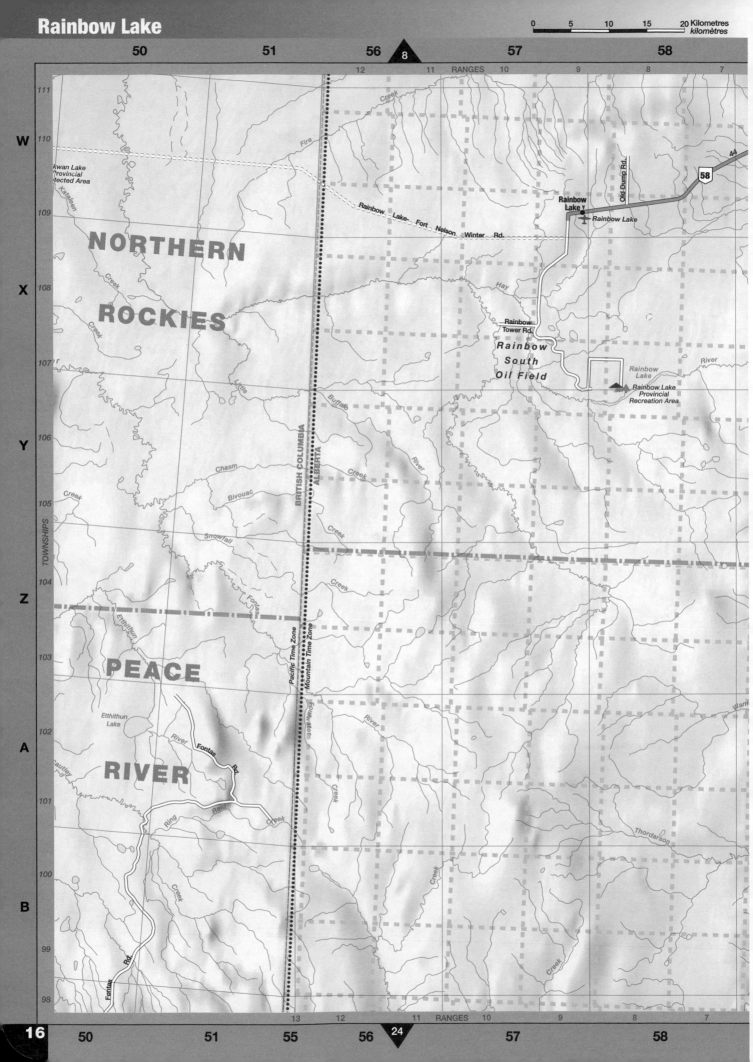

50   51   56   **8**   57   58

12   11   RANGES   10   9   8   7

111

W 110

44

Old Dump Rd.

58

kwan Lake
Provincial
Protected Area

Rainbow
Lake ▼

Rainbow Lake

Kataleen

Creek

Rainbow Lake Fort Nelson Winter Rd.

NORTHERN

Hay

109

X 108

Creek

Creek

Rainbow
Tower Rd.

Rainbow
South
Oil Field

Rainbow
Lake

River

ROCKIES

107

Little

Buffalo

Rainbow Lake
Provincial
Recreation Area

Y 106

Chasm

Creek

River

Creek

BRITISH COLUMBIA

ALBERTA

Bivouac

105

TOWNSHIPS

Snowfall

Creek

104

Z

Fontas

Creek

103

Ethithun

PEACE

Pacific Time Zone

Mountain Time Zone

102

Etthithun
Lake

River

Fontas

Fontas River

River

River

Wan

A

Gautley

RIVER

Rd.

101

Ring

Reid

Creek

Creek

Thordarson

100

Creek

Creek

B 99

Fontas

Creek

98

Rd.

50   51   55   56   **24**   57   58

13   12   11   RANGES   10   9   8   7

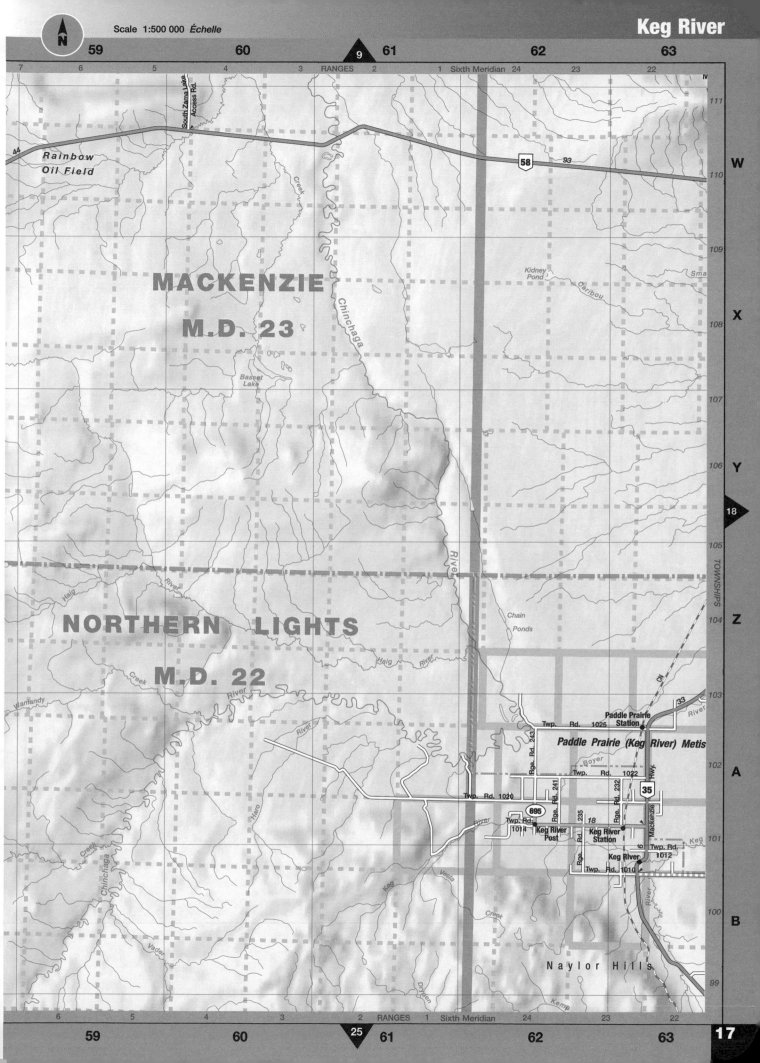

Scale 1:500 000 *Échelle*

N

59   60   9   61   62   63

7   6   5   4   3   RANGES   2   1   Sixth Meridian   24   23   22

111

Rainbow
Oil Field

58   93

W

110

109

MACKENZIE

Kidney
Pond

Caribou

Sma

X

108

M.D. 23

Chinchaga

Basset
Lake

107

River

Y

106

18

105

River

Chain
Ponds

Heig

River

NORTHERN   LIGHTS

TOWNSHIPS

Z

104

Creek

Haig   River

M.D. 22

River

33   103

Paddle Prairie
Station

Wanfandy

Twp. Rd. 1025

Paddle Prairie (Keg River) Metis

Haro

River

Boyer

102

Twp.   Rd.   1022

Rge. Rd. 243

Rge. Rd. 241

Rge. Rd. 232

35

A

Twp. Rd. 1020

Hwy.

Mackenzie

Chinchaga

Creek

695

Rge. Rd. 235

18

Keg

Twp. Rd.
1014

Keg River
Post

Keg River
Station

6

101

Vesta

Twp. Rd.
1012

Keg River

Rge. Rd.

Twp. Rd. 1010

Keg

River

B

Keg

100

Creek

Naylor Hills

Chinchaga

Vader

Dryden

Kemp

River

99

6   5   4   3   RANGES   2   1   Sixth Meridian   24   23   22

59   60   25   61   62   63

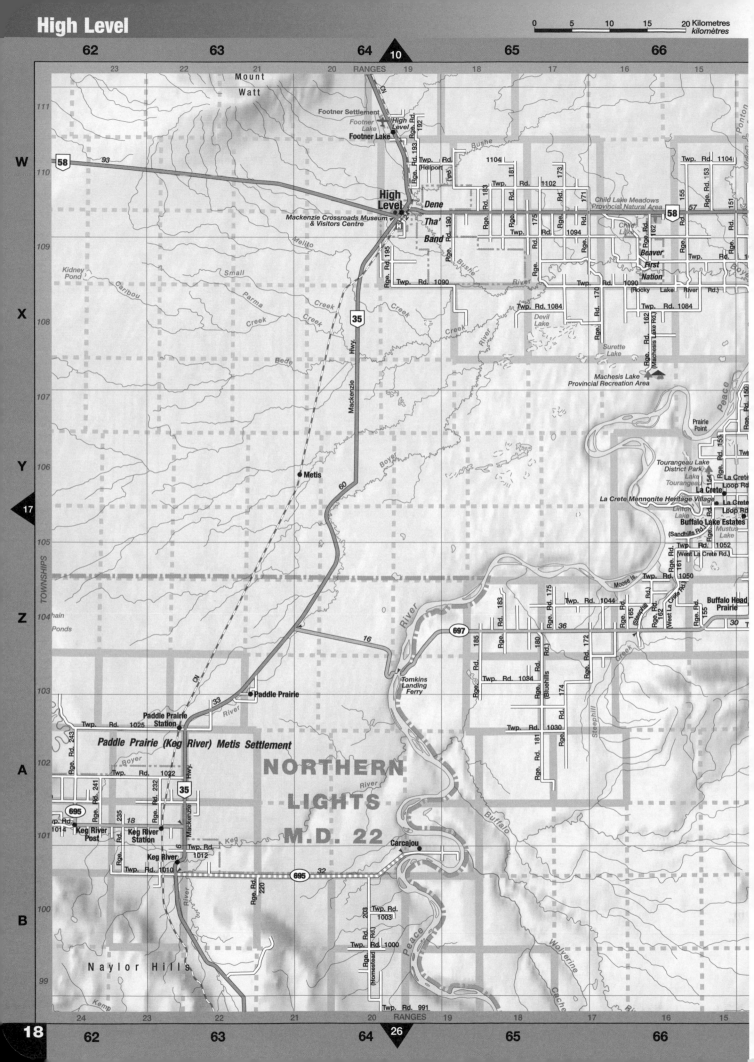

62   63   64   **10**   65   66

RANGES

W   58   93

Mount
Watt

Footner Settlement
Footner Lake
High Level
Footner Lake

High
Level

Dene
Tha'
Band

Mackenzie Crossroads Museum
& Visitors Centre

Child Lake Meadows
Provincial Natural Area

58   57

Beaver

First

Nation

Kidney Pond

Small

Caribou

Parma

Melito

Creek

Creek

Creek

Bushe

River

(Rocky   Lake   River   Rd.)

X   108

Devil
Lake

Bede

Creek

Creek

River

Surette
Lake

Machesis Lake
Provincial Recreation Area

Prairie
Point

Y   106   Metis

Boyer

Peace

Tourangeau Lake
District Park
Lake
Tourangeau

La Crete

La Crete Mennonite Heritage Village

Buffalo Lake Estates

(Sandhills Rd.)

Linton
Lake

Mustus
Lake

Loop Rd

17

TOWNSHIPS

Z   104   Chain
Ponds

16

697

Moose Is.

Buffalo Head

Prairie

Tomkins
Landing
Ferry

CN

33   Paddle Prairie

Paddle Prairie
Station

Twp.   Rd.   1025

Paddle Prairie (Keg River) Metis Settlement

Boyer

Twp.   Rd.   1022

NORTHERN

LIGHTS

M.D. 22

A   102

River

695

35   Hwy.

18

Keg River
Post

Keg River
Station

Keg   Keg River

Carcajou

695   32

Mackenzie

Twp.   Rd.   1012

Twp.   Rd.   1010

Peace

B   100

Naylor Hills

Kemp

Wolverine

24   23   22   21   20   19   18   17   16   15

RANGES

26

62   63   64   65   66

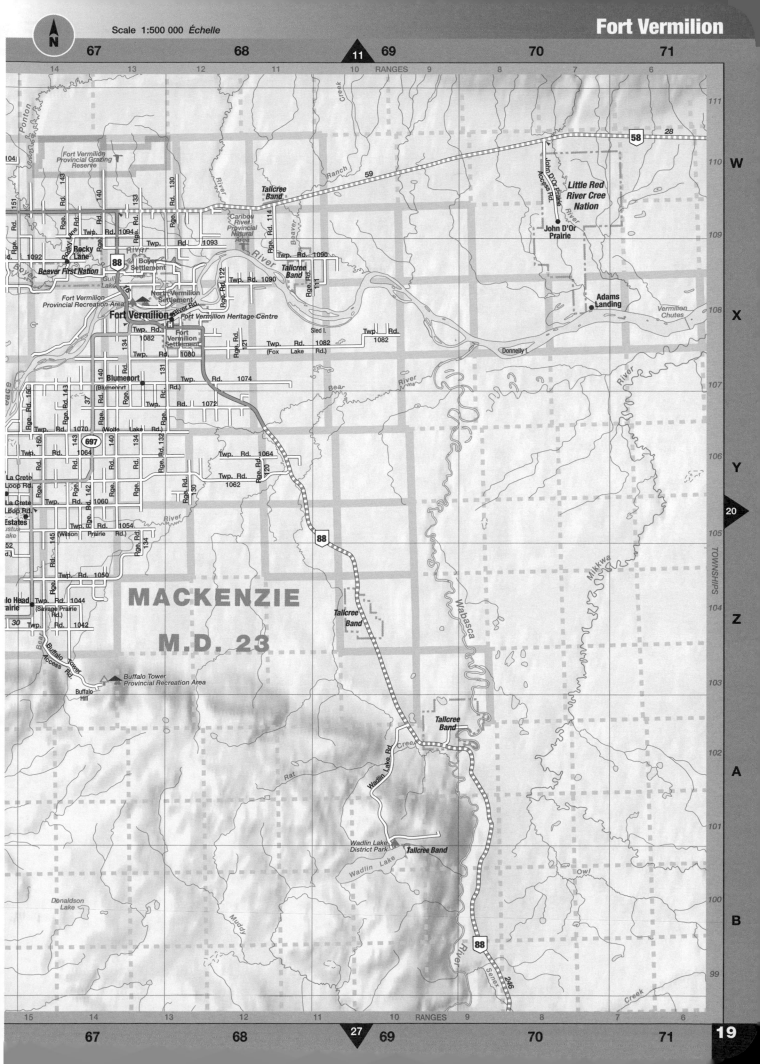

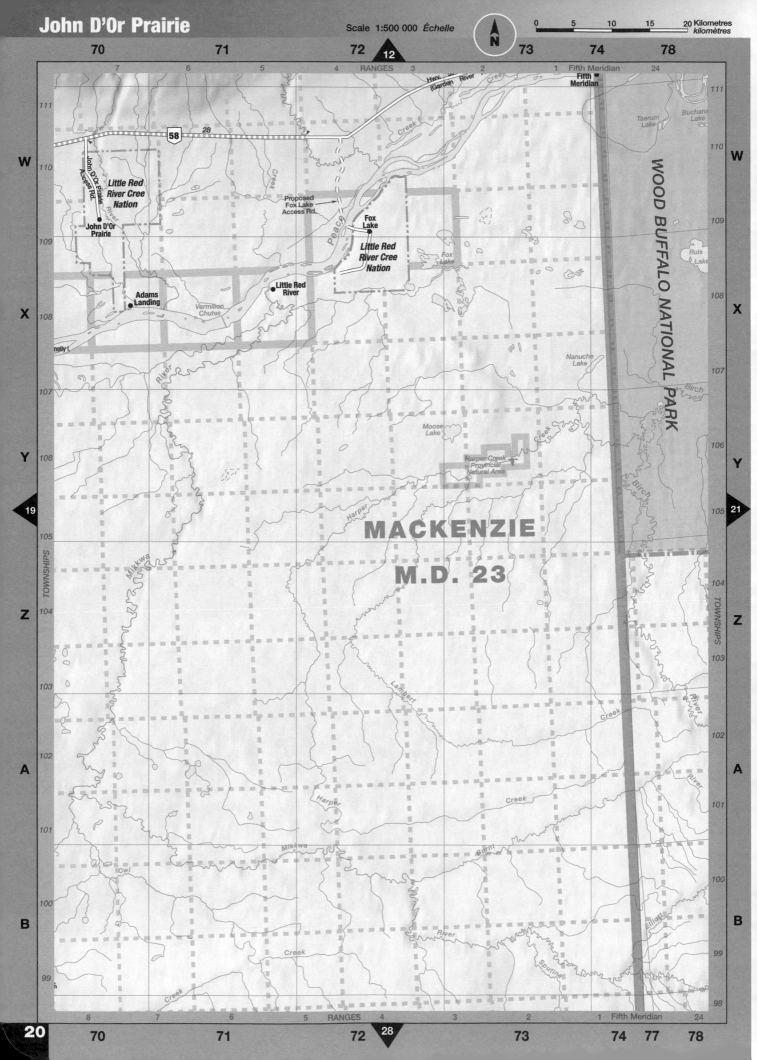

0 5 10 15 20 Kilometres
kilomètres

70 71 72 **12** 73 74 78

7 6 5 4 RANGES 3 2 1 Fifth Meridian 24

111

Hwy. (Garden River
Creek

Fifth Meridian

111

W

58 28

110

W

Taerum Lake

Buchana Lake

John D'Or Prairie Access Rd.

Little Red River Cree Nation

Creek

Creek

110

Proposed Fox Lake Access Rd.

Fox Lake

109

John D'Or Prairie

Peace

Little Red River Cree Nation

Fox Lake

Ruis Lake

109

X

River

Adams Landing

Vermilion Chutes

Little Red River

X

108

nelly I.

108

River

Nanuche Lake

Birch

107

107

Moose Lake

Creek

106

Y

Harper Creek Provincial Natural Area

Birch

106

Y

19

Harper

21

105

MACKENZIE

105

TOWNSHIPS

Mikkwa

M.D. 23

River

TOWNSHIPS

Z

104

104

Z

103

Lambert

103

A

Harper

Creek

River

102

102

A

101

Creek

101

B

Mikkwa

Burnt

River

100

Owl

100

B

Elliott

River

99

99

Creek

Spurting

98

8 7 6 5 RANGES 4 3 2 1 Fifth Meridian 24

70 71 72 **28** 73 74 77 78

WOOD BUFFALO NATIONAL PARK

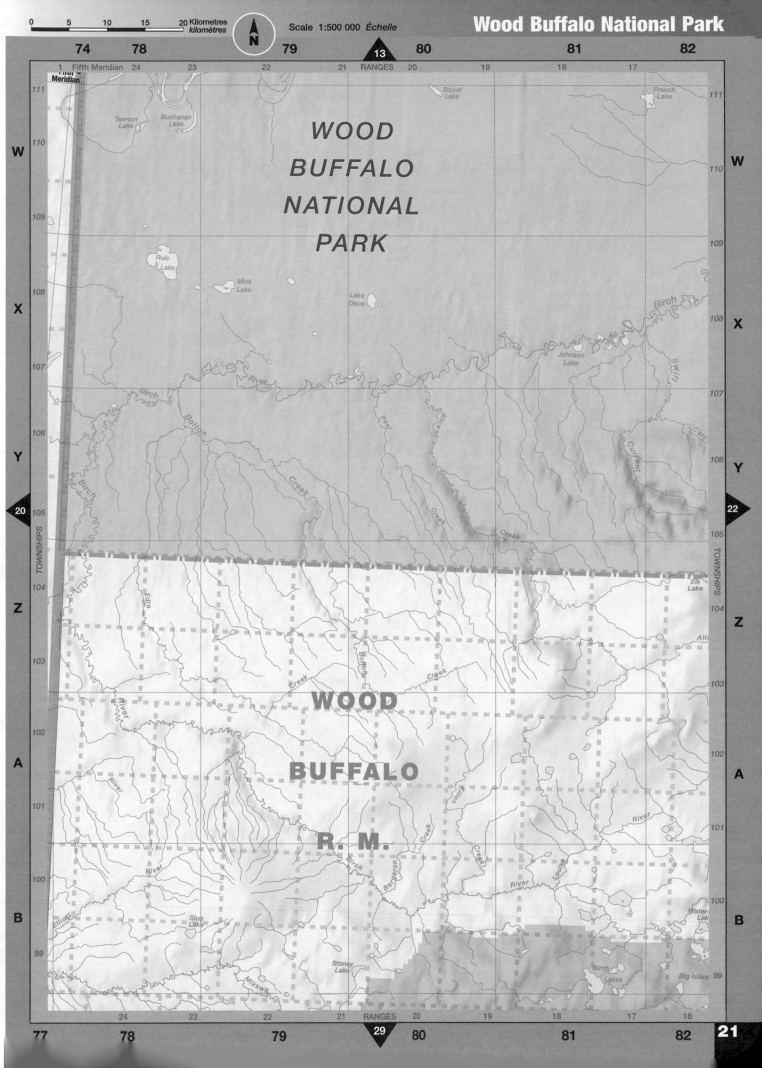

Scale 1:500 000 *Échelle*

20 Kilometres
kilomètres

N

WOOD
BUFFALO
NATIONAL
PARK

WOOD

BUFFALO

R. M.

Fifth Meridian

First
Meridian

TOWNSHIPS

TOWNSHIPS

RANGES

RANGES

Taerum Lake

Buchanan Lake

Ruis Lake

Mink Lake

Lake Dene

Stovel Lake

French Lake

Birch

Johnson Lake

Swift

Current

Carol

Birch

Bolton

Creek

Peel

Alice

Creek

Creek

Creek

Elk Lake

Edra

Bolton

Creek

Creek

Alic

River

Creek

River

River

Elliott

Creek

Birch

Bergeron

Creek

Elliott

River

Louise

River

Water Lake

Slug Lake

Stoney Lake

Mikkwa

Birch Lakes

Big Island

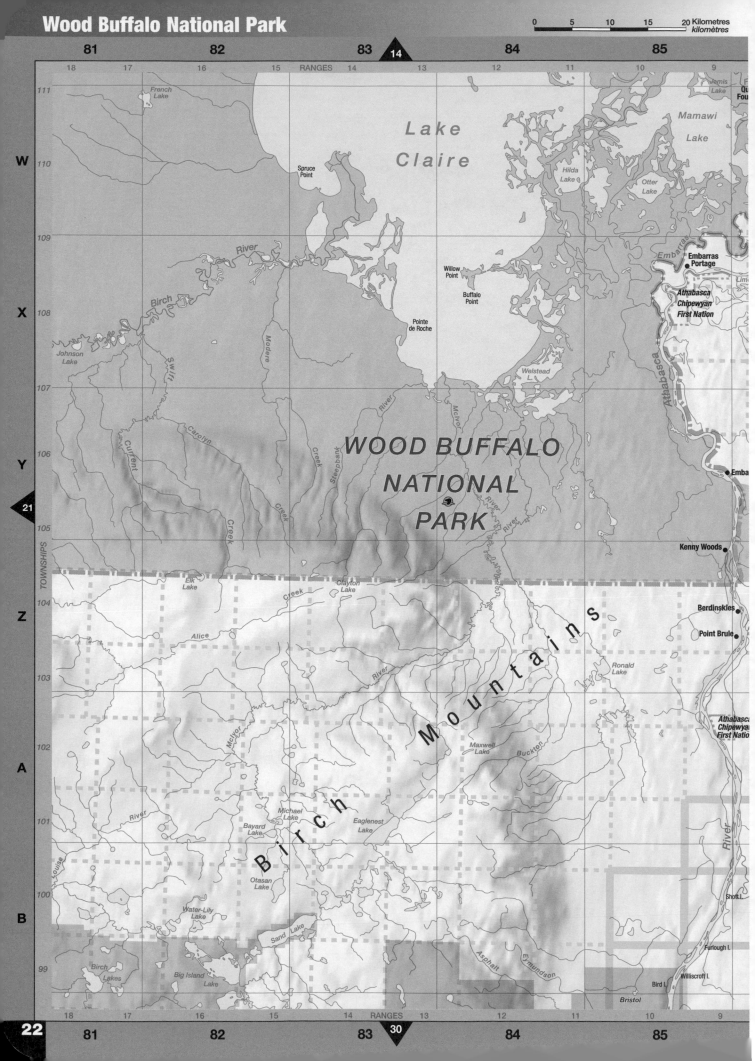

0   5   10   15   20 Kilometres
kilomètres

81   82   83 ▼14   84   85

18   17   16   15   RANGES   14   13   12   11   10   9

111

French
Lake

*Lake
Claire*

Jemis
Lake

Qu
Fou

W   110

Spruce
Point

*Mamawi
Lake*

Hilda
Lake

Otter
Lake

River

109

Embarras

Embarras
Portage

Birch

Willow
Point

Buffalo
Point

*Athabasca
Chipewyan
First Nation*

X   108

Johnson
Lake

Swift

Modere

Pointe
de Roche

Lim

107

McIvor

Welstead
L.

Carolyn

River

Athabasca

Curfent

Creek

Steepbank

WOOD BUFFALO

Y   106

NATIONAL

Emba

Creek

River

21

PARK

River

105

Creek

Kenny Woods

TOWNSHIPS

Elk
Lake

Glayton
Lake

Berdinskies

Z   104

Creek

Point Brule

Alice

Ronald
Lake

*Athabasca
Chipewya
First Natio*

103

River

M   o   u   n   t   a   i   n   s

McIvor

102

Maxwell
Lake

Buckton

A

B   i   r   c   h

River

Michael
Lake

Eaglenest
Lake

101

Bayard
Lake

Shot L.

Louise

Otasan
Lake

100

Furlough I.

B

Water-Lily
Lake

Sand   Lake

99

Birch
Lakes

Big Island
Lake

Asphalt

Ermundson

Williscroft I.

River

Bird I.

Bristol

18   17   16   15   14   RANGES   13   12   11   10   9

81   82   83 ▼30   84   85

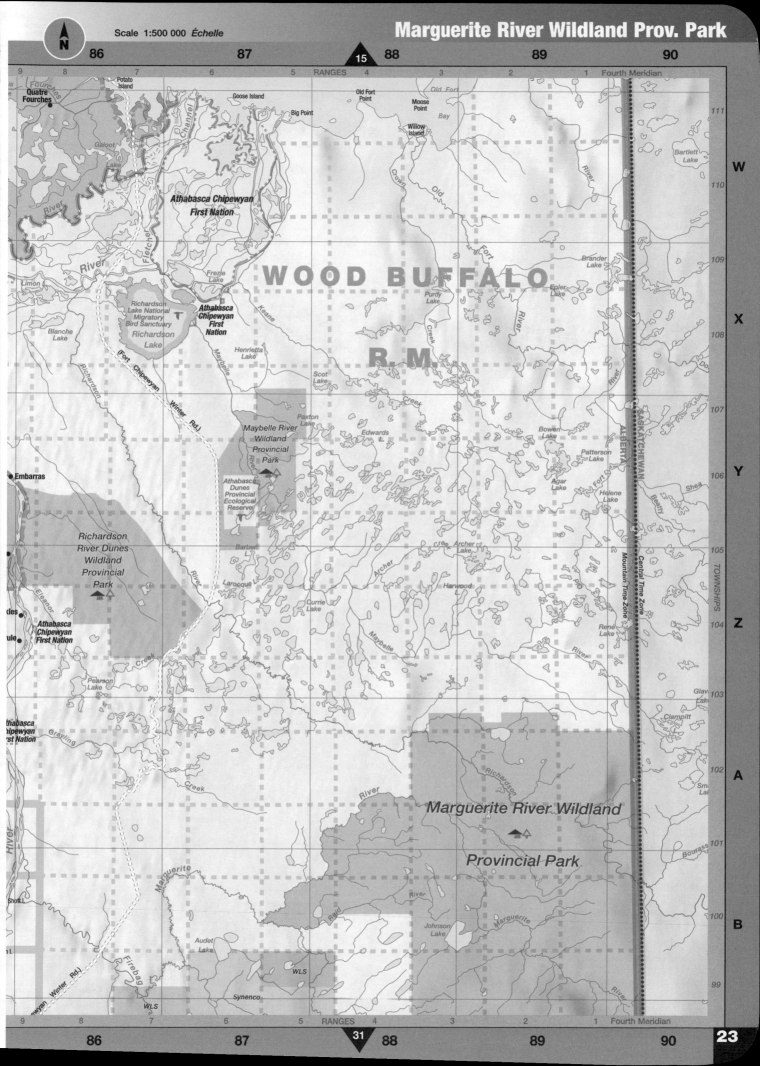

Scale 1:500 000 Échelle

N

86   87   15   88   89   90

9   8   7   6   5   RANGES   4   3   2   1   Fourth Meridian

Quatre
Fourches

Fourches

Potato
Island

Goose Island

Old Fort
Point

Old Fort

Moose
Point

Willow
Island

Big Point

Bay

111

Bartlett
Lake

W

110

Galoot
Lake

River

Channel

Fletcher

Athabasca Chipewyan
First Nation

Crown

Old

Fort

River

Brander
Lake

109

River

Limon l.

River

Frezie
Lake

WOOD BUFFALO

Purdy
Lake

Epler
Lake

X

108

Blanche
Lake

Richardson
Lake National
Migratory
Bird Sanctuary

Richardson
Lake

Athabasca
Chipewyan
First
Nation

Keane

R.M.

Richardson

Maybelle

Henrietta
Lake

Scot
Lake

Creek

107

(Fort Chipewyan

Winter Rd.)

Maybelle River
Wildland
Provincial
Park

Paxton
Lake

Edwards
L.

Bowen
Lake

Patterson
Lake

Y

106

Embarras

River

Athabasca
Dunes
Provincial
Ecological
Reserve

Agar
Lake

Fort

Helene
Lake

Shea

ALBERTA

SASKATCHEWAN

Richardson
River Dunes
Wildland
Provincial
Park

River

Barber

Larocque l.

Cree

Archer
Lake

Archer

Harwood

Old

Beatty

Mountain Time Zone

Central Time Zone

105

Eleanor

River

Currie
Lake

Marbelle

Rene
Lake

TOWNSHIPS

Z

104

des

Athabasca
Chipewyan
First Nation

ule

Creek

River

103

Grayling

Glau
Lake

Clampitt

thabasca
hipewyan
rst Nation

102

Marguerite River Wildland

Richardson

A

Creek

River

Bourass

101

River

Provincial Park

Marguerite

Sm
La

Shott l.

River

River

Marguerite

100

Marguerite

Reid

Johnson
Lake

B

99

Audet
Lake

Firebag

WLS

hipewyan Winter Rd.)

WLS

Synenco

River

9   8   7   6   5   RANGES   4   3   2   1   Fourth Meridian

86   87   31   88   89   90

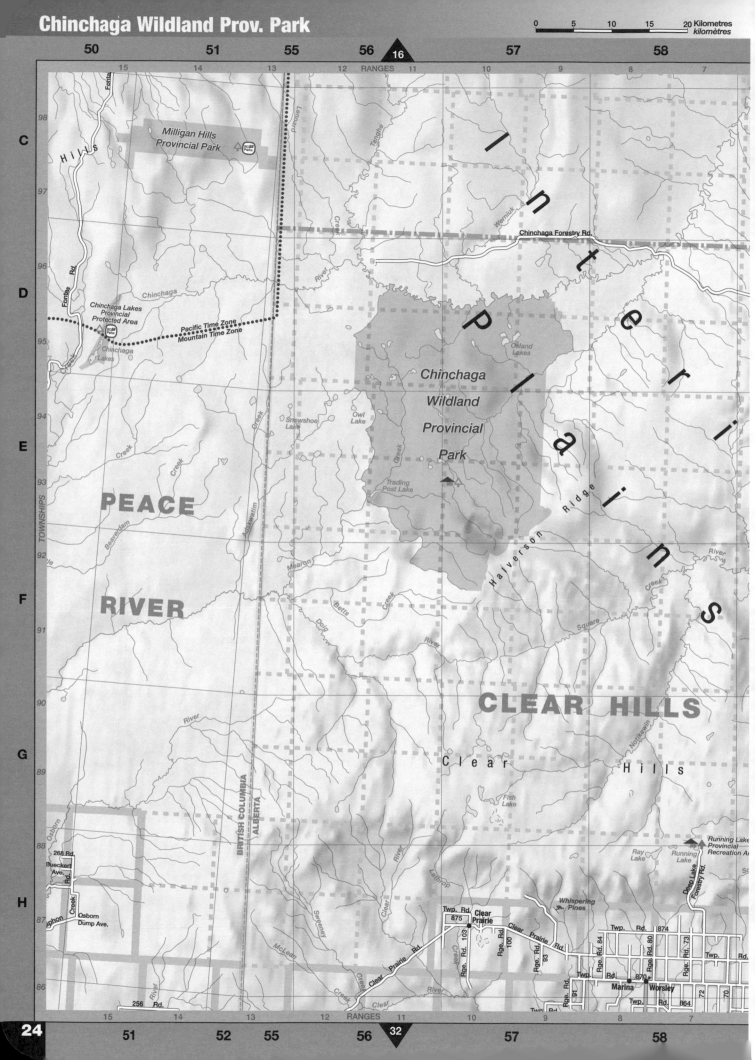

Milligan Hills
Provincial Park

Chinchaga Forestry Rd.

Chinchaga Lakes
Provincial
Protected Area

Pacific Time Zone
Mountain Time Zone

Chinchaga
Lakes

Osland
Lakes

Chinchaga

Wildland

Provincial

Park

Snowshoe
Lake

Owl
Lake

Trading
Post Lake

I n t e r i o r   P l a i n s

PEACE

RIVER

Halverson   Ridge

CLEAR HILLS

C l e a r   H i l l s

Fish
Lake

Running Lake
Provincial
Recreation Ar

Ray
Lake

Running
Lake

Whispering
Pines

Clear
Prairie

Marina   Worsley

BRITISH COLUMBIA
ALBERTA

268 Rd.

Bueckert
Ave.

Osborn
Dump Ave.

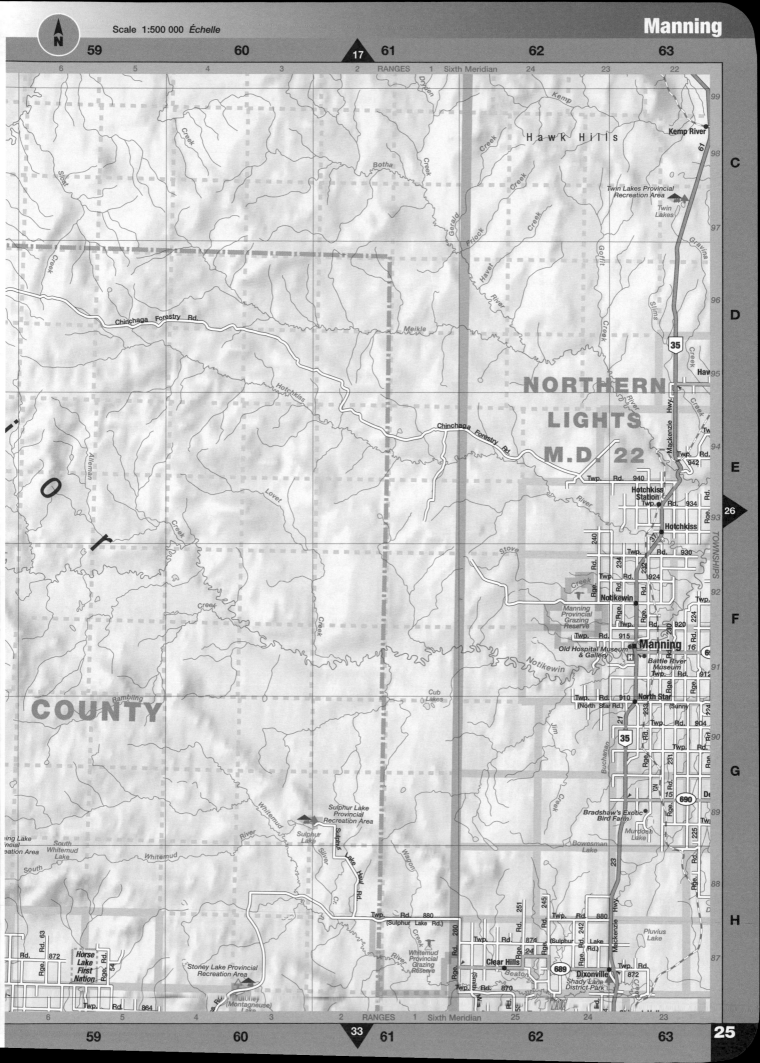

Scale 1:500 000 *Échelle*

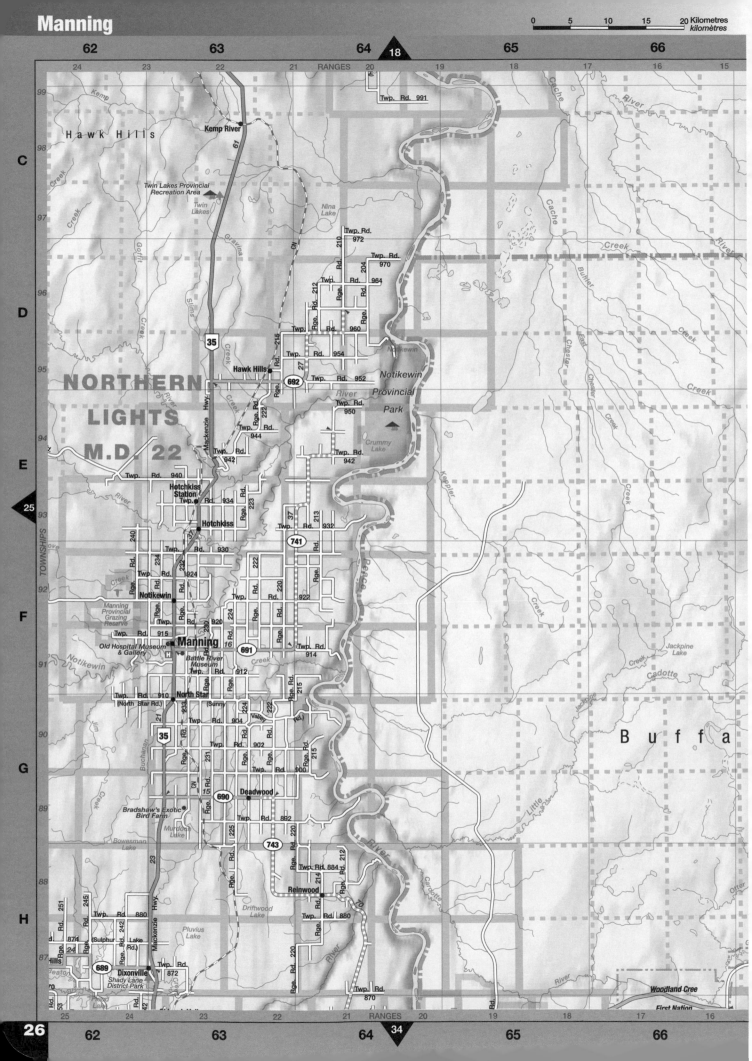

0   5   10   15   20 Kilometres
kilomètres

62   63   64   18   65   66

24   23   22   21 RANGES 20   19   18   17   16 Woodland Cree   15

Kemp River

Hawk Hills

C

Twin Lakes Provincial
Recreation Area

Twin Lakes

Nina Lake

Twp. Rd. 991

Cache River

D

NORTHERN

LIGHTS

M.D. 22

35

Hawk Hills

692

Notikewin River

Notikewin
Provincial
Park

Crummy Lake

Twp. Rd. 972
Twp. Rd. 970
964
960
954
952
Twp. Rd. 950
Twp. Rd. 942

E

25

Hotchkiss Station

Hotchkiss

Twp. Rd. 940
Twp. Rd. 934
930

741

932

TOWNSHIPS

F

Notikewin

Manning Provincial Grazing Reserve

Old Hospital Museum & Gallery

Manning

691

Battle River Museum

North Star

924
920
915
912
910
904
902
900

922

G

35

690

Deadwood

Bradshaw's Exotic Bird Farm

Murdoch Lake

Bowesman Lake

743

882

B u f f a l o

Jackpine Lake

Cadotte River

H

251
245

Reinwood

Twp. Rd. 884
Twp. Rd. 880

870

689

Dixonville

Shady Lane District Park

872

Driftwood Lake

Pluvius Lake

Woodland Cree
First Nation

62   63   64   34   65   66

25   24   23   22 RANGES 21   20   19   18   17   16

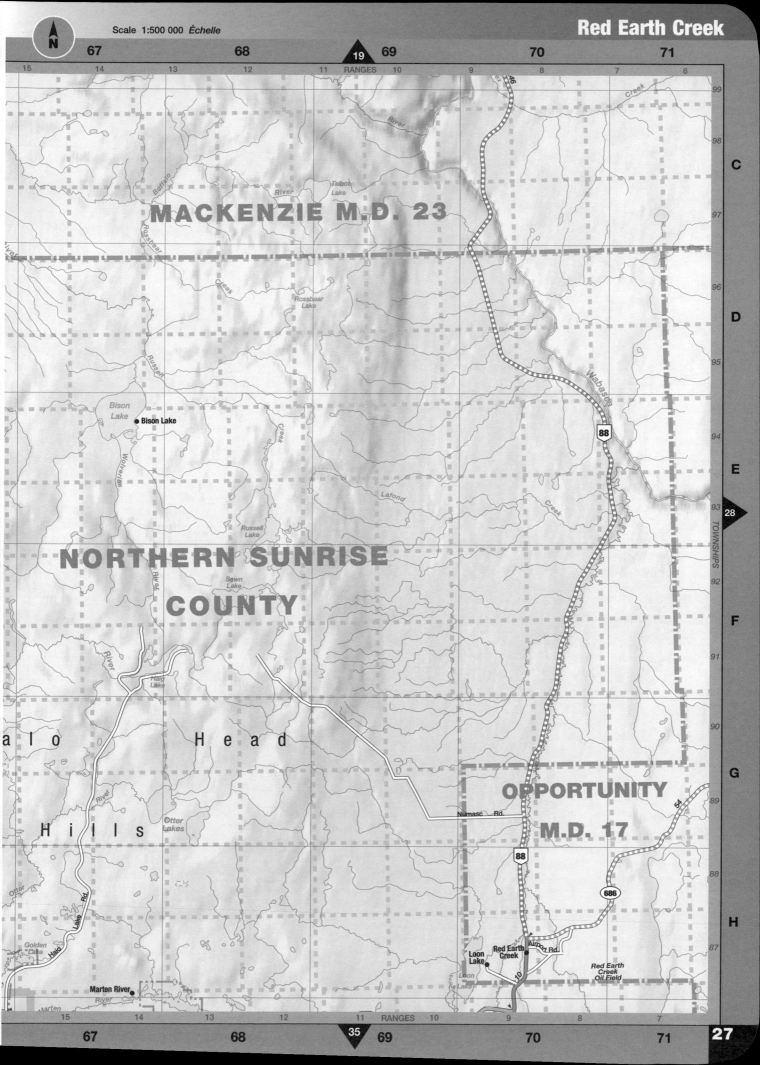

N

67   68   19   69   70   71
RANGES

15   14   13   12   11   10   9   8   7   6

99

C

97

MACKENZIE M.D. 23

96

D

95

88

94

E

93   28

TOWNSHIPS

92

NORTHERN SUNRISE

COUNTY

91

F

Bison Lake • Bison Lake

Rossbear Lake

Talbot Lake

River

Russell Lake

Sawn Lake

Lafond

Wabasca

90

G

OPPORTUNITY

M.D. 17

Haig Lake

alo   H e a d

Numasc Rd.

54

89

H i l l s   Otter Lakes

88   686

88

H

Golden Lake   Haig   Lake Rd.

Loon Lake   Red Earth Creek   Airport Rd.

Red Earth Creek Oil Field

87

Marten River •

River

Loon Lake

15   14   13   12   11   10   9   8   7
RANGES

67   68   35   69   70   71

27

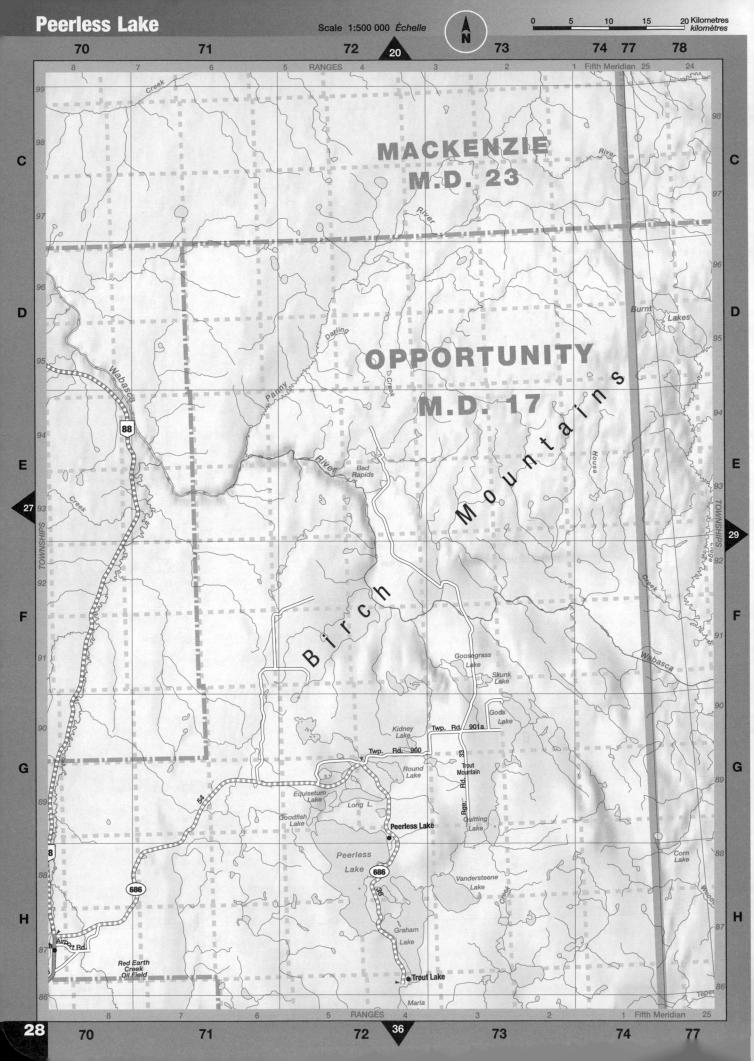

MACKENZIE
M.D. 23

OPPORTUNITY

M.D. 17

Birch Mountains

Wabasca

88

Creek

Darling

Panny

River

Bad
Rapids

Goosegrass
Lake

Skunk
Lake

Gods
Lake

Kidney
Lake

Twp. Rd. 901a

Twp. Rd. 900

Round
Lake

Trout
Mountain

Equisetum
Lake

Long L.

Goodfish
Lake

Peerless Lake

Quitting
Lake

Peerless
Lake

686

Vandersteene
Lake

Corn
Lake

54

686

8

Airport Rd.

Red Earth
Creek
Oil Field

Graham
Lake

36

Trout Lake

Maria

Burnt Lakes

House

Wabasca

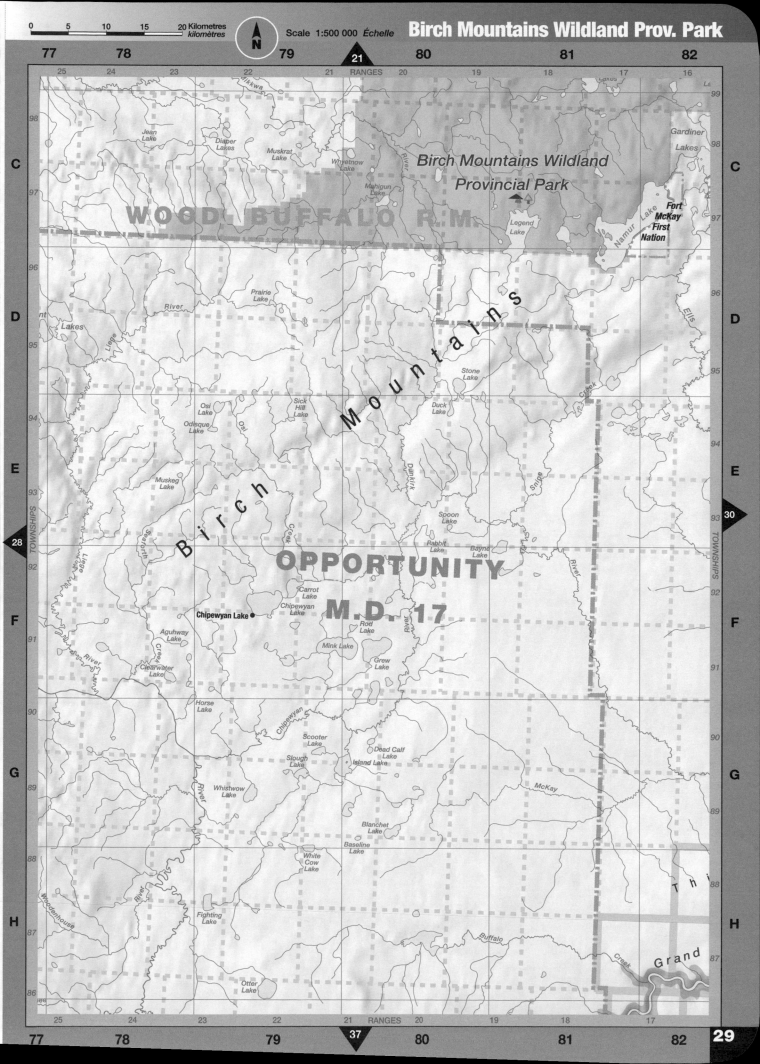

0 5 10 15 20 Kilometres
kilomètres

N

Scale 1:500 000 Échelle

77   78   79   21   80   81   82
RANGES

25 24 23 22 21 20 19 18 17 16

99

98

Jean
Lake

Diaper
Lakes

Muskrat
Lake

Whretnow
Lake

River

Birch Mountains Wildland
Provincial Park

Gardiner
Lakes

98

C

C

Mahigun
Lake

Legend
Lake

Namur
Lake

Fort
McKay
First
Nation

97

WOOD BUFFALO R.M.

97

96

96

Prairie
Lake

River

Ells

D

nt
Lakes

Liege

River

Mountains

D

95

95

Stone
Lake

Creek

E

Osi
Lake

Odisque
Lake

Osi

Sick
Hill
Lake

Duck
Lake

94

94

Muskeg
Lake

Birch

Dunkirk

Snive

E

93

Spoon
Lake

93   30

TOWNSHIPS

28

Seaforth

Liege

Creek

Rabbit
Lake

Bayne
Lake

River

TOWNSHIPS

92

OPPORTUNITY

92

Carrot
Lake

Chipewyan
Lake

M.D. 17

F

Chipewyan Lake

Rod
Lake

River

F

91

Aguhway
Lake

Mink Lake

91

Creek

River

Clearwater
Lake

Grew
Lake

G

Horse
Lake

Chipewyan

90

90

Scooter
Lake

Dead Calf
Lake

G

River

Whistwow
Lake

Island Lake

Slough
Lake

McKay

89

89

Blanchet
Lake

H

Baseline
Lake

Thi

88

Woodenhouse

White
Cow
Lake

88

River

H

87

Fighting
Lake

Buffalo

Grand

87

Creek

86

Otter
Lake

86

77   78   79   37   80   81   82
RANGES

25 24 23 22 21 20 19 18 17

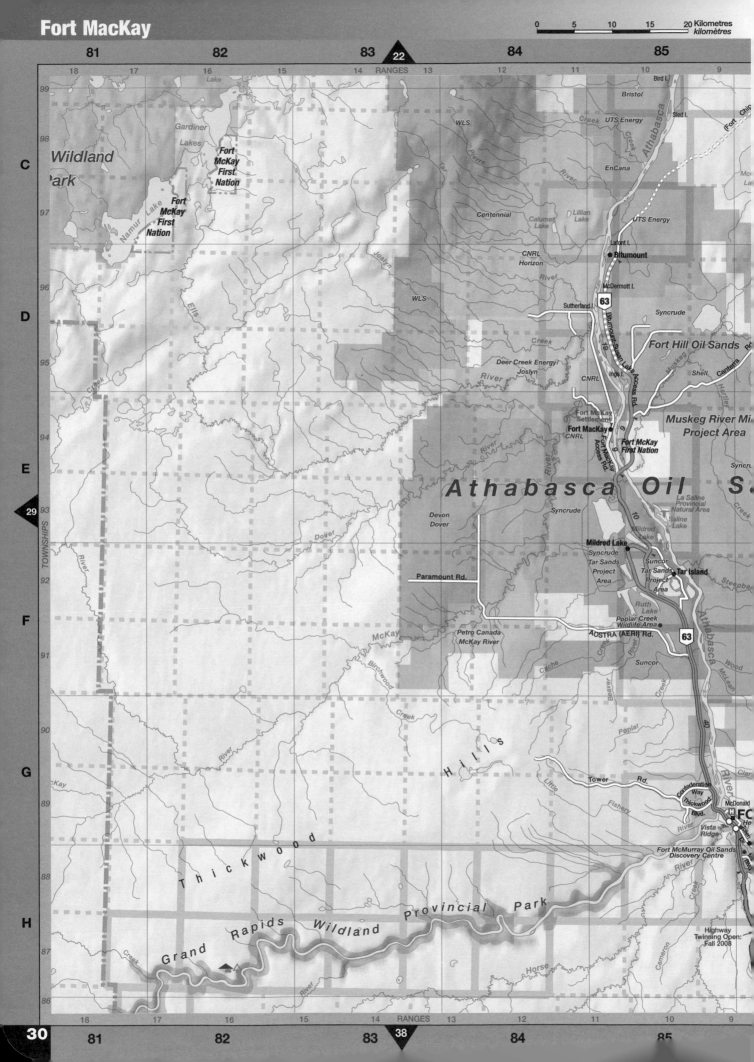

0   5   10   15   20 **Kilometres**
kilomètres

81   **82**   **83** ▼ 22   **84**   **85**

18   17   16   15   14 RANGES 13   12   11   10   9

99

C   Wildland
Park

98   *Gardiner
Lakes*

Fort
McKay
First
Nation

WLS

Bristol

Bird I.

UTS Energy

EnCana

Mcl

97   Namur Lake   Fort
McKay
First
Nation

Centennial   Calumet
Lake   Lillian
Lake

UTS Energy

Lafont I.

● **Bitumount**

Sled I.

D

96   Ells   Joslyn   WLS

CNRL
Horizon

McDermott I.

Sutherland I.

63

Syncrude

95   Creek   River

Deer Creek Energy/
Joslyn   CNRL

Ings. I.

Fort Hill Oil Sands

Shell   Cantera

Muskeg   Hartley

E

94   River   River

Fort McKay
Settlement
Fort MacKay ●
CNRL   Fort McKay
First Nation

**Muskeg River Mi
Project Area**

29 ◄   93   River

Devon
Dover

Syncrude

Athabasca Oil S

La Saline
Provincial
Natural Area

Saline
Lake

Syncr

F

92   Dover   Mildred
Lake

Paramount Rd.

● **Mildred Lake**
Syncrude
Tar Sands
Project
Area

Tar Sands
Project
Area   ● **Tar Island**

Steepbar

91   McKay   Birchwood

Petro Canada
McKay River

AOSTRA (AERI) Rd.

Ruth
Lake

Poplar Creek
Wildlife Area

Suncor

63

Athabasca   Wood

G   90   River   Creek   Cache   Creek   Beaver   River

Poplar

Mclean

H i l l s

89   McKay   Little

Tower   Rd.

Thickwood   Fishery   Blvd.

Confederation
Way

McDonald

FC
He

H

88   Thickwood   Vista
Ridge

Fort McMurray Oil Sands
Discovery Centre

87   Grand   Rapids   Wildland   Provincial   Park

Creek

Horse   Cameron   Creek

Highway
Twinning Open:
Fall 2008

86   River   ○ 22

18   17   16   15   14 RANGES 13   12   11   10   9

30   **81**   **82**   **83** ▼ 38   **84**   **85**

TOWNSHIPS

63

10

40

River

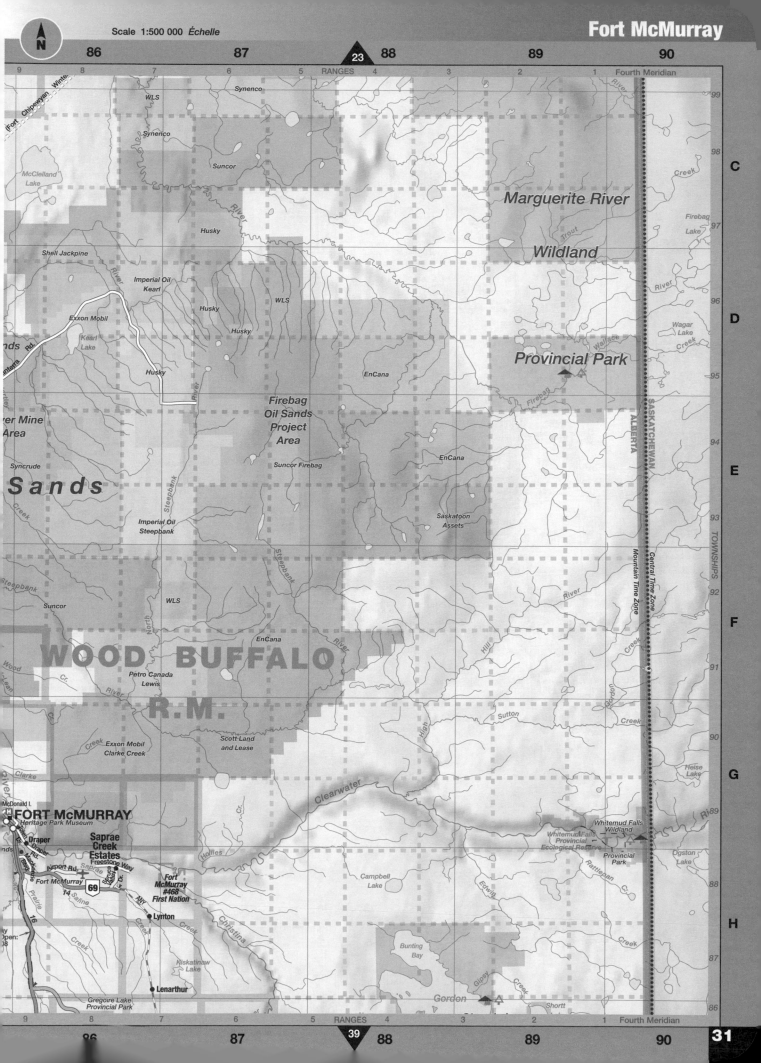

Scale 1:500 000 *Échelle*

N

RANGES

Fourth Meridian

Synenco

WLS

Synenco

Synenco

Suncor

McClelland Lake

Marguerite River

Creek

Firebag Lake

Husky

Wildland

Shell Jackpine

River

Imperial Oil Kearl

Husky

WLS

Exxon Mobil

Husky

Wagar Lake Creek

Kearl Lake

Husky

Provincial Park

ds Rd.

Husky

EnCana

Firebag

River

er Mine Area

Firebag Oil Sands Project Area

S a n d s

Syncrude

Suncor Firebag

EnCana

ALBERTA

SASKATCHEWAN

Central Time Zone

Mountain Time Zone

TOWNSHIPS

Imperial Oil Steepbank

Steepbank

Saskatoon Assets

Steepbank

Steepbank

WLS

River

Suncor

North

WOOD BUFFALO

Wood

Cr.

River

Petro Canada Lewis

EnCana

River

Hill

Sutton

Creek

R.M.

High

Clearwater

Creek

Exxon Mobil Clarke Creek

Scott Land and Lease

Clarke

Creek

Heise Lake

River

McDonald I.

FORT McMURRAY

Heritage Park Museum

Whitemud Falls Wildland

Whitemud Falls Provincial Ecological Reserve

Ogston Lake

Draper

Saprae Creek Estates

Freestone Way

Holfes

Rattlesnan

Provincial Park

Rd.

Airport Rd.

Saprae Dr.

Fort McMurray

69

14 Saline

Fort McMurray #468 First Nation

Campbell Lake

Edwin

Gipsy Cr.

Creek

Prairie

16

Lynton

Creek

Christina

Bunting Bay

Creek

ay Open:

08

Creek

Riskatinaw Lake

Lenarthur

Gregoire Lake Provincial Park

Gordon

Gipsy

Creek

Shortt

RANGES

Fourth Meridian

0   5   10   15   20 Kilometres
kilomètres

51   52   55   56   24   57   58

J

K

L

PEACE

RIVER

M

To Fort St. John

TOWNSHIPS

To Chetwynd

N

O

32

51   52   55   56   41   57   42   58

BRITISH COLUMBIA   ALBERTA

Marina   Worsley
726

Cleardale
64   64

Many Islands
Many Islands District Park

Dunvegan West Wildland Provincial Park

Silver Valley Provincial Ecological Reserve

Dunvegan West Wildland Provincial Park

Dunvegan West Wildland Provincial Park

Cotillon County Recreation Area

Bear Canyon
717

Cherry Point

Clayhurst

Goodlow

Cecil Lake

Flatrock

Boundary Lake

Ole's Lake Provincial Recreation Area

Bear Canyon Provincial Grazing Reserve

Cotillion

Silver Valley   Savanna
681

Blueberry Mountain Provincial Grazing Reserve

SADDLE   HILLS

681   725

Blueberry Mountain
680

Poplar Ridge

Ksituan

Moonshine Lake Provincial Park

Whitburn

COUNTY

Bonanza

719

Bay Tree
49

Dawson Creek

Pouce Coupe

2

Gundy

Tomslake

Tupper

Demmitt

43

52

Gordondale

Ksituan Lake

Happy Valley

727

49

Spirit Ridge

White Mountain

Bridgevi

Westmark   677

Northma

Hilltop Lake County Campground

Homestead

Silverwing

724

Blooming Valley

Valhalla

Valhalla Centre

Melsness Mercantile Historic Site

La Glace

59   721

Peace River Corridor Provincial Park

East Doe River

Doe River

Valley View

Rolla

Seven Mile Corner   Sweetwater

Kilkerran

Briar Ridge

Pouce Coupe

Swan Lake Provincial Park

Cutbank Lake

Pouce   Coupe   River

Boone

Jackfish Lake

Boone Lake

Spring Lake

Saddle

Demmitt County Park

Dickson Lake   Ponita

Albright Lake

Updike Lake

Brainard

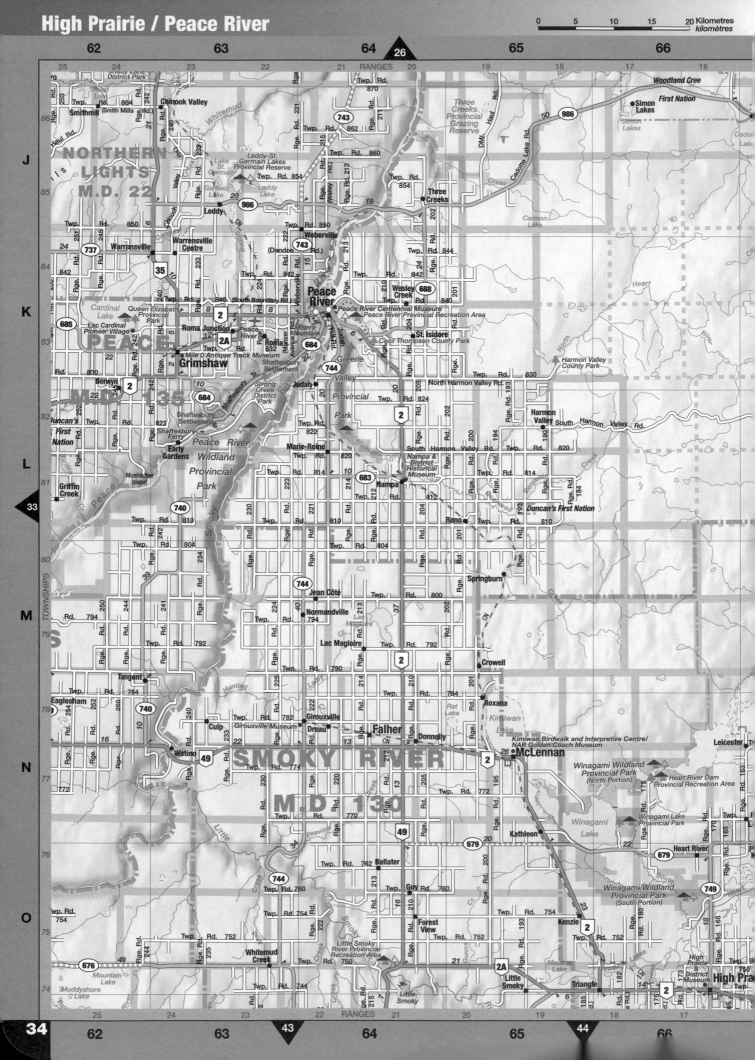

0 5 10 15 20 Kilometres
kilomètres

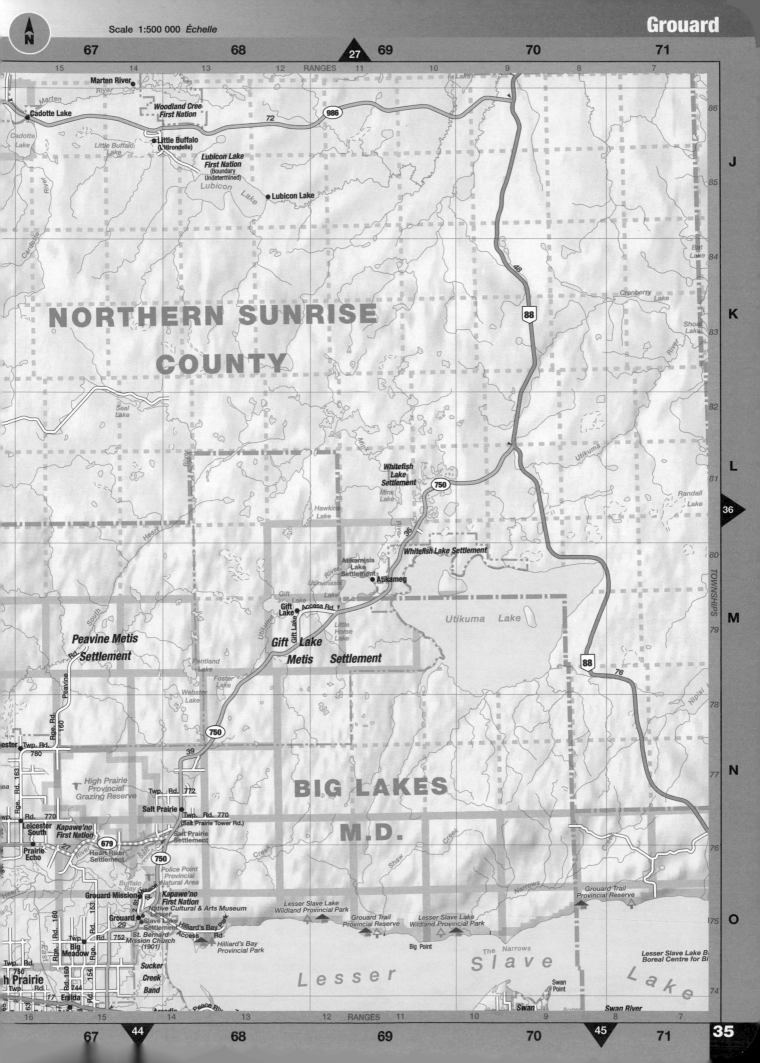

Scale 1:500 000 Échelle

N

RANGES

15   14   13   12   11   10   9   8   7

Marten River

Woodland Cree First Nation

Marten River

Cadotte Lake

986

72

J

86

Little Buffalo (L'Hirondelle)

Little Buffalo Lake

Lubicon Lake First Nation (Boundary Undetermined)

Lubicon Lake

Lubicon Lake

Cadotte Lake

Cadotte River

Lake

85

Bat Lake

84

48

Cranberry Lake

88

K

83

Shoal Lake

NORTHERN SUNRISE

COUNTY

82

Seal Lake

L

81

Whitefish Lake Settlement

750

Randall Lake

36

TOWNSHIPS

Hawkins Lake

Mink Lake

River

Heart River

Whitefish Lake Settlement

80

Atikamisis Lake Settlement

Atikameg

Gift Lake

Gift Lake   Access Rd.

M

79

Utikuma   Lake

Peavine Metis Settlement

Peavine Rd.

Pentland Lake

Gift   Lake Metis   Settlement

Little Horse Lake

Utikuma River

Foster Lake

Webster Lake

88

76

78

Rge. Rd. 160

750

39

Nipisi

N

77

Twp. Rd.

780

High Prairie Provincial Grazing Reserve

Twp. Rd. 772

BIG LAKES

Rge. Rd. 163

Salt Prairie

Twp. Rd. 770 (Salt Prairie Tower Rd.)

M.D.

Shaw Creek

Rd.   770

Leicester South

Kapawe'no First Nation

679

27

Heart River

Salt

Salt Prairie Settlement

750

Creek

76

Prairie Echo

Heart River Settlement

Buffalo Bay

Police Point Provincial Natural Area

The Narrows

Grouard Trail Provincial Reserve

Heart

Grouard Mission

Mission

Lesser Slave Lake

Kapawe'no First Nation

Native Cultural & Arts Museum

Lesser Slave Lake Wildland Provincial Park

Grouard Trail Provincial Reserve

Lesser Slave Lake Wildland Provincial Park

O

75

Rge. Rd. 160

Twp. Rd.

153

Grouard   29

Slave Lake Settlement

Hilliard's Bay Access   Rd.

St. Bernard Mission Church (1901)

752

Big Meadow

Hilliard's Bay Provincial Park

Big Point

Lesser Slave Lake Boreal Centre for Bi...

Twp. Rd. 750

Sucker Creek Band

Lesser

Slave

Lake

74

h Prairie

Twp. Rd.

154

744   Emida

77

Peace River

Swan Point

Swan

Swan River

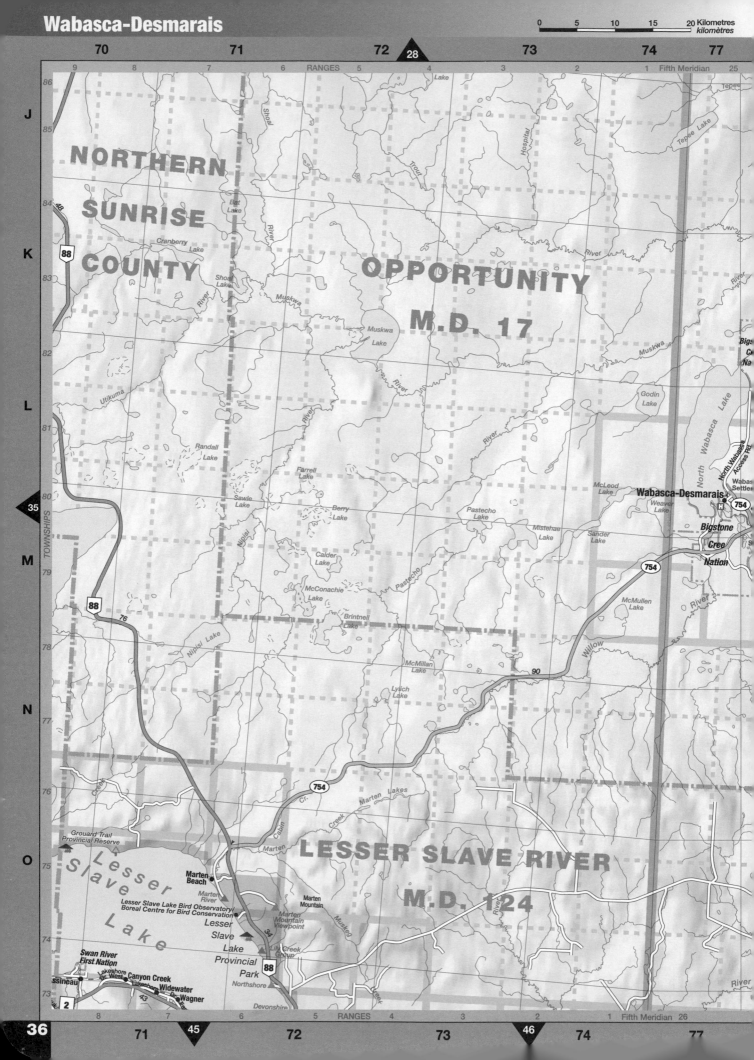

0   5   10   15   20 Kilometres
kilomètres

70   71   72   28   73   74   77

9   8   7   6 RANGES 5   4   3   2   1 Fifth Meridian 25

86

J
85

NORTHERN

84   48

K
83

SUNRISE

Cranberry
Lake

COUNTY

88

Shoal
Lake

OPPORTUNITY

82

Muskwa

M.D. 17

Muskwa
Lake

Godin
Lake

L
81

Utikuma

Bigs
C
Na

Muskwa

River

Randall
Lake

River

McLeod
Lake

Wabasca-Desmarais

80

Farrell
Lake

754

35 TOWNSHIPS

Sawle
Lake

Berry
Lake

Pastecho
Lake

Weaver
Lake

Mistehae
Lake

Sander
Lake

Bigstone

M
79

Nipisi

88   76

Calder
Lake

Pastecho

McMullen
Lake

754

Cree

Nation

River

McConachie
Lake

Brintnell
Lake

Nipisi Lake

McMillan
Lake

90   Willow

754

N
77

Lylich
Lake

Grouard Trail
Provincial Reserve

Creek

76

754

Marten   Lakes

LESSER SLAVE RIVER

O
75

Lesser
Slave

Cabin

Creek

Marten

Marten Beach

M.D. 124

Marten
River

Lesser Slave Lake Bird Observatory/
Boreal Centre for Bird Conservation

Marten
Mountain

Marten
Mountain
Viewpoint

Musteg

River

Lake

74

Lesser
Slave

34

Lily Creek
Group

Swan River
First Nation

Lake

Provincial
Park

88

Lakeshore
Dr. West Canyon Creek

ssineau

Lakeshore   Widewater

Northshore

Wagner

2   43   Devonshire

73

36   8   7   6 RANGES 5   4   3   2   1 Fifth Meridian 26

71   45   72   73   46   74   77

WOOD BUFFALO R.M.

Grand Rapids Wildland Provincial Park

House River Indian Cemetery

Bigstone Cree Nation

Kamistikowik Lake

Diaper Lake

Wood Buffalo Lake

Horsetail Lake

Wabasca Access Rd.

Wabasca Settlement

754

Bigstone Cree Nation

Wabasca Settlement

813   36

Island L.

Bigstone Cree Nation

South Wabasca Lake

Sandy Lake

Sandy Lake

Pelican Lake

Muskeg

Athabasca

Boivin

Loon

Deadman

House

Pelican Portage

Agnes Lake

Drowned

Horse

Pelican Mountain

Long Lake

Pelican Creek

LAC LA BICHE COUNTY

May Hill

Crooked River

Rock Island Lake Rd.

Rock Island Lake

Tanasiuk Provincial Recreation Area

Orloff Lake Rd.   57

813

Otter-Orloff Lakes

Orloff

Parallel

McMillan Lake

River

63

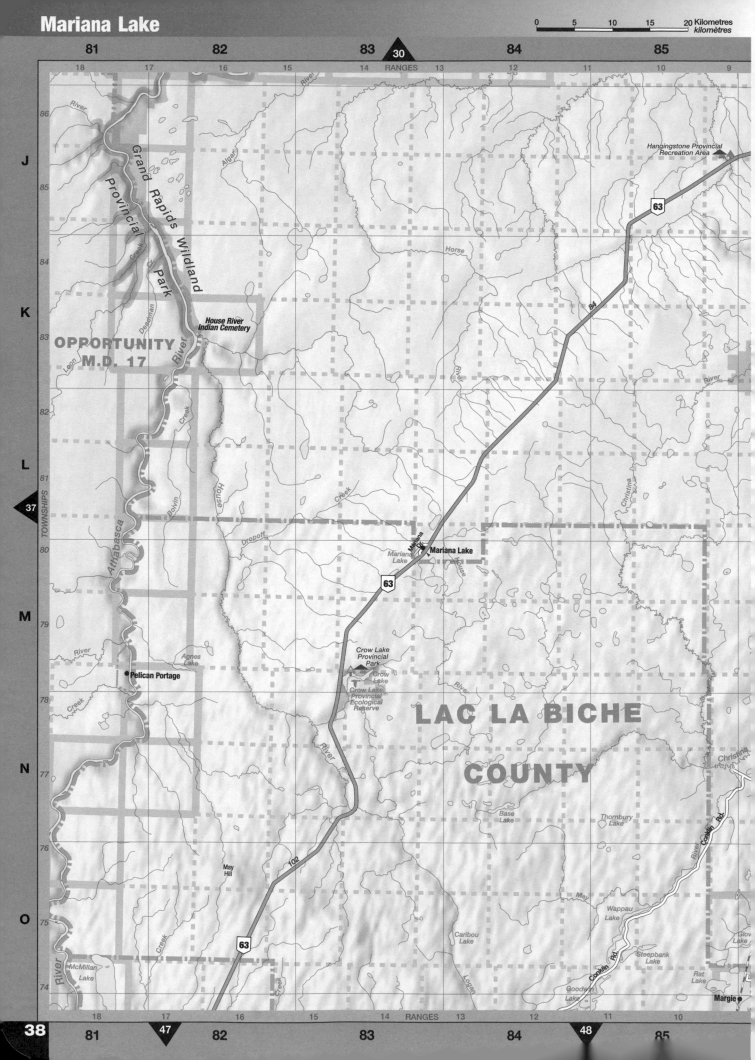

0   5   10   15   20 **Kilometres**
kilomètres

81   82   **83** 30   84   85

18   17   16   15   14 RANGES   13   12   11   10   9

J

86

River

Grand Rapids

85

Provincial

K

84

Wildland

Park

Deadman

Leon

Cr

OPPORTUNITY
M.D. 17

83

House River
Indian Cemetery

Horse

River

82

Creek

Bolwin

House

L   81   37

TOWNSHIPS

80

Dropoff

Algar

Creek

River

Christina

River

Mariana
PS.

Mariana
Lake

Mariana Lake

House

63

84

63

Hangingstone Provincial
Recreation Area

M   79

River

Agnes
Lake

Crow Lake
Provincial
Park

Crow
Lake

Crow Lake
Provincial
Ecological
Reserve

River

Pelican Portage

N   78

Creek

LAC LA BICHE

77

River

COUNTY

Base
Lake

Thornbury
Lake

River

Conklin Rd.

76

May
Hill

102

May

Wappau
Lake

Christina

O   75

McMillan
Lake

Caribou
Lake

Conklin Rd.

Steepbank
Lake

Glov
Lake

63

Creek

River

74

River

Creek

Goodwin
Lake

Margie

Rat
Lake

18   17   16   15   14 RANGES   13   12   11   10

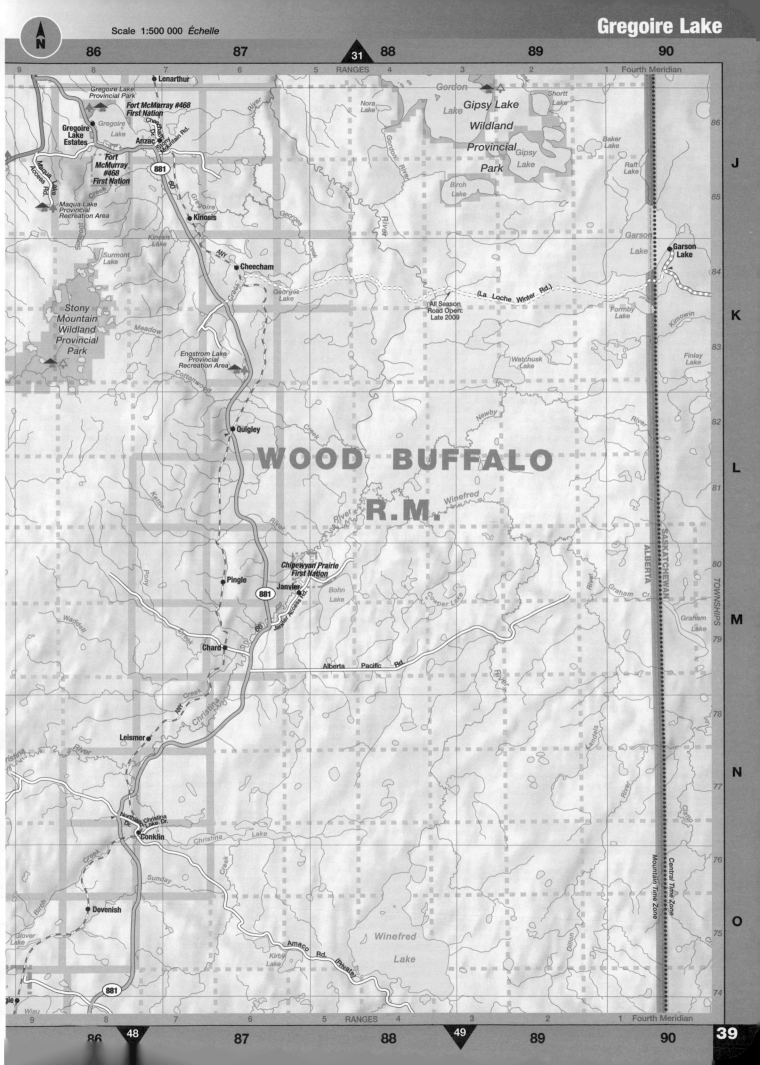

Scale 1:500 000 *Échelle*

N

Airports

Airdrie 70 M-N76
Athabasca 47 S79-80
Barrhead 56 W73
Bassano 77 P81-82
Beiseker 70 M78
Bonnyville 59 V87
Brooks 78 Q83
Calgary International 70 N75-76
Camrose 65 C80-81
Cardston 82 Y78
Castor 66 G83
Claresholm Industrial 76 T77
Cold Lake Regional 49 U89
Consort 73 H-J88
Cooking Lake 57 A79-80
Coronation 72 H85
Drayton Valley 55 A72 63 B72
Drumheller 71 L80
Edmonton International 56 A78
Edson 54 Z66
Elk Point 59 X87
Empress 79 O90
Foremost 84 W-X85
Forestburg 66 E83
Fort Chipewyan 14 V86
Fort McMurray 31 H86
Glendon 58 V86
Grande Cache 52 X58
Grande Prairie 42 Q58-59
Hanna 72 L83-84
Hardisty 66 E85
High Level 18 W64
High River 76 R76
Innisfail 70 H75
Jasper-Hinton 53 A62
Josephburg 57 Y80
Killam-Sedgewick 66 D84
Lac La Biche 47 S83
Lacombe 64 F77
Lethbridge County 83 W80
Lloydminster 59 A90
Mayerthorpe 55 X70-71
McNeill Petrocan 79 Q90
Medicine Hat 85 U87-88
Milk River 84 Y-Z83
Mistahiya 67 C87
Olds-Didsbury 70 K75
Oyen 73 M88
Peace River 34 K63
Pincher Creek 82 W76
Ponoka Industrial (Labrie Field) 64 E77-78
Provost 67 G89
Red Deer Airport 64 G76-77
Rocky Mountain House 63 F72
St. Paul 58 W85
Slave Lake 45 P72
South Calgary 76 P76
Springbank 70 N74
Stettler 65 G80-81
Sundre 69 K73
Taber 83 V82
Three Hills 71 K79
Tofield 57 A81
Two Hills 58 Y84
Vauxhall 78 T83
Vegreville 58 Z83
Vermilion 59 A87-88
Viking 66 B83-84
Villeneuve 56 Y77
Vulcan 76 R78
Wainwright 67 D87
Westlock 56 V-W77
Wetaskiwin 64 C78
Whitecourt 55 W69

Bird Sanctuaries

Birch Lake Provincial 58 A85
Ministik Lake Game 57 A80
Red Deer National Migratory 64 G77
Richardson Lake National Migratory 23 X86-87
Saskatoon Lake National Migratory 42 Q57-58

Higher Learning

Lethbridge College 83 V-W80
Maskwachees Cultural College 64 D78
Mt. Royal College 76 O75
Olds Agricultural College 70 K75
NAIT 56 Z78
Red Deer College 64 G77
University of Alberta 56 Z78
University of Calgary 70 N75
University of Lethbrige 83 V79-80

Museums

Alberta Beach & District 56 Y74
Alberta Forest Service 53 A62-63
Alix Wagon Wheel 65 F79
Alliance & District 66 F84
Andrew & District Local History 57 X82
Anthony Henday 65 G79
Appaloosa Horse 76 T77-78
Arrowwood Country Store 77 Q79
Atlas Coal Mine 71 M81
Barrhead Centennial 56 W73-74
Basilian Fathers 57 Z82-83
Battle River 26 F63
Bentley 64 F75
Big Valley Station & Museum 71 H80-81
Bonnyville & District 59 V87-88
Bowden Pioneer 70 J75
Breton & District Historical 63 B73
Brooks & District 78 R83
Brownvale North Peace Agricultural 33 L61-62
Camrose & District Centennial 65 C80-81
Canmore Museum 74 O70
Card Pioneer Home 82 Y78
Caroline Wheels of Time 69 H72-73
Castor & District 66 G83
Cereal Prairie Pioneer 73 M87-88
Claresholm 76 T77
Climb Through Time 67 C89
Court House 82 Y77-78
Crossroads 73 M88
Crowsnest 81 W74
Crowsnest Pass Ecomuseum 81 W74
Danish Canadian National 70 H74
DeBolt & District Pioneer 43 Q61
Delia & District Dawson Historical 71 L82
Devil's Coulee Dinosaur and Heritage 83 X-Y82
Dewberry Valley 59 Z88
Dickson Store 70 H74
Didsbury & District 70 K74-75
Dinosaur & Fossil 71 L-M81
Dr. Woods House 56 A78 64 B78
Dr. George / Kemp House 70 H75-76
Donalda & District 65 E81
Drayton Valley & District Historical 63 B71-72
East Coulee School 71 M81-82
Edgerton & District 67 D89
Enchant & District 77 T81
End of Steel Heritage 33 K60
Field Station of the Royal Tyrrell 78 P-Q85
Forestburg & District 66 E83
Fort Museum of the North West Mounted Police 82 V78
Fort Chipewyan Bicentennial 14 V86
Fort Ostell 64 E78
Fort Saskatchewan 57 Y79
Fort Vermilion Heritage Centre 19 X68
Galloway Station 54 Z67
Gem of the West 83 V80-81
Gibbons 57 X79
Girouxville 34 N63-64
Glenbow 76 O75
Gopher Hole 70 K77
Grande Prairie 42 Q58-59
Grizzly Bear Prairie 33 N60
Hanna & District Pioneer 72 K83-84
Heritage Park 56 Y-Z78
Heritage Park 31 G86
High Prairie & District 34 O66
Historic Markerville Creamery 70 H75
Historical Village & Pioneer Museum at Shandro 58 X83
Holden Historical 65 B82
Homestead 71 L81
Iron Creek 66 D85
Irrigation Impact 84 V83
Jasper-Yellowhead 60 D61
Kinosayo 45 P70
Kneehill Historical 70 K78 71 K79
Kootenai Brown Pioneer Village 82 W76
Lac Ste. Anne Pioneer 55 X71
Lakusta Heritage 57 Z82-83
Mackenzie Crossroads Museum & Visitors Centre 18 W63-64
Mallaig & District 58 V85
Medicine Hat Museum & Art Gallery 85 U87-88
Michener House 64 F77-78
Mile 0 Antique Truck 34 K63
Millet & District 64 B78
Mirror & District 65 F79-80
Morrison Museum of the Country School 59 A88
Mountain View 70 K74-75
Museum of the Highwood 76 Q76
Nanton Lancaster Air 76 R-S77
NAR Golden Coach 34 N65
Nampa & District Historical 34 L64
Native Cultural & Arts 35 O67
Native Cultural Arts 48 S83
Nose Creek Valley 70 M75-76
Old Hospital Museum & Gallery 25 F62-63
Okotoks 76 P76
Pas-Ka-Poo 64 E74
Peace River Centennial 34 K64
Pembina Lobstick Historical 55 Y71
Pioneer Acres 70 M77
Prairie Acres Heritage Village & Museum 83 U80
Prairie Elevator 73 N89
Prairie Memories 85 U89
Prairie Panorama 67 F87
Raymond 83 W-X80
RCMP Centennial 33 L60-61
Red Brick Arts Centre & Museum 54 Z67
Redcliff 79 T87
Redwater & District 57 X79
Remington Carriage 82 Y77-78
Reynolds-Alberta 64 C78
Rocky Mountain House 63 F72
Rosebud Centennial 71 M80
Roulston 70 L75
Royal Tyrrell 71 L80-81
Saddle Lake Cultural 58 X84-85
St. Ann Ranch Museum & Centre 70 J-K78 71 J-K79
St. Paul Historical 58 W-X86
Scandia Eastern Irrigation District 77 S82-83
Seba Beach Heritage 55 Z72-73
Sexsmith Blacksmith Shop 42 P59
Siksika Nation Museum 77 P79
Smithson International Truck 64 E74
Smoky Lake 57 W81-82
Sodbusters Archives & Museum 65 D83
South Peace Centennial 41 P-Q56
Spirit River & District 33 M59
Stavely & District 76 T77
Stettler Town & Country 65 G80-81
Stony Plain Pioneer 56 Z75
Strathcona County 57 Z79
Sundre Pioneer Village 69 J-K73
Taber & District 83 V82-83
Thorhild & District 57 V80
Three River's Rock & Fossil 82 W75-76
Tofield 57 A81
Tri-Town 49 U89
Trochu & District 70 J-K78 71 J-K79
Two Hills & District 58 Y84
Vegreville Regional 57 Z82-83
Vermilion Heritage 59 A87
Veteran 72 J86-87
Viking Historical 66 B84
Wainwright & District 67 D87
Waterton Lakes Park Natural History 82 Z76
Westlock & District Historical 56 V77
Wetaskiwin & District 64 C78
YesterYear 71 K80-81

National Historic Sites

Athabasca Pass 60 F60-61
Banff Park Museum 69 N70
Bar U Ranch 75 R74-75
Cave & Basin 68 N69 69 N70
First Oil Well in Western Canada 82 Z76
Frog Lake Massacre 59 X-Y89
Henry House 60 C61
Howse Pass 68 K65-66
Jasper House 60 B61
Jasper Park Information Centre 60 D60-61
Rocky Mountain House 63 F-G72
Skoki Ski Lodge 68 L68
Sulphur Mountain Cosmic Ray Station 69 N70
Yellowhead Pass 60 C-D60

Oil Fields / Oil Sands

Athabasca Oil Sands 30 E84-85
Firebag Oil Sands Project Area 31 E87
Fort Hill Oil Sands 30 D85
Rainbow Oil Field 17 W59
Rainbow South Oil Field 16 X57
Red Earth Creek Oil Field 27 H70-71
Suncor Tar Sands Project Area 30 F85
Syncrude Tar Sands Project Area 30 F85
Zama Oil Field 9 T59-60

Points of Interest

1910 CPR Station Complex 70 M78
Agriculture Canada Onefour Research Substation 85 Z89
Alberta Birds of Prey Centre 83 V80-81
Alberta Central Railway 65 C-D79
Alberta Fairytale Grounds 56 Z75
Alberta Heritage Exposition Park 56 A78 64 B78
Andrew Interpretive Grain Elevator 57 X82
Barr Colony Heritage Cultural Centre 59 A90
Battle River (Fabyan) Railway Trestle 66 D86
Blackfoot Crossing Historical Park 77 P80
Boreal Centre for Bird Conservation 36 O71
Bow Island 84 U85-86
Bradshaw's Exotic Bird Farm 25 G62-63
Bruderheim Moravian Church (1895) 57 X80-81
Calaway Park 70 N74
Camp Wainwright (DND) 66 D-E86 67 D-E87
Canada'a Aviation Hall of Fame 64 C78
Canadian Forces Base Suffield 79 R87-88
Canadian Petroleum Discovery Centre 56 A77-78
CFB Cold Lake 49 U89
CFB Edmonton 56 Y78
Canadian National Historic Wind Power Centre 84 X86
Cluny Earthlodge Village 77 P80
Cochrane Ranche 69 W73-74
Cold Lake Air Weapons Range 49 Q87-90
Cultural Heritage Centre 56 Z75
Devonian Botanic Garden 56 A77
Diplomat Interpretive Centre 65 F82
Doug's Exotic Zoo Farm 64 F78
Ellis Bird Farm 64 F77
Em-Tee Town 63 C71-72
Fort George 59 X87
Fort Macleod 82 V78
Fort McMurray Oil Sands Discovery Centre 31 G-H86
Fort Normandeau 64 G76-77
Fort Whoop-Up 83 V80
Galt Historic Railway Park 83 W81
George Pegg Historic Garden 56 Y73
GuZoo Animal Farm 71 K79
Historic Fort Dunvegan 33 M60
Historic Main St. 64 F77
Historic Station & Grain Elevator 65 E80-81
Horseshoe Canyon Centre 71 M80
Innisfail Historical Village 70 H75-76
Jessie Lake Wetlands 59 V87-88
Jimmy Lake Range 49 R90
k.d. lang hometown 73 H87
Kimiwan Birdwalk and Interpretive Centre 34 N65
Kinosoo Totem Poles 49 U89-90
La Crete Mennonite Heritage Village 18 Y66
Lac Cardinal Pioneer Village 33 K62-63
Lac La Biche Mission 48 S83
Lesser Slave Lake Bird Observatory 36 O71
Medalta Clay Products Interpretive Centre 85 U88
Medicine River Wildlife Centre 69 H73-74
Millarville Racetrack 75 P74
Melsness Mercantile Historic Site 32 O57
Morrin Sod House & Historical Park 71 K80
Museum of Miniatures 82 Y77-78
Muskeg River Mine Project Area 30 D85
Nakoda Institute 69 N72-73
Newbrook Observatory 57 V80
Nordegg Interpretive Centre 62 F68
Northwest Mounted Police 1884 Barracks Historic Site 82 V78
Okotoks Erratic 75 Q75
Old Woman's Buffalo Jump 76 R76
Peter Fidler Statue 59 X87
Piikani Lodge Interpretive Centre 82 W76
Poplar Creek Wildlife Area 30 F85
Primrose Lake Evaluation Range 49 S90
Pysanka 58 Z83
Ram River Falls 68 H69
Ribstones Historic Site 66 C84
St. Bernard Mission Church (1901) 35 O67-68
St. Edmund's Church (1916) 71 H80-81
Sedgewick Archives & Gallery 66 D84-85
Shaftesbury Ferry 34 L63
Starship Enterprise FX6-1995-A 76 R78-79
Steen River Meteorite Impact Crater 10 R63
Tallcreek Raceway 65 F79
Tomkins Landing Ferry 18 Z64
Trek Station 76 R78-79
UFO Landing Pad 58 W-X86
Ukrainian Cultural Heritage Village 57 Z81
Wainwright Railway Preservation 67 D87
Western Heritage Centre 69 N73-74
Whitecourt Forest Interpretive Centre 55 W69
Whyte Museum of the Canadian Rockies 68 N69
World's Largest Dinosaur 71 L-M81
World's Largest Mallard Duck 57 X82
World's Largest Softball 67 E90
Yellowhead Raceway 53 A62-63

Provincial Historic Sites

Brooks Aqueduct 78 R84
Buckingham House 59 X87
Carmangay Tipi Rings 76 T78 77 T79
Father Lacombe Chapel 56 Y77-78
Frank Slide 81 W74-75
Head-Smashed-In Buffalo Jump 82 V77
Leitch Collieries 81 W74-75
St. Ann Ranch 71 J79
Stephansson House 64 G74
Stirling Agricultural Village 83 W81
Turner Valley Gas Plant 76 Q74-75
Victoria Settlement 57 W81-82

Skiing

Canada Olympic Park 70 N75
Canyon 64 G77
Castle Mountain 81 X74-75
Drayton Valley & Brazeau 63 B72
Drumheller Valley 71 M80
Fortress 75 P71
Grizzly Ridge 45 Q71
Gwynne Valley 65 C79
Hidden Valley 85 W89-90
Innisfail 70 H75
Kinosoo Ridge 49 U90
Lake Louise 68 M67-68
Little Smoky 34 O64 43 P64
Long Lake Ski Area 47 U81
Marmot Basin 60 D61
Medicine Lodge 64 F74
Misery Mountain 34 K63-64
Misty Ridge 46 U73
Mount Joy 67 B-C90
Mount Norquay 69 N70
Nakiska 75 O71
Nitehawk 42 R59
Pass Powder Keg 81 W74
Spring Lake 32 O56
Sunshine Village 74 O69
Swan Ridge 45 S70
Tawatinaw Valley 56 V78
Vista Ridge 30 G85
Whispering Pines 24 H57
Whitecourt 55 W69

Wildlife Areas

Blue Quills National 58 W85
CFB Suffield National Wildlife Area 79 Q89 R88-89 S87-88
Meanook National 47 T79
Siffleur Provincial 68 J67
Spiers Lake National 71 J82
White Goat Provincial 61 G65

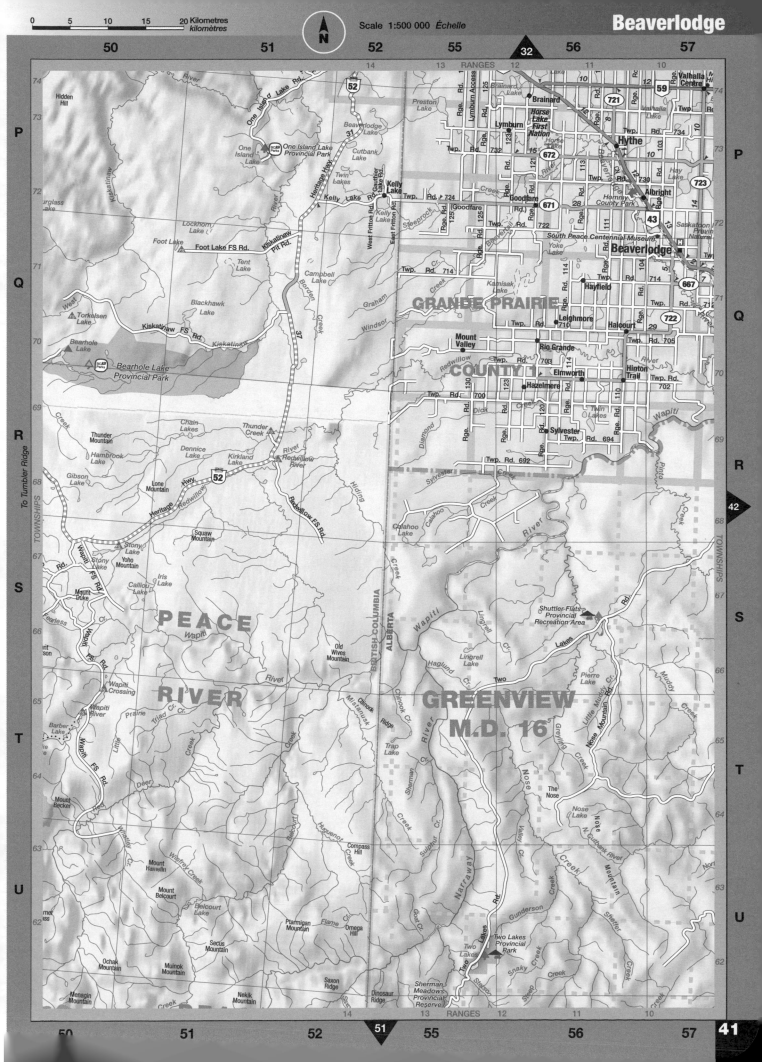

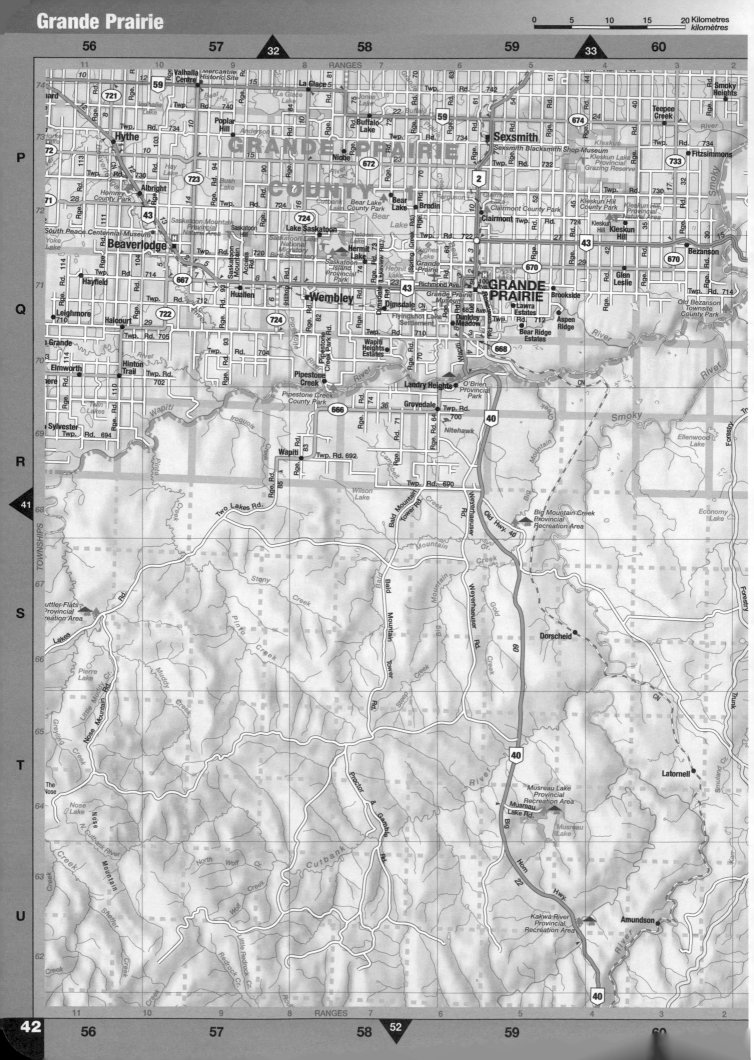

0 5 10 15 20 Kilometres
kilomètres

56 57 32 58 59 33 60

11 10 Rge. 9 RANGES 8 7 6 5 4 3 2

74

P

Valhalla Mercantile Centre
Historic Site
721 Valhalla Lake 59
Valhalla
Rge. Rd. 740 La Glace 5
73 Hythe 734 Poplar Hill La Glace La Glace Lake
Twp. Rd. 103 Anderson Niobe Jones Lake 22 Buffalo 59
72 72 Albright Hay Lake GRANDE PRAIRIE 59
723 Bush Lake 672 Sexsmith
71 71 Beaverlodge COUNTY Sexsmith Blacksmith Shop Museum 733 Fitzsimmons
South Peace Centennial Museum Saskatoon Mountain 724 Bear Bear Lake Bredin Kleskun Lake Smoky
43 Provincial Nature Area Saskatoon Lake County Park Clairmont County Park Provincial Grazing Reserve Teepee Creek

Q

667 Hayfield Lake Saskatoon 724 Clairmont 43 Kleskun Hill Bezanson
Leighmore Halcourt 722 Huallen Saskatoon Island Provincial Park Hermit Lake 43 Grande Prairie Museum GRANDE PRAIRIE 670 Glen Leslie 670
Grande Wembley 724 Dimsdale Lawra Estates Brookside
Elmworth Hinton Trail Pipestone Creek Dunkley Meadow Aspen Ridge Old Bezanson Townsite County Park
Twin Lakes Wapiti Heights Estates Bear Ridge Estates 668

R

Sylvester 666 Landry Heights O'Brien Provincial Park Smoky
41 Wapiti Grovedale 40 Big Mountain Creek Provincial Recreation Area Economy Lake
Nitehawk Ellenwood Lake

S

Cuttler Flats Provincial Recreation Area Stony Creek Dorscheid

T

40 Latornell
Musreau Lake Provincial Recreation Area

U

40 Kakwa River Provincial Recreation Area Amundson

56 57 58 52 59 60

Scale 1:500 000 *Échelle*

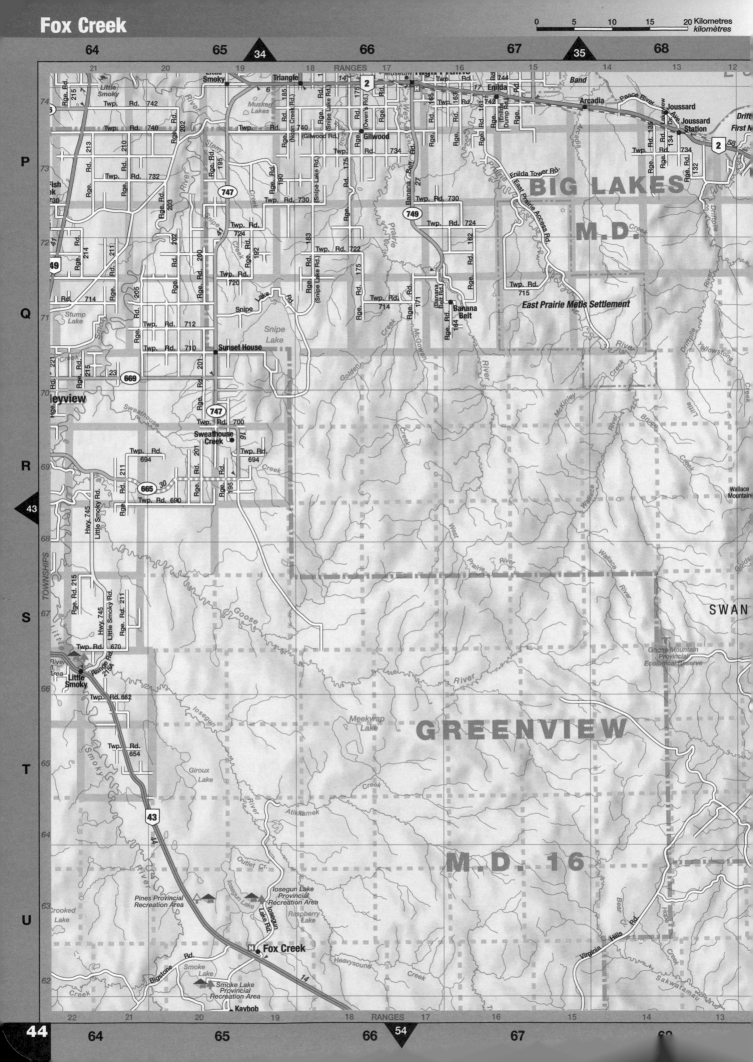

Kilometres
kilomètres
0 5 10 15 20

64 **34** 65 66 **35** 67 68

RANGES

21 20 19 18 17 16 15 14 13 12

P

Little Smoky
Rge. Rd. 215
Rge. Rd. 215
Twp. Rd. 742
Twp. Rd. 740
Rge. Rd. 213
Rge. Rd. 210
Twp. Rd. 732
Rge. Rd. 214
Rge. Rd. 211
Fish ek 730
Rge. Rd.
749

Little Smoky
Triangle
Muskeg Lakes
Museum
High Plains Twp.
Enilda
744
Arcadia
Peace River
Band
Joussard
Joussard Station
Drift First N
2

BIG LAKES

M.D.

East Prairie Metis Settlement

Q

Stump Lake
Rge. Rd. 221
Rge. Rd. 215
Rge. 205
Twp. Rd. 712
Twp. Rd. 710
Rge. Rd. 714
669
Snipe
Snipe Lake
Sunset House
Banana Belt

eyview

R

43

Sweathouse Creek
Sweathouse Creek
747
Twp. Rd. 700
Twp. Rd. 694
Rge. Rd. 211
665
Twp. Rd. 690
Twp. Rd. 694

Wallace Mountain

S

TOWNSHIPS

Hwy. 745
Little Smoky Rd.
Rge. Rd. 215
Hwy. 745
Little Smoky Rd.
Rge. Rd. 211
Twp. Rd. 670
Range Rd. 214
Little Smoky
Twp. Rd. 662

Goose

SWAN

Goose Mountain Provincial Ecological Reserve

T

Iosegun
Twp. Rd. 654
Giroux Lake

River

Meekwap Lake
Creek

GREENVIEW

43

U

Crooked Lake
Pines Provincial Recreation Area
Iosegun Lake
Iosegun Lake Provincial Recreation Area
Raspberry Lake
Outlet Cr.

M.D. 16

Bear Cr. Rd.
Virginia Hills

Smoke Lake
Smoke Lake Provincial Recreation Area
Fox Creek
Bigstone Rd.
Kaybob
Heavysoune Creek
Sakwatamau

RANGES

22 21 20 19 18 17 16 15 14 13

64 65 66 **54** 67 68

Scale 1:500 000 *Échelle*

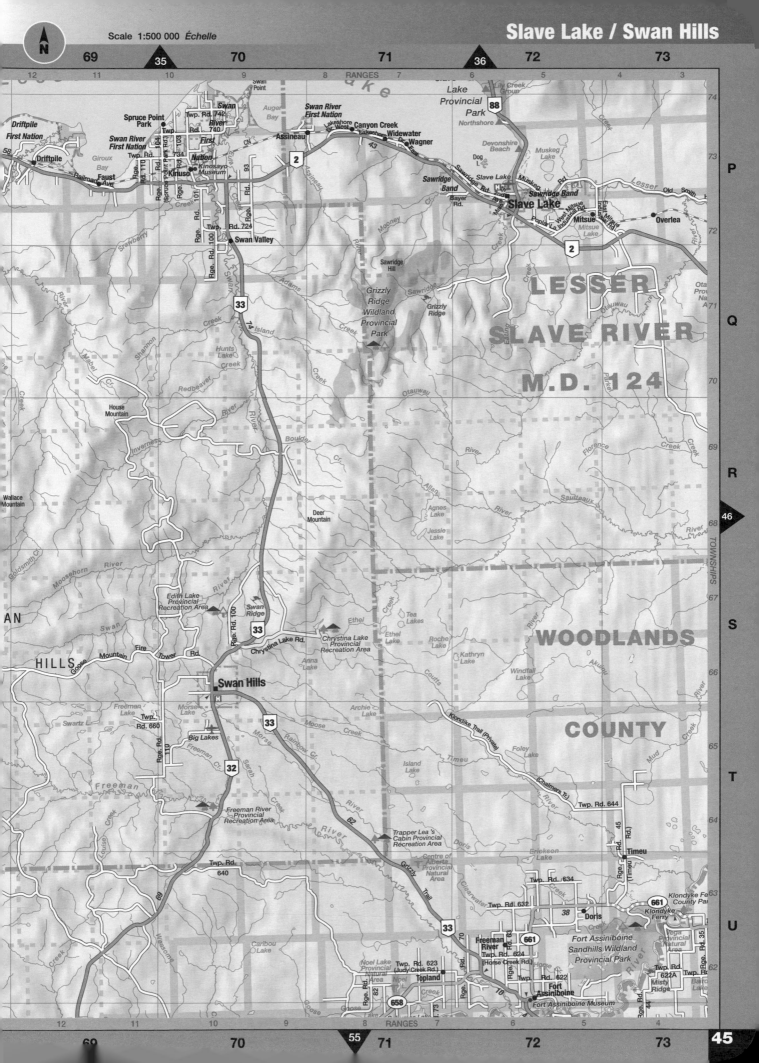

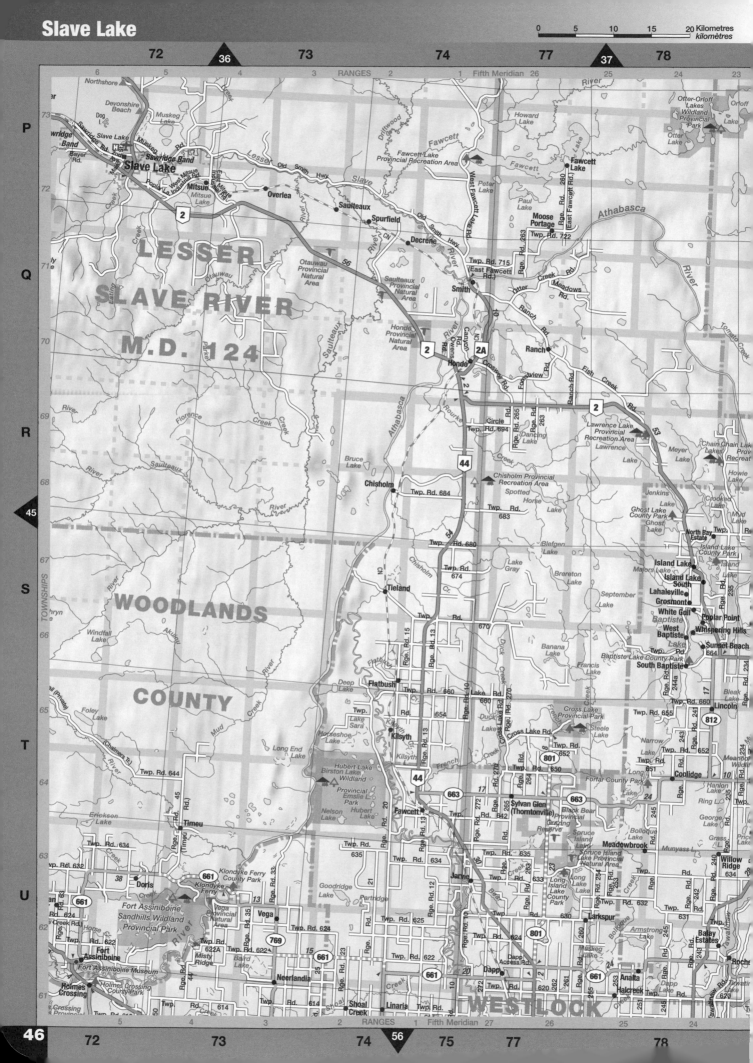

0   5   10   15   20 Kilometres
kilomètres

72   36   73   74   77   37   78

P   Q   R   S   T   U

RANGES   Fifth Meridian

LESSER
SLAVE RIVER
M.D. 124

WOODLANDS

COUNTY

Northshore
Devonshire Beach
Slave Lake
Sawridge Band
Mitsue
Overlea
Saulteaux
Spurfield
Decrene
Smith
Hondo
Ranch
Fawcett Lake
Moose Portage
Chisholm
Tieland
Flatbush
Kilsyth
Fawcett
Doris
Vega
Neerlandia
Fort Assiniboine
Holmes Crossing
Timeu
Jarvie
Sylvan Glen (Thorntonville)
Larkspur
Dapp
Linaria
Shoal Creek

Island Lake
Island Lake South
Lahaleville
Grosmont
White Gull
West Baptiste
South Baptiste
Poplar Point
Whispering Hills
Sunset Beach
Lincoln
Coolidge
Meadowbrook
Willow Ridge
Balay Estates
Analta
Halcreek

WESTLOCK

RANGES   Fifth Meridian

Scale 1:500 000 *Échelle*

N

OPPORTUNITY M.D. 17

LAC LA BICHE COUNTY

ATHABASCA COUNTY 12

SMOKY LAKE COUNTY

Calling Lake

Calling Lake Provincial Park

Bigstone Cree Nation

Calling Lake

Calling River

Wandering River

Breynat

Amesbury

Avenir

La Biche River Wildland Provincial Park

Poachers' Landing Provincial Recreation Area

Chain Lakes (Lower) Provincial Recreation Area

Deep Creek

Pleasant View

Richmond Park

Big Coulee

Sawdy

Jumping Deer Estate

Deer Ridge Estate

Athabasca Landing Settlement

Athabasca

Athabascan Acres

Century Estates

Colinton

Meanook

Perryvale

Mystic Meadows

Rochester

O'Morrow

Spruce Valley

Grassland

Atmore

Plamondon

Bayview Beach

Poplar Point

Lac La Biche Mission

Old Mission

Egg Lake

Donatville

Amber Valley

Paxson

Kinikinik

Boyle

Blue Heron Estate

Paradise Valley

Pickeral Point

Perch Cove Estates

North Skeleton Beach Estates

Mewatha Beach

Pelican Beach

Bondiss

Golden Nodding Acres

Caslan

Noral

Hylo

Venice

Christy

Ellscott

Stronach Lake

Buffalo Lake Metis Settlement

Alpen

Alpen Siding

Danube

Newbrook

Newbrook Observatory

Kikino

Kikino Metis Settlement

Kikino Lone Pine

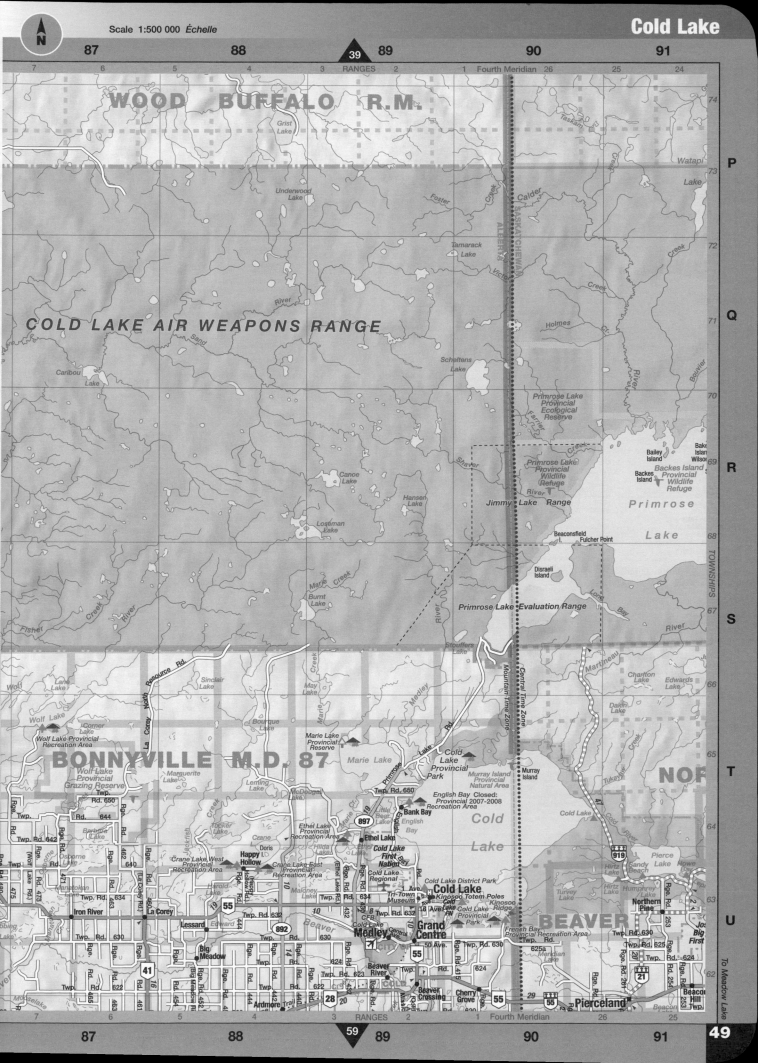

N

WOOD BUFFALO R.M.

Grist Lake

COLD LAKE AIR WEAPONS RANGE

Underwood Lake

Tamarack Lake

Foster Creek

Calder Creek

Watapi Lake

Taskan Creek

Victoria Creek

Holmes Cr.

Scheltens Lake

Caribou Lake

Canoe Lake

Loseman Lake

Hansen Lake

Primrose Lake Provincial Ecological Reserve

Bailey Island

Backes Island

Backes Island Provincial Wildlife Refuge

Primrose Lake Provincial Wildlife Refuge

Primrose Lake

Jimmy Lake Range

Beaconsfield

Fulcher Point

Disraeli Island

Long Bay

Primrose Lake Evaluation Range

Burnt Lake

Marie Creek

Stouffers Lake

Martineau River

Charlton Lake

Edwards Lake

Dakin Lake

Fisher Creek River

Sinclair Lake

May Lake

Medley Lake Rd.

Central Time Zone

Mountain Time Zone

Lane Lake

Wolf Lake

Corner Lake

Wolf Lake Provincial Recreation Area

BONNYVILLE M.D. 87

Wolf Lake Provincial Grazing Reserve

Marguerite Lake

Bourque Lake

Leming Lake

McDougal Lake

Marie Lake Provincial Reserve

Marie Lake

Cold Lake Provincial Park

Murray Island Provincial Natural Area

Murray Island

NOR

Twp. Rd. 650

Twp. Rd. 650

Cold Lake

Pierce Lake

Sandy Beach

Howe Bay

Hirtz Lake

Humphrey Lake

Northern Pine

Turvey Lake

Hirtz Lake

Tucker Lake

Crane Lake

Doris Lake

Hilda Lake

Ethel Lake

English Bay

Little Bear Lake

Bank Bay

English Bay Closed: Provincial 2007-2008 Recreation Area

Crane Lake West Provincial Recreation Area

Happy Hollow

Crane Lake East Provincial Recreation Area

Ethel Lake Provincial Recreation Area

Maloney Lake

Cold Lake First Nation

Cold Lake Regional

Kinosoo Totem Poles

Cold Lake District Park

Cold Lake

Cold Lake Provincial Park

BEAVER

Iron River

La Corey

Lessard

Harold Lake

Edward

Tri-Town Museum

Cold Lake FN

Kinosoo Ridge

French Bay Provincial Recreation Area

Meridian Lake

Jos Big First

Big Meadow

Medley

Grand Centre

50 Ave.

Twp. Rd. 630

Twp. Rd. 630

Beaver River

Beaver Crossing

Cherry Grove

Ardmore Trail

Pierceland

Beacon Hill Twp.

To Meadow Lake

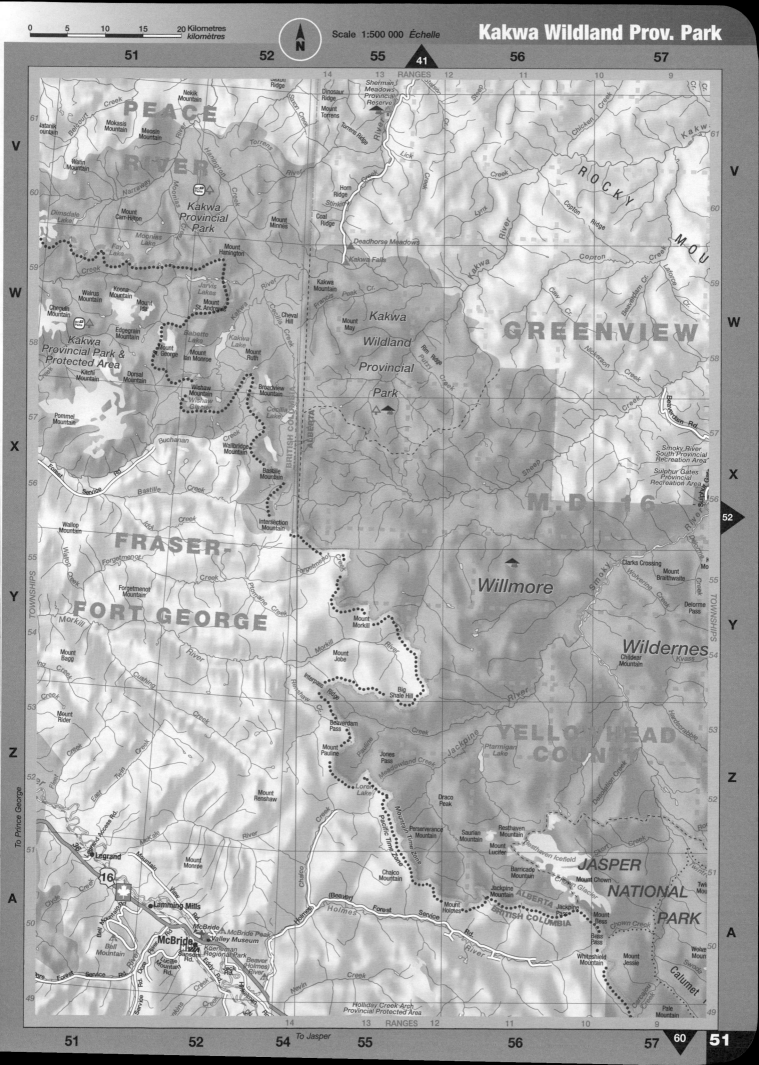

Scale 1:500 000 *Échelle*

0 5 10 15 20 Kilometres / kilomètres

N

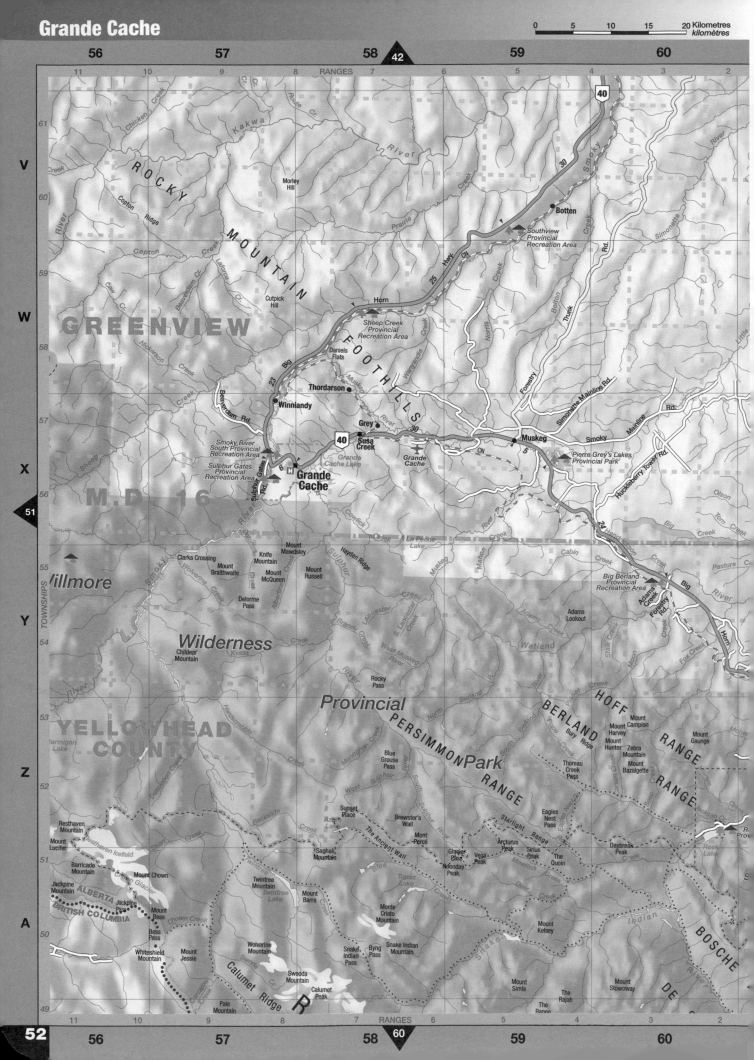

0 5 10 15 20 Kilometres
kilomètres

56 **57** **58** **42** **59** **60**

11 10 9 8 RANGES 7 6 5 4 3 2

V

61

ROCKY

Morley
Hill

W

60

Copton
Ridge

Kakwa

River

River

Botten

Southview
Provincial
Recreation
Area

59

Copton

Creek

MOUNTAIN

Cutpick
Hill

Hwy.

30

Smoky

Rd.

W

58

GREENVIEW

Nickerson

Beaverdam Cr.

Clay Cr.

Laforce Cr.

Creek

Horn

Sheep Creek
Provincial
Recreation Area

FOOTHILLS

Daniels
Flats

Big

25

Wanyandie

Creek

Norris

Creek

Bolton

Trunk

Simonette

Forestry

Simonette Mainline Rd.

Rd.

X

57

Sheep

Creek

Beaverdam Rd.

23

Thordarson

Winniandy

River

Grey

Susa
Creek

30

40

Muskeg

5

Smoky

Mainline

Rd.

Little

51

X

56

M.D. 16

Smoky River
South Provincial
Recreation Area

Sulphur Gates
Provincial
Recreation Area

Sulphur Gates Rd.

River

40

Grande
Cache Lake

H

Grande
Cache

Grande
Cache

CN

Pierre Grey's Lakes
Provincial Park

Huckleberry Tower Rd.

Olson

Creek

Tom Creek

Y

55

Willmore

Clarks Crossing

Mount
Braithwaite

Knife
Mountain

Mount
McQueen

Mount
Mawdsley

Mount
Russell

Hayden Ridge

Sulphur

Cowlick

Creek

La Peche
Lake

Mahon

River

Muskeg

Creek

Cabin

Creek

24

Henderson

Big

Creek

Creek

Big Berland
Provincial
Recreation Area

Adams
Creek

Big

Forestry
Rd.

Pasture

River

54

Delorme
Pass

Wolverine

Albertine

Creek

Creek

Wilderness

Childear
Mountain

Kvass

Creek

Lancaster

St. Lancaster
Creek

Brandy

Creek

West Muskeg

River

Berland

Adams
Creek

Wetland

Adams
Lookout

Stalk Creek

Moon

Creek

Fox Creek

Horn

53

Ptarmigan
Lake

YELLOWHEAD

COUNTY

Hardscrabble

Creek

Smoky

Rocky
Pass

River

North

Berland

River

Persimmon

Pope

Creek

Creek

BERLAND

Mount
Harvey

Mount
Hunter

Mount
Campion

Bury Ridge

Thoreau
Creek
Pass

HOFF

Mount
Gaunge

RANGE

Z

52

Manoghen Creek

West

Sulphur

South

Provincial

PERSIMMON

Blue
Grouse
Pass

Sulphur

South

River

Creek

Berland

Zebra
Mountain

Mount
Bazalgette

RANGE

Rockslide

Creek

Dawson Creek

River

Park

RANGE

Sunset
Place

Azure
Lake

Brewster's
Wall

Mont
Percé

The Ancient Wall

Blue

Sulphur

River

Starlight
Range

Glacier
Pass

Vega
Peak

Noonday
Peak

Arcturus
Peak

Sirius
Peak

Eagles
Nest Pass

Eagles Nest

The
Quoin

Mowitch Creek

Daybreak
Peak

Rock
Prov

51

Resthaven
Mountain

Mount
Lucifer

Resthaven Icefield

Barricade
Mountain

Chown Glacier

Mount Chown

ALBERTA

BRITISH COLUMBIA

Jackpine
Pass

Twintree
Mountain

Twintree
Lake

Saghall
Mountain

Mont
Barra

Topaz

Creek

Indian

River

Creek

A

50

Jackpine
Mountain

Mount
Bess

Bess
Pass

Chown Creek

Mount
Cristo
Mountain

Monte
Cristo
Mountain

Snake Indian

River

Mount
Kelsey

Mount
Simla

BOSCHE

Indian

River

DE

Whiteshield
Mountain

Mount
Jessie

Wolverine
Mountain

Swoda Cr.

Swooda
Mountain

Snake
Indian
Pass

Byng
Pass

Snake Indian
Mountain

Mount
Stowoway

The
Rajah

Mobrer

49

Pale
Mountain

Calumet
Peak

Calumet Ridge

R

The
Range

52

11 10 9 8 RANGES 7 6 5 4 3 2

TOWNSHIPS

56 **57** **58** **60** **59** **60**

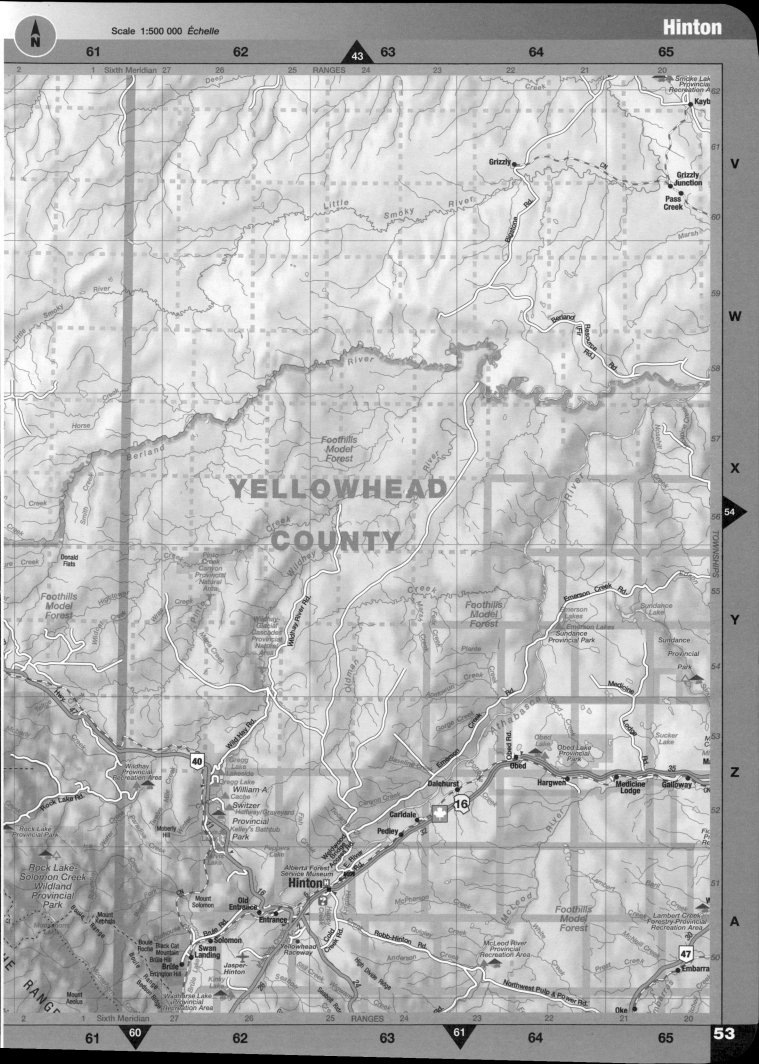

Scale 1:500 000 *Échelle*

N

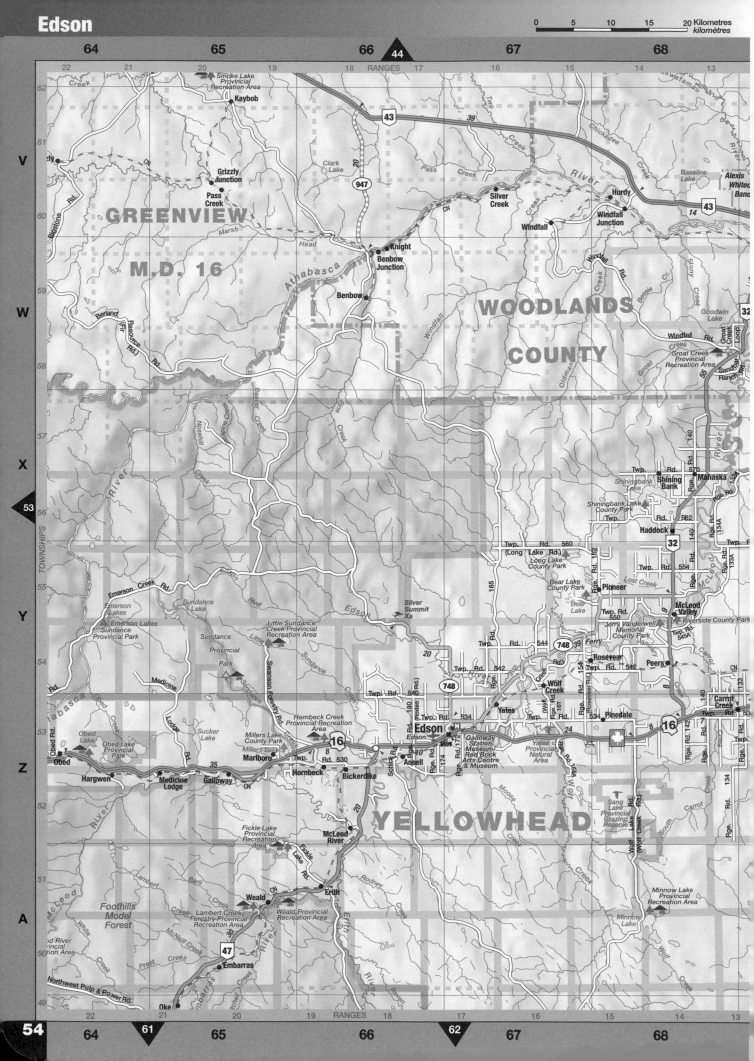

20 Kilometres
kilomètres

0   5   10   15   20

Top margin
64   65   66   **44**   67   68

RANGES

22 21 20 19 18 17 16 15 14 13

62

Left margin labels
V
W
X
Y
Z
A

TOWNSHIPS

61
60
59
58
57
56 **53**
55
54
53
52
51
49

Place names and features

Smoke Lake Provincial Recreation Area

Kaybob

Berdy

GREENVIEW

Grizzly Junction

Pass Creek

M.D. 16

Berland (Fir Resource Rd.)

Clark Lake

947

Head

Marsh

Athabasca

Silver Creek

Windfall

Hurdy

Windfall Junction

43

14   43

32

Knight

Benbow Junction

Benbow

WOODLANDS

COUNTY

Goodwin Lake

Windfall

Groat Creek Provincial Recreation Area

Sandstone Ranch

Athabasca River

Nosehill Creek

Beaver Creek

Pine Creek

Windfall Creek

Oldman Creek

Groat Creek

Bessie Cr.

Stony Creek

Baseline Lake

Alexis Whitec Band

Shiningbank Lake

Shining Bank

Mahaska

570

140

Shiningbank Lake County Park

562

Haddock

32

134A

133A

Emerson Creek Rd.

Emerson Lakes

Emerson Lakes Sundance Provincial Park

Sundance Lake

Sundance River

Little Sundance Creek Provincial Recreation Area

Silver Summit Xa

Edson River

Twp. Rd. 560

(Long Lake Rd.)
Long Lake County Park

Bear Lake County Park

Pioneer

Bear Lake

McLeod Valley

Riverside County Park

Jerry Vandenwell Memorial County Park

550

545A

165

Twp. Rd. 554

Twp. Rd. 550

McLeod River

748

39

Ferry

Rosevear

Peers

133

CN

Sundance Provincial Park

Medicine

Sundance Provincial Park

Swanson Forestry Rd.

Little Sundance Creek

Hornbeck Creek Provincial Recreation Area

Millers Lake County Park

Millers Lake

Twp. Rd. 544

Twp. Rd. 542

748

Twp. Rd. 542

Wolf Creek

Pinedale

Carrot Creek

Athabasca River

Obed Lake

Obed Lake Provincial Park

Obed Rd.

Obed

Hargwen

Medicine Lodge

Galloway

Lodge Rd.

Sucker Lake

Marlboro

Twp. Rd. 530

Hornbeck

Bickerdike

16

8

35

1

20

Schick Rd.

Ansell

Edson

Yates

748

Twp. Rd. 540

Twp. Rd. 542

Twp. Rd. 544

Twp. Rd. 534

540

534

Galloway Station Museum, Red Brick Arts Centre & Museum

VIA

Yates Creek Provincial Natural Area

24

16

Rge. Rd. 142

Rge. Rd. 134

CN

Moose Creek

Sang Lake Provincial Grazing Reserve

YELLOWHEAD

Fickle Lake Provincial Recreation Area

McLeod River

Fickle Lake Rd.

Weald

Weald Provincial Recreation Area

Erith

Rodney Creek

Minnow Lake Provincial Recreation Area

Minnow Lake

Foothills Model Forest

Lambert Creek

Beril Creek

McNeill Creek

Lambert Creek Forestry Provincial Recreation Area

47

Embarras

Oke

Northwest Pulp & Power Rd.

Embarras River

Prest Creek

White Creek

McLeod River

...d River ...vincial ...ction Area

Bottom margin
54   64   **61**   65   66   **62**   67   68

RANGES

22 21 20 19 18 17 16 15 14 13

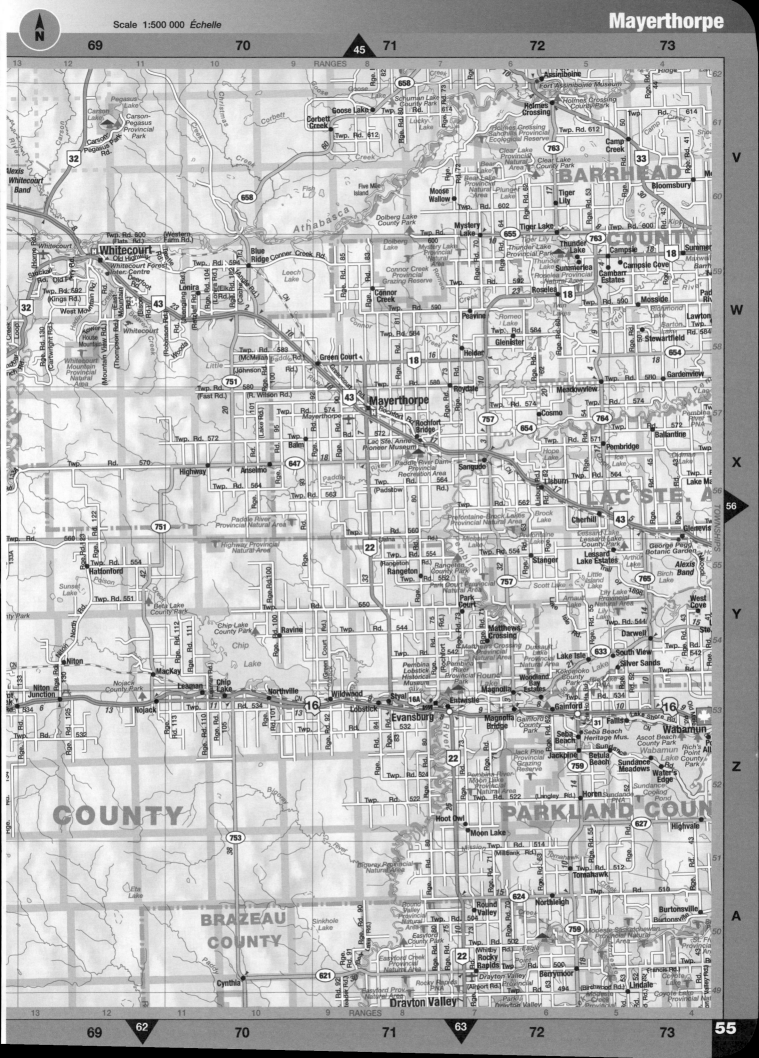

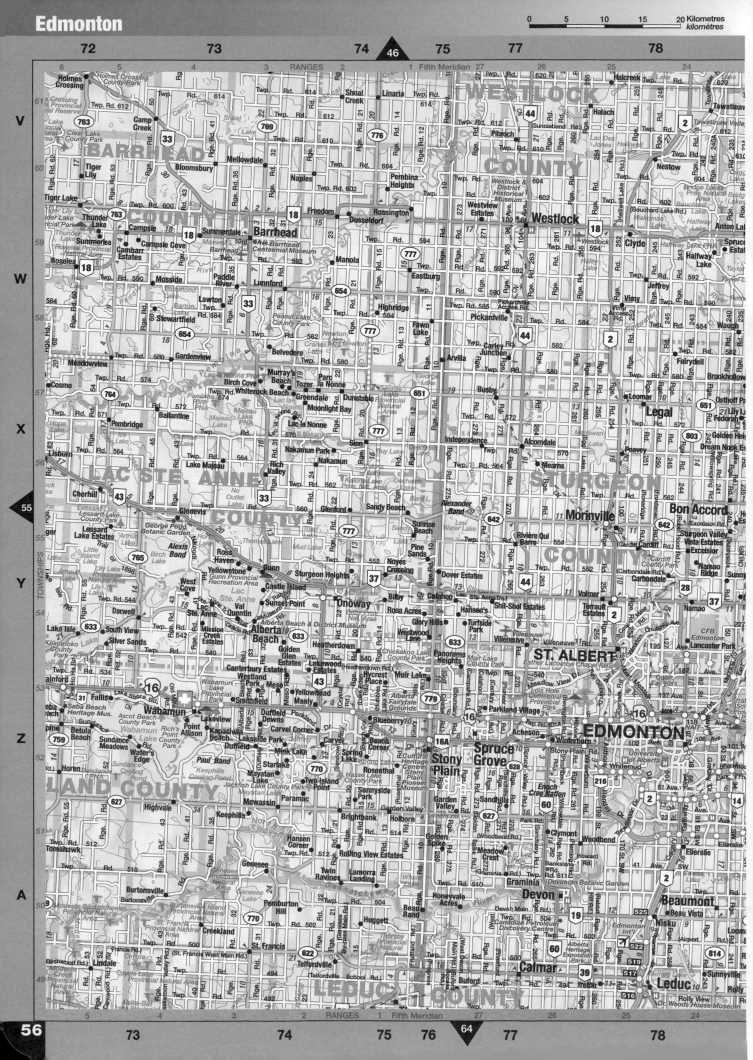

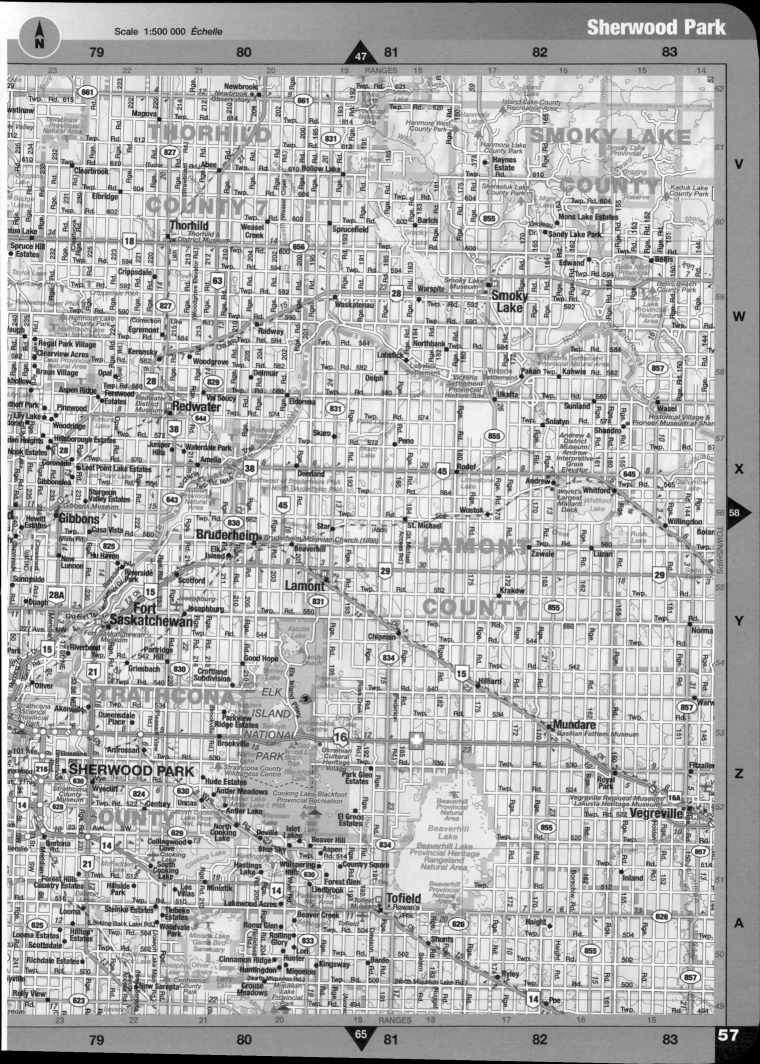

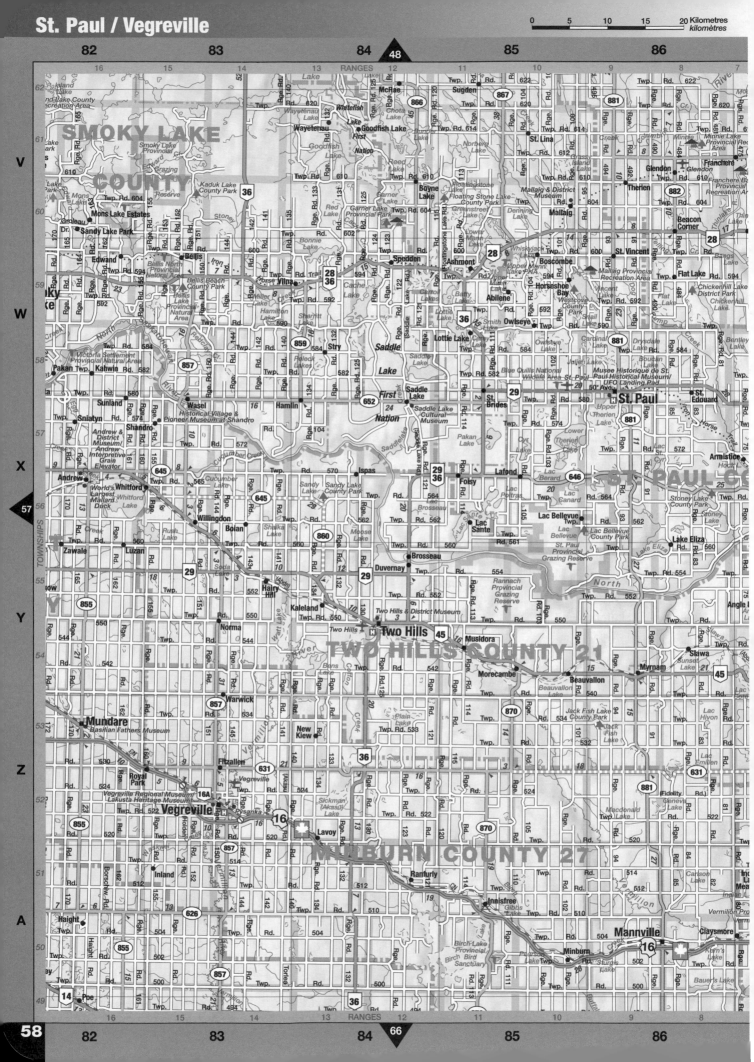

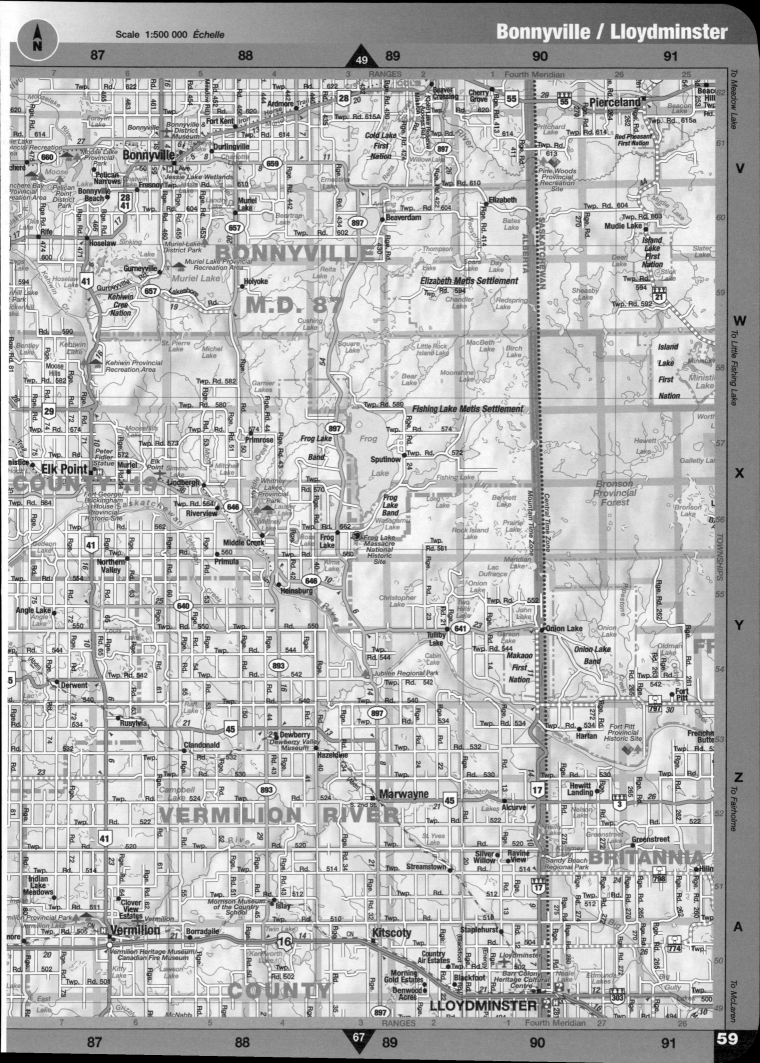

Scale 1:500 000 Échelle

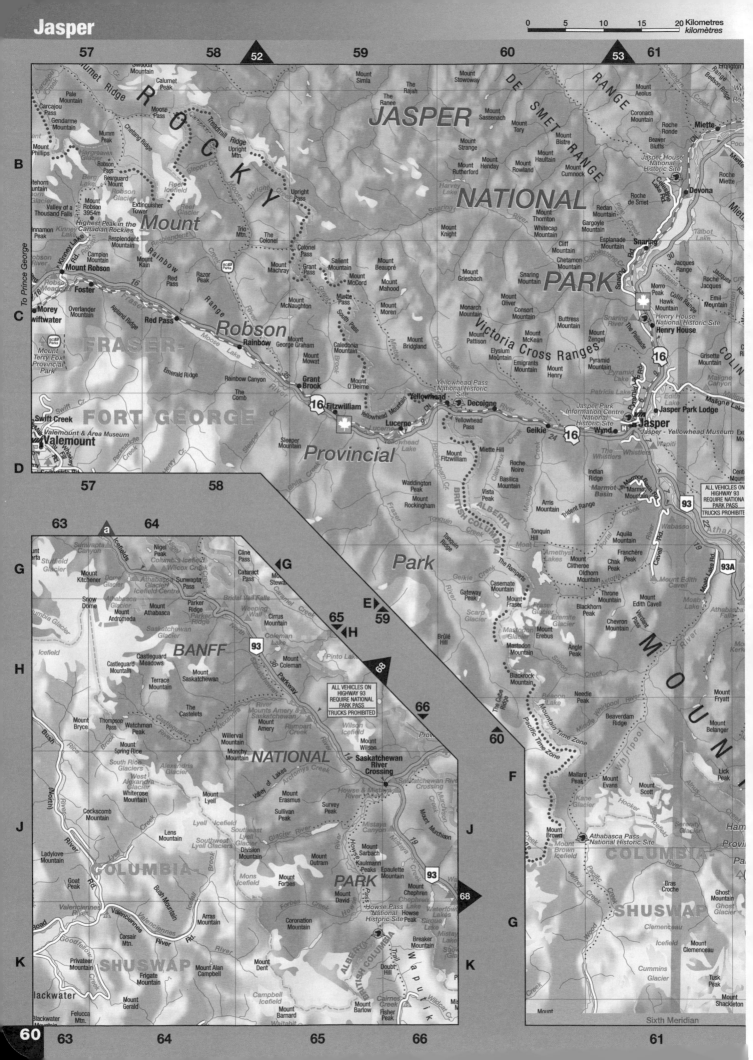

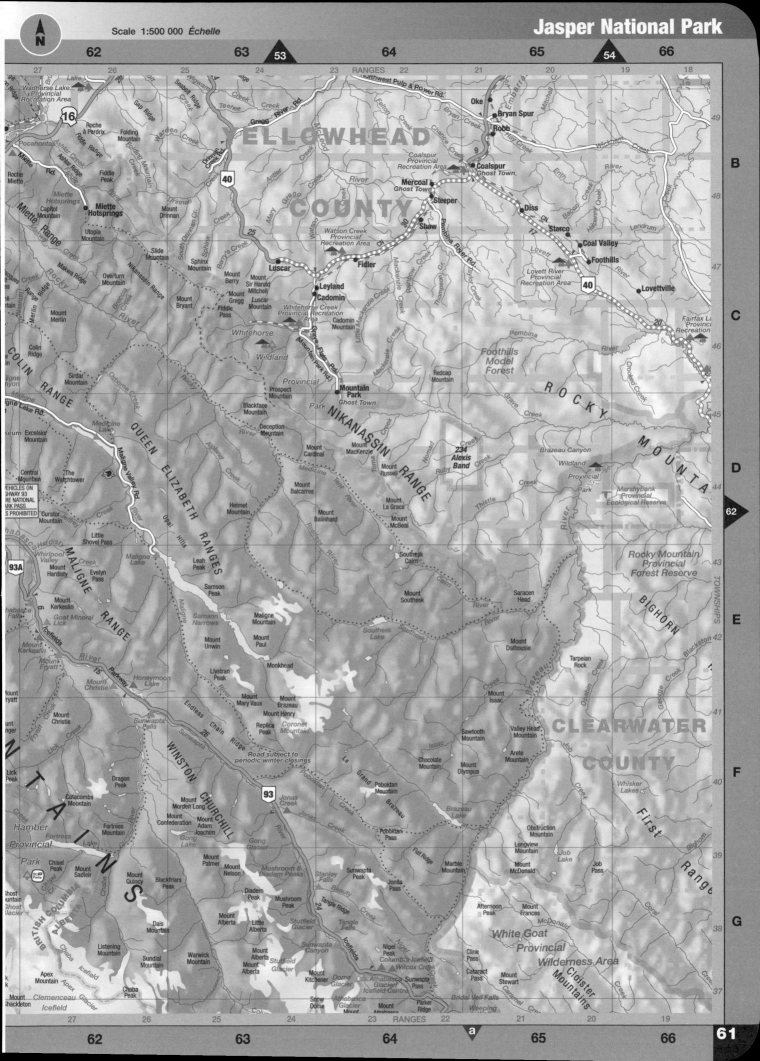

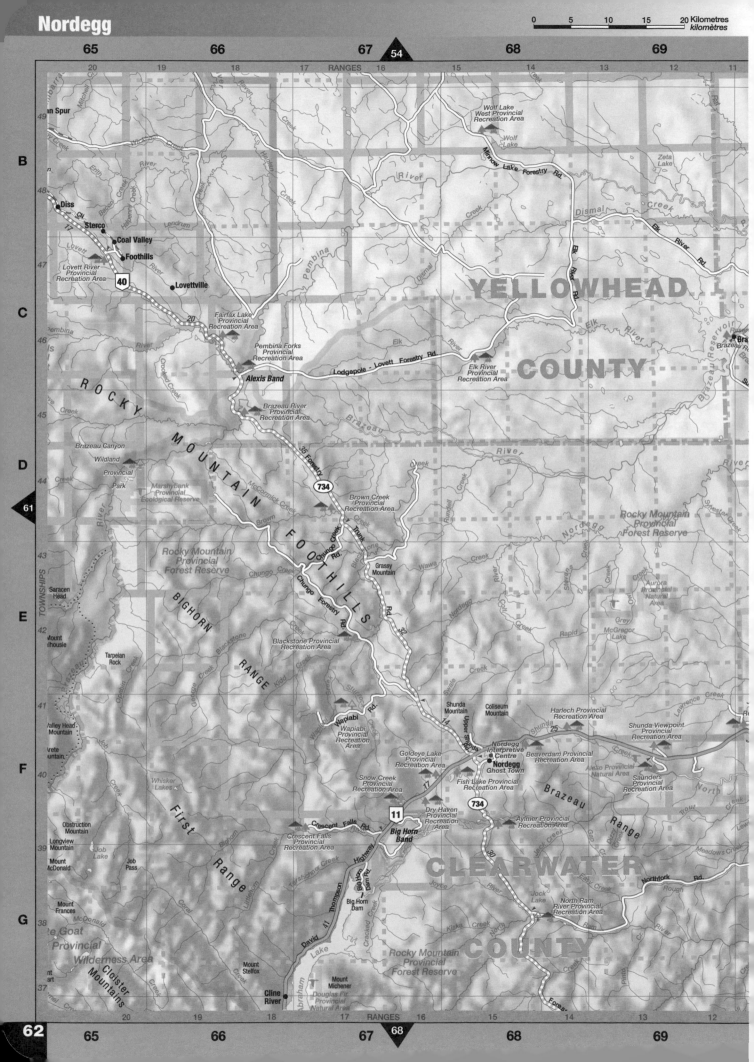

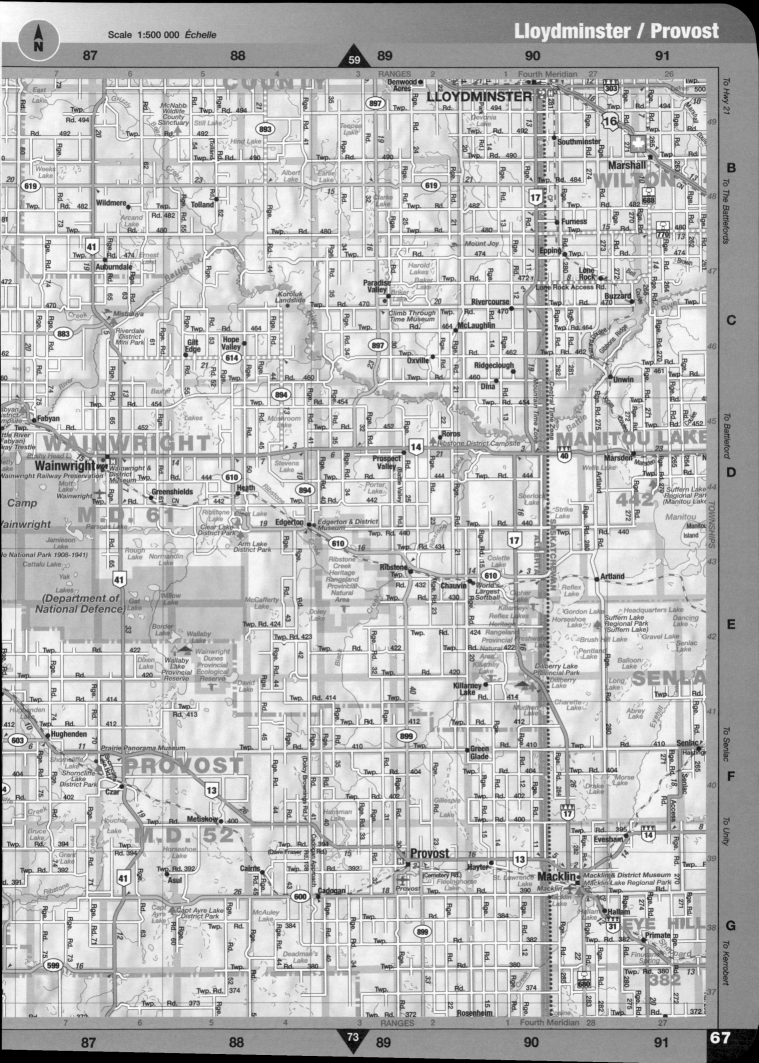

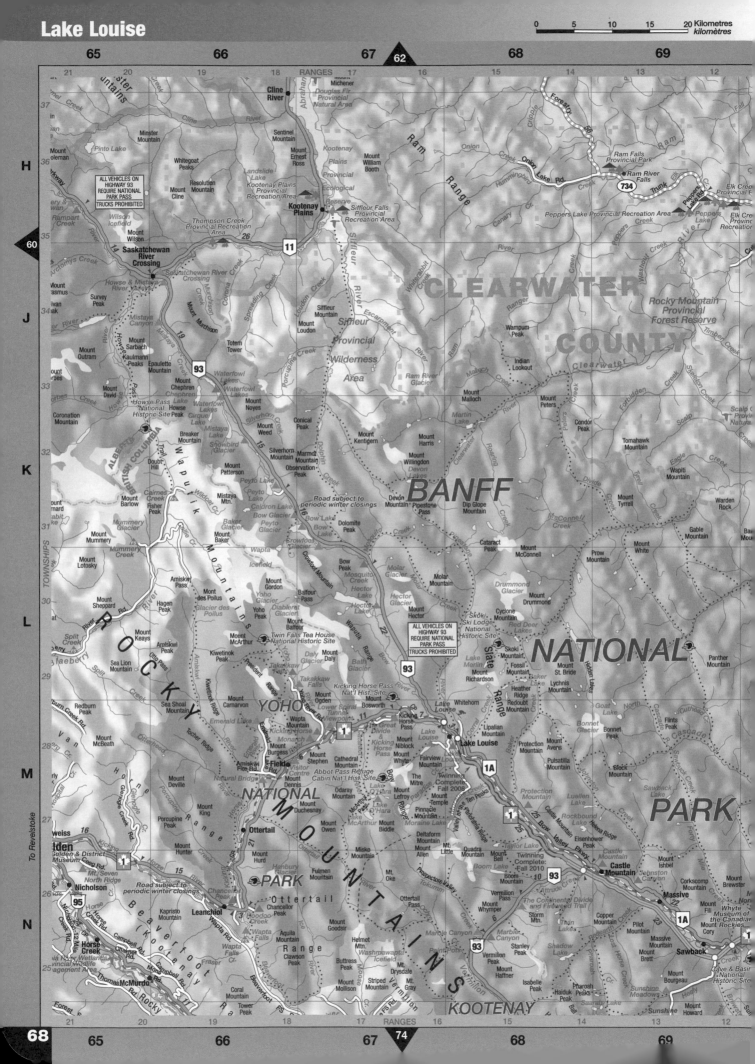

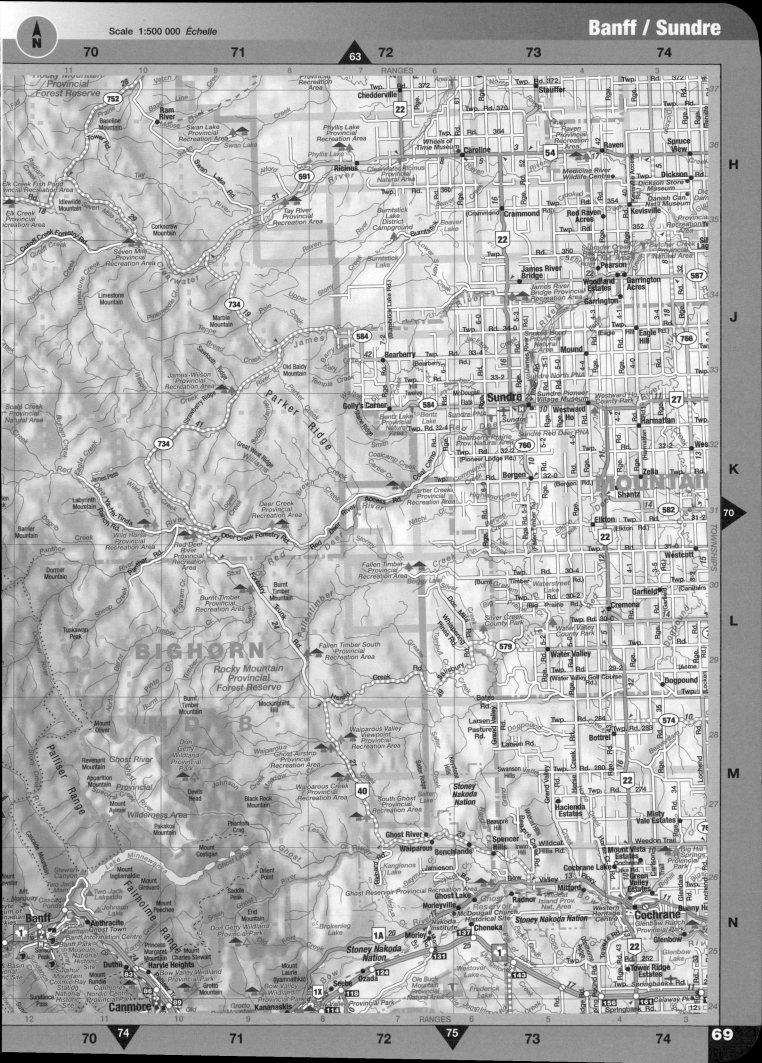

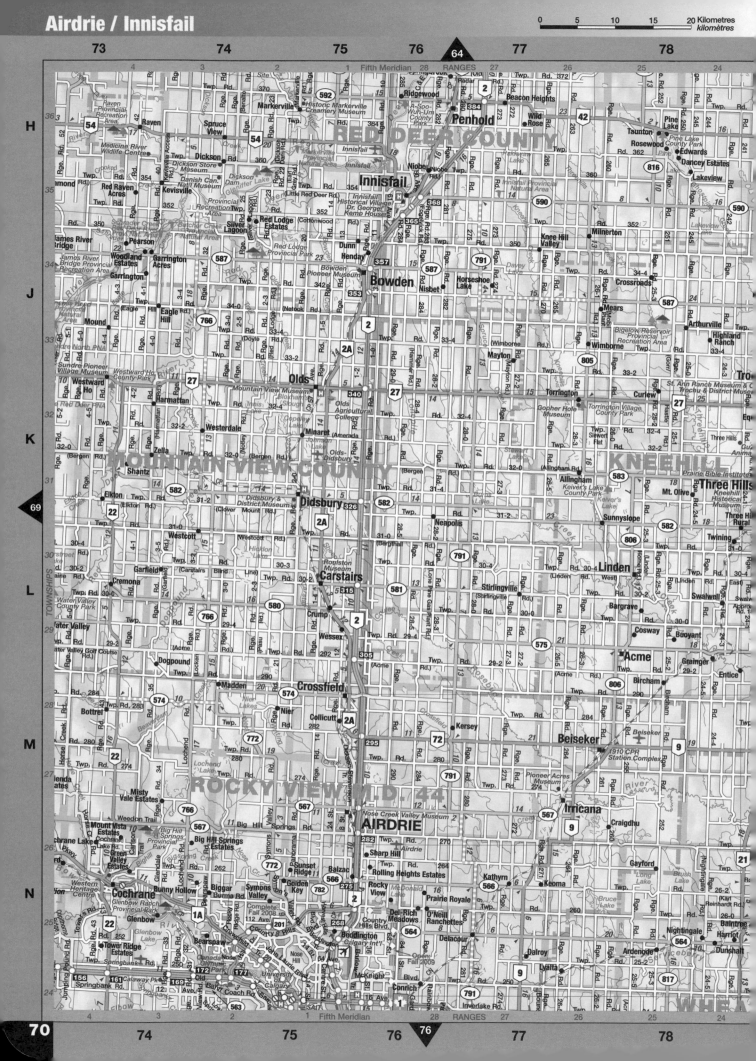

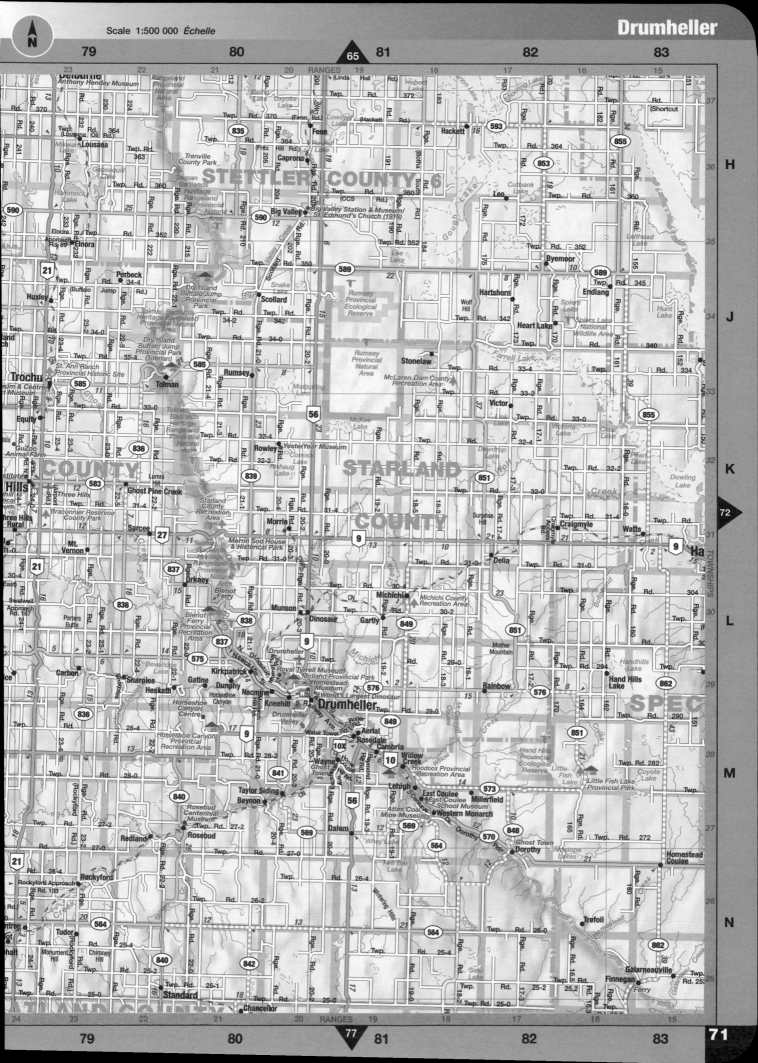

Kilometres
0   5   10   15   20 Kilometres
kilomètres

PAINTEARTH
COUNTY 18

SPECIAL AREA No. 2

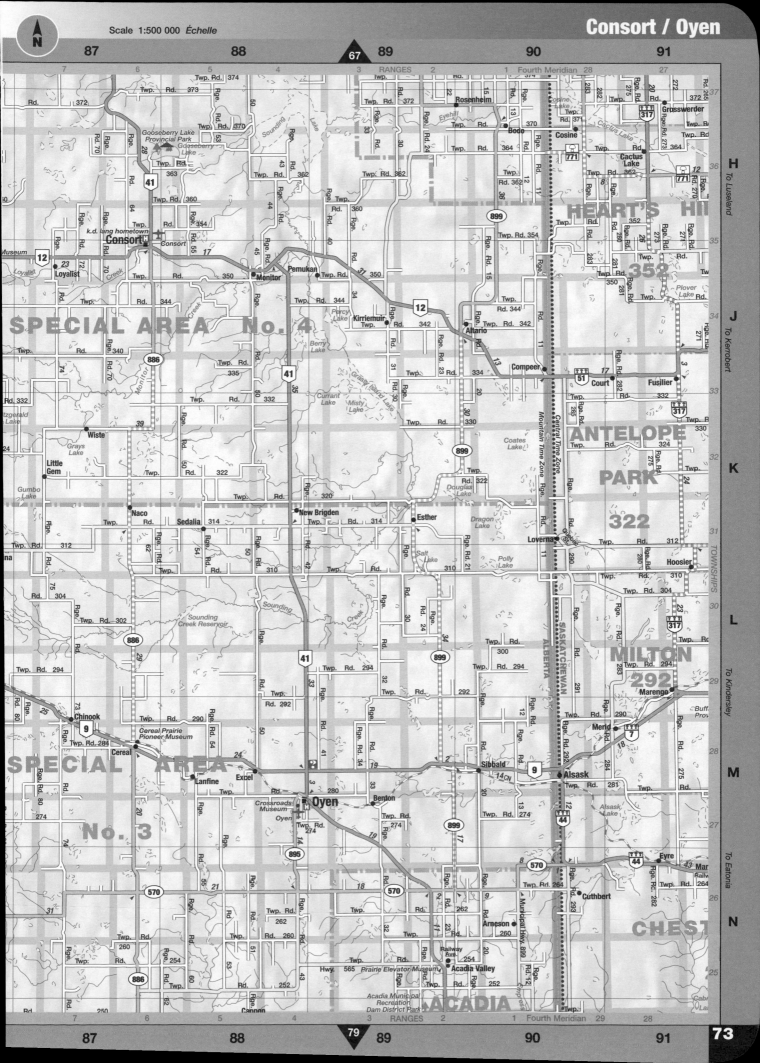

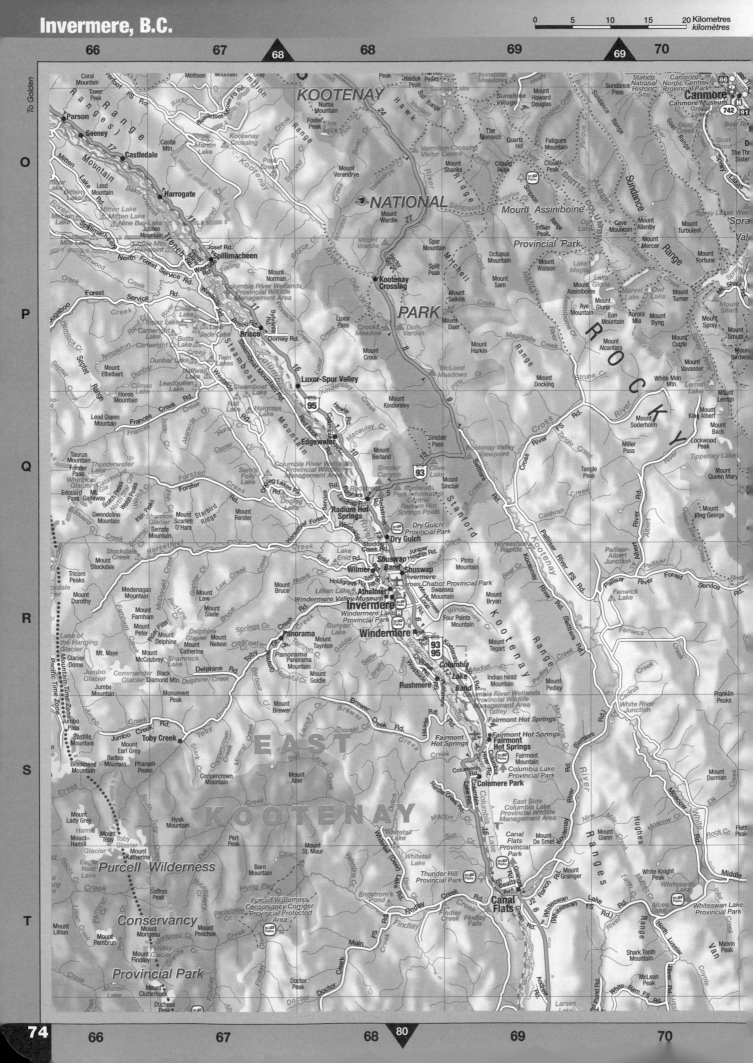

20 Kilometres
kilomètres

0 5 10 15

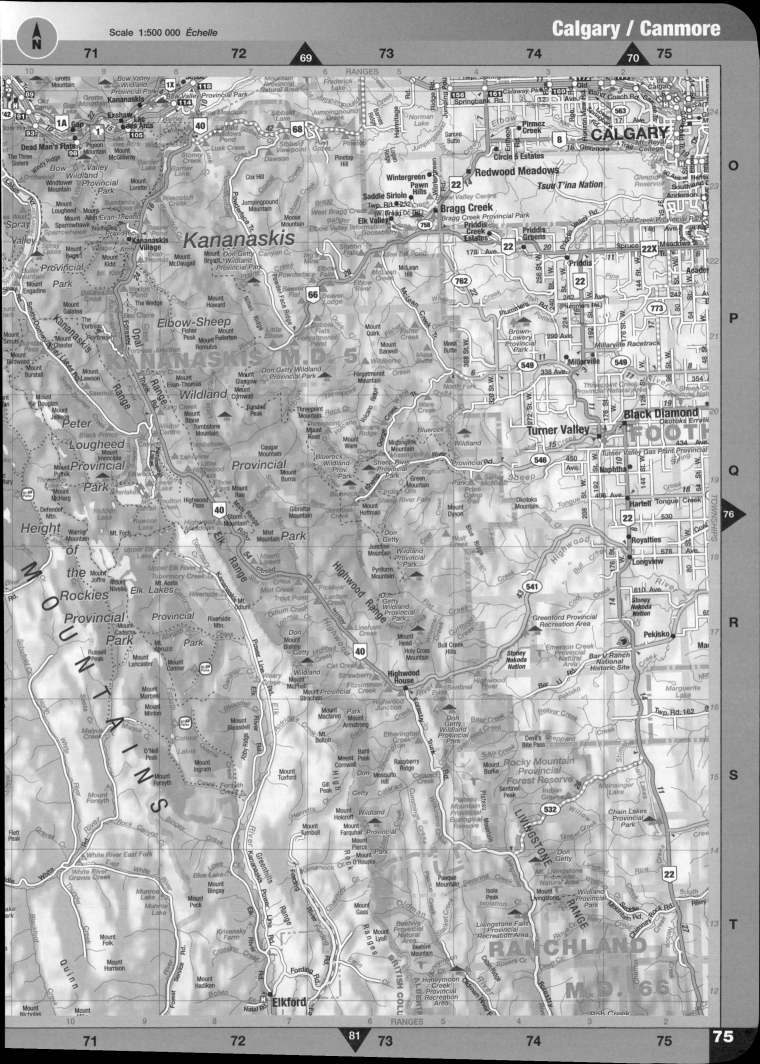

Kilometres
kilomètres
0 5 10 15 20

82 83 84 **72** 85 86

O

Pollockville

Bullpound

36

561 561

Cessford
Rge. Rd. 234

O

556
862
Gem

Wardlow

Howie

P

Mallow

Matzhiwin

876
Steveville

Halsbury

Countess

884

Rosemary

550
Duchess

Dinosaur
Provincial Park
Iddesleigh Jenner

NEWELL

544
Millicent

Patricia

Princess
544

Q

COUNTY 4

36
Brooks
873

Cassils
542
Brooks
Macbeth

77

Tillebrook
Provincial Park

876

R

539
873

Bow
City

Bantry

875
Tilley

884

535
Mesekum

Kininvie
1

S

Rainier
873

36

Scandia

530
Alderson

Ralston

T

Rolling
Hills

525
Suffield

875

TABER
M.D.
524

524
Hays

Cecil

Ronalane
524

Vauxhall
864
Grantham

Bow Island
Provincial
Grazing
Reserve

Saskatchewan

82 83 84 **84** 85 86

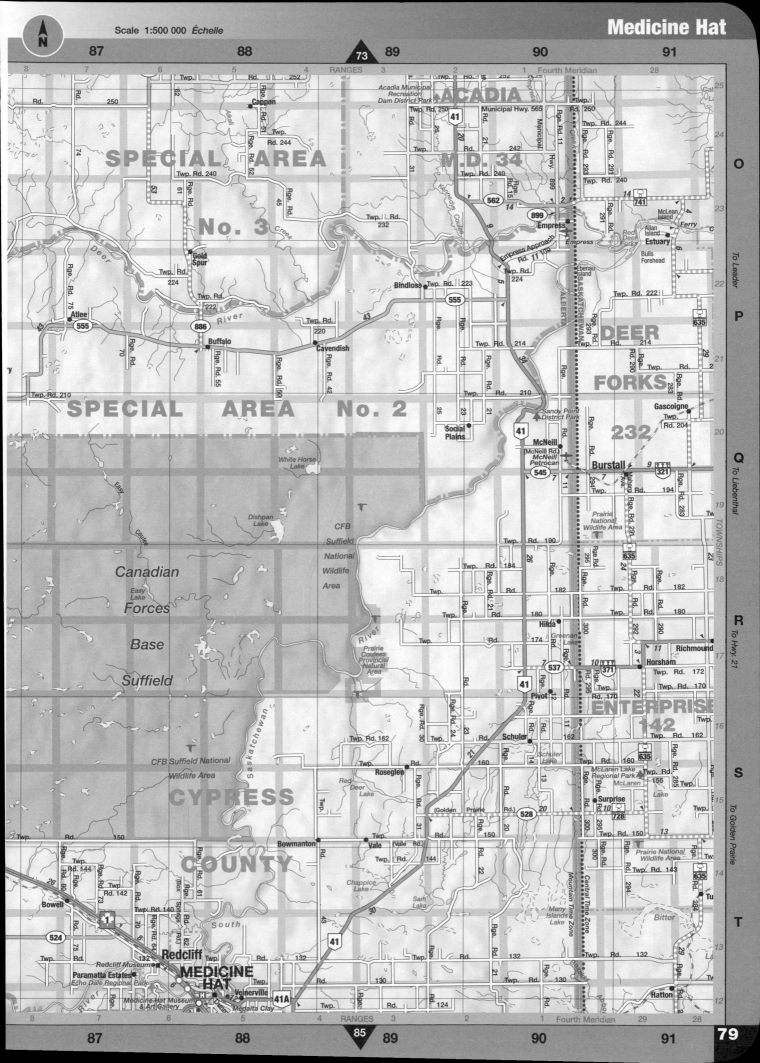

N

87 88 73 89 90 91

RANGES

SPECIAL AREA

No. 3

ACADIA

M.D. 34

SPECIAL AREA No. 2

DEER FORKS 232

Canadian Forces Base Suffield

CFB Suffield National Wildlife Area

ENTERPRISE 142

CYPRESS COUNTY

MEDICINE HAT

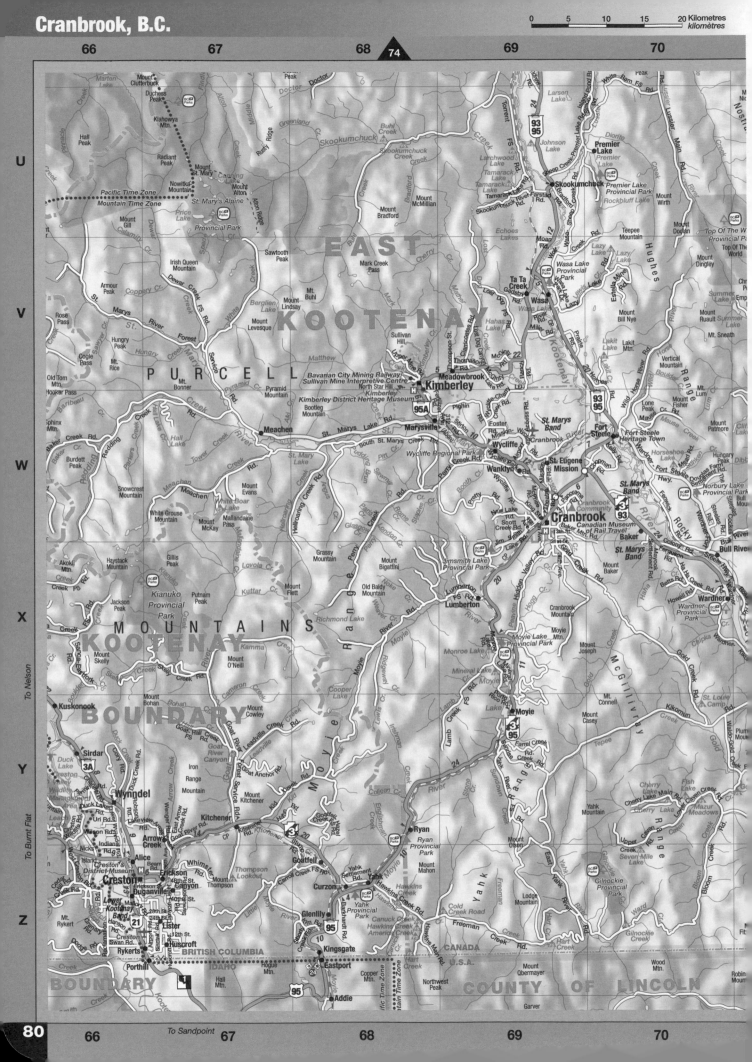

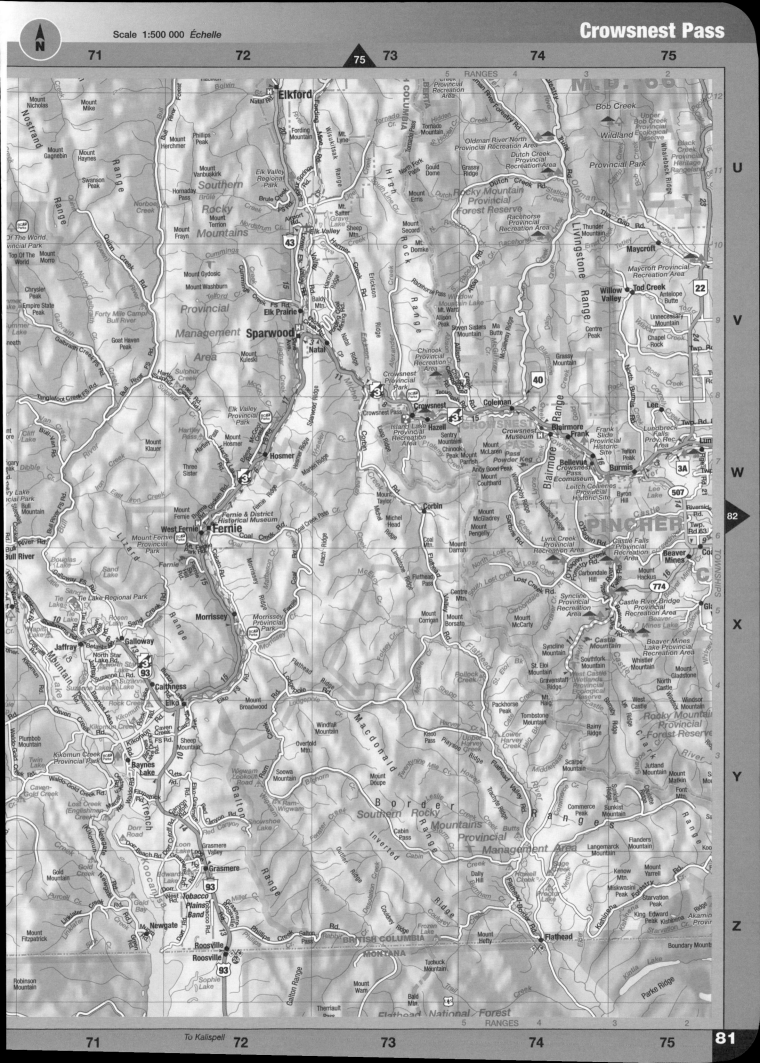

0 5 10 15 20 Kilometres
kilomètres

74   75   76   76   77   78
RANGES

Fifth Meridian

U
Bob Creek
Upper Bob Creek Provincial Ecological Reserve
Black Creek Heritage Rangeland
Dry Coulee
Trout Creek Rd.
520
Furman
Claresholm Industrial
520
Claresholm
Woodhouse
WILLOW

Trunk Rd.
Oldman
Rocky Mountain Provincial Forest Reserve
Meadow Creek
CREEK
Granum
519

V
Thunder Mountain
Maycroft
22
Tod Creek
Willow Valley
North Fork
Olin Creek
Peigan Nation
Spring Point
Head-Smashed-In Buffalo Jump Provincial Historic Site
2
Nolan
M D 26
Fort Macleod
811
Pearce
3
Orton
511

W
Blairmore
Frank
Bellevue
Burmis
3A
Lundbreck
Cowley
510
785
Summer-view
Oldman Dam Provincial Recreation Area
3
Chokio
810
Peigan Nation
Brocket
786
Ardenville

81
PINCHER
Beaver Mines
Coalfield
775
Pincher Station
785
Pincher Creek
507
Stand Off
810

X
774
507
CREEK
Gladstone Valley
6
Fishburn
Hartleyville
Glenwood
505
505

Y
Rocky Mountain Provincial Forest Reserve
Pecten
505
Drywood
Yarrow
Twin Butte
Hill Spring
Parkbend
Ninastoko
Remington Carriage Museum/Card Pioneer Home
800
Cardston
2
Raley
501
503

Z
WATERTON LAKES NATIONAL PARK
WATERTON-GLACIER INTERNATIONAL PEACE PARK
Waterton Townsite
Park View
Mountain View
5
Blood Tribe
Payne Lake Provincial Recreation Area
Beazer
501
Aetna
Kimball
501

GLACIER NATIONAL PARK
Chief Mountain
Port of Chief Mountain
17
Port of Piegan
89
Garway

82   75   76   77   To Browning   78

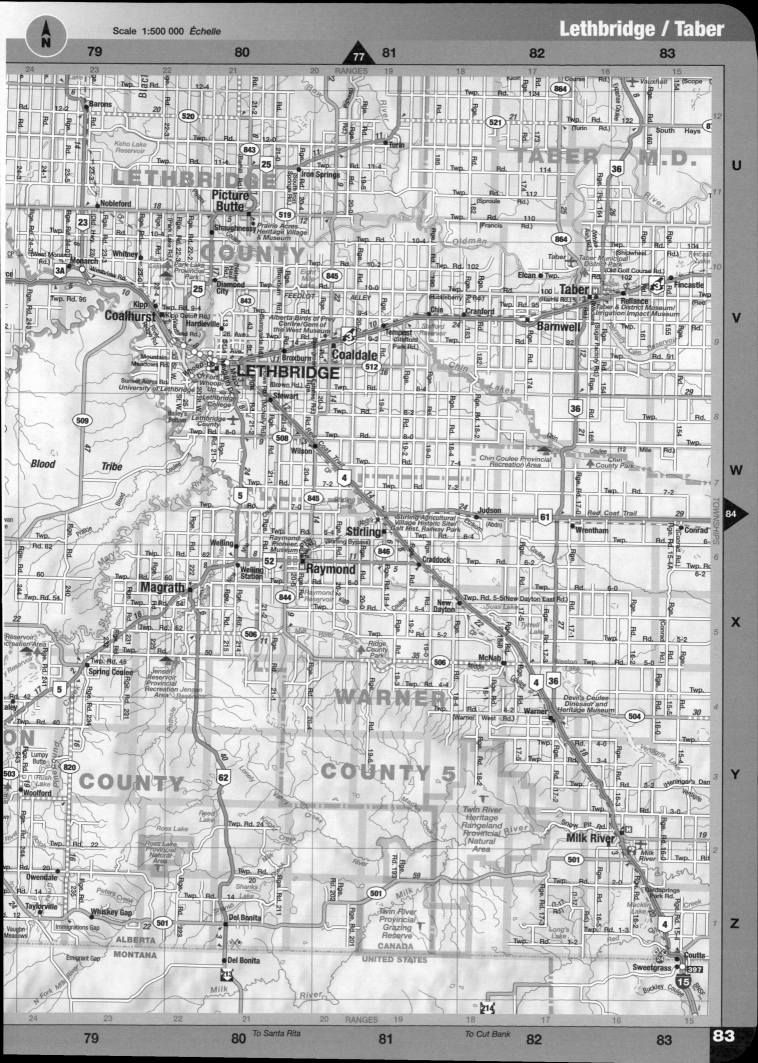

0 5 10 15 20 Kilometres
kilomètres

82   83   84   78   85   86

TABER M.D.

Taber

Barnwell

Reliance

Fincastle

Purple Springs

Antonio

Grassy Lake

Juno

Burdett

Bow Island

Winnifred

Whitla

FORTY MILE

Wrentham

Conrad

Skiff

Legend

Foremost

Nemiskam

Etzikom

COUNTY 8

The Canadian National Historic Wind Power Centre

Warner

WARNER

COUNTY 5

Milk River

Coutts

Sweetgrass

Writing-on-Stone Provincial Park

Aden

Port of Aden

Port of Whitlash

CANADA
U.S.A.

Sweet Grass Hills

To Great Falls

84

82   83   84   85   86

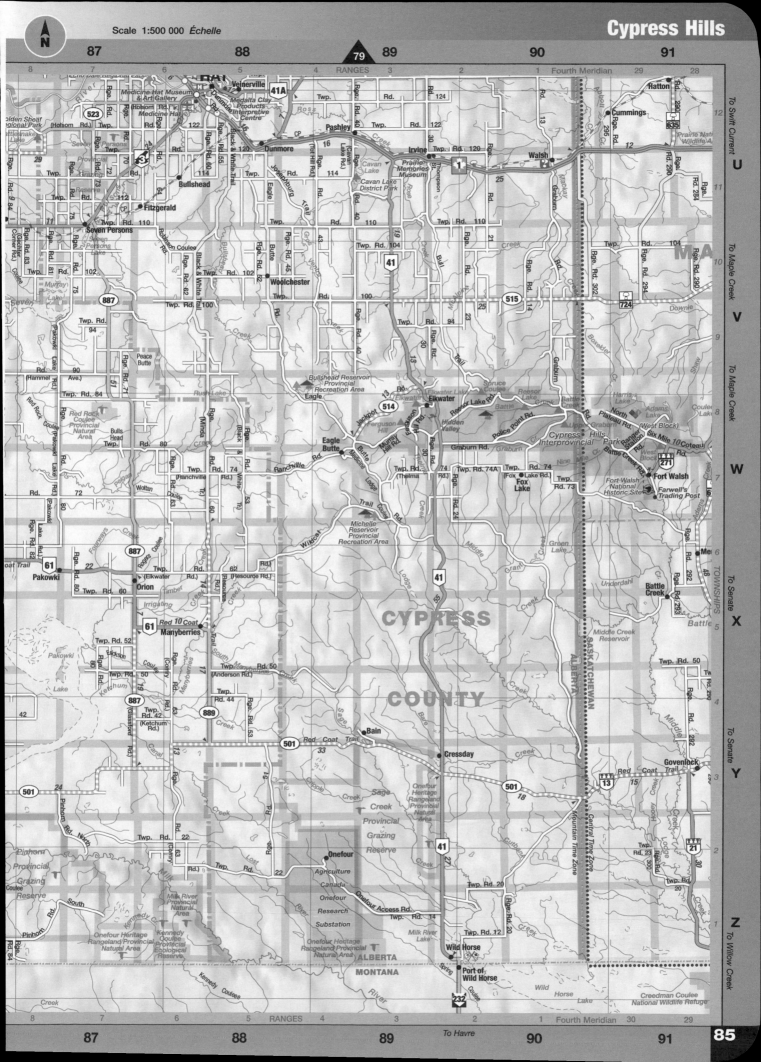

0   20   40   60   80   100 km

To Hay River

N.W.T.

CAMERON HILLS

60th Parallel Territorial Park

Indian Cabins

Highway

35

Steen River

Buchan Lake

Thinahtea North Provincial Protected Area

Thinahtea South Provincial Protected Area

Thinahtea Lake

Petitot River

Thurston Lake

Beatty Lake

Bistcho Lake

Lutose

Mackenzie

•1022m

Caribou Wi Provi

CARIBOU MOUNTAINS

735m

Kotcho Lake Village Provincial Park

Kwokullie Lake

Kotcho Lake

Thelaandoa Creek

Zama City

Slavey Creek

Meander River

Melvin River

Margaret Lake

Pitch L

Eva Lake

Hay River Provincial Protected Area

Mega River

Zama Lake

Hay Lake

Habay

Hay-Zama Lakes Wildland Provincial Park

Chateh (Assumption)

Tugate

Hutch Lake

35

Bushe River

MacKenzie Crossroads Museum   57

Rocky Lane

Boyer

58   59

John D' Prairie

Kyklo Cr.

(Winter Road)

Ekwan Lake Provincial Protected Area

Rainbow Lake

141

58

High Level

Fort Vermilion

North Vermilion Fort Vermilion

88

INTERIOR

Fontas River

Ini Old owth ial Park

Rainbow Lake

Bede River

70

625

Machesis Lake

La Crete

697

Bear River

BRITISH

COLUMBIA

Milligan Hills Provincial Park

1082m

Chinchaga River

Key River

697

Buffalo Head Prairie

Paddle Prairie

Ferry

Keg River

695

River

Carcajou

Wadin Lake

Milikwa

Chinchaga Lakes Provincial Protected Area

Chinchaga Wildland Provincial Park

PLAINS

Meikle River

Kemp R.

Kemp River

126

Twin Lakes

35

Wolverine River

BUFFALO

HEAD

HILLS

Prespatou

Altona

Doig River

Notikewin River

Twin Lakes

692

Notikewin Provincial Park

Bison Lake

738m

Lafond Cr.

Rose Prairie

Montney

North Pine

1120m

CLEAR HILLS

Running Lake

Worsley

Whitemud River

Sulphur Lake

Hotchkiss

Mackenzie

741

Notikewin

Manning

691

Swan Lake

Hay Lake

88

St. John

Charlie Lake

Beatton Provincial Park

Goodlow

Ole's Lake

Cleardale

726

Eureka River

730

689

Dixonville

Highway

35

690

Deadwood

North Star

743

Cadotte Lake

Loon Lake

Red Earth Creek

Taylor

Baldonnel

Cecil Lake

Clayhurst

717

Bear Canyon

PEACE

64

Silver Valley

Wildland

685

Hines Creek

Figure Eight Lake

Queen Elizabeth Provincial Park

737

986

Chinook Valley

Cadotte River

Little Buffalo

986

Lubicon Lake

97

Taylor Landing Provincial Park

Doe River

RIVER

Dunvegan

729

682

732

735

Whitelaw

Bluesky

Berwyn

2

Brownvale

685

684

2A

Grimshaw

19

688

Peace River

St. Isidore

Greene Valley Provincial Park

Heart River

Kiskatinaw Provincial Park

Farmington

Bonanza

Rolla

719

VALLEY

Silver Valley

725

Blueberry Mountain

680

Dunvegan

Fairview

64A

Historic Fort Dunvegan

740

Peace River Wildland Provincial Park

Shaftesbury Ferry

683

Marie-Reine

Nampa

Reno

Atikameg

Gift Lake

Atikamisis Lake

125

Sunset Prairie

Progress

Arras

Dawson Creek

49

Pouce Coupe

Bay Tree

105

Gordondale

49

727

Rycroft

739

2

Dunvegan Provincial Park

Tangent

Jean Côté

744

2

Kimiwan Lake

Winagami

Atikameg

750

98

Mile 0 Alaska Highway

Tomslake

Swan Lake Provincial Park

Spirit River

731

Woking

677

733

Peoria

Eaglesham

104

Watino

Girouxville

Falher

Donnelly

49

McLennan

2

Winagami Lake Prov. Park

Heart River

Salt Prairie

52

Tupper

62

Demmitt

Valhalla Centre

59

721

43

La Glace

63

Buffalo Lake

2

724

Teepee Creek

676

744

Guy

49

Kathleen

679

Winagami Wildland Provincial Park

2A

749

Big Prairie

Grouard Mission

Grouard

Hilliard's Bay Provincial Park

Lesser Slave Lake Wildland Provincial Park

Scale 1:2 000 000 *Échelle*

N

To Hay River

Falls Territorial Park
Salt River
Northern Life Museum
Fort Smith
5
Queen Elizabeth Territorial Park Closed in Winter
Wood Buffalo National Park Fort Smith Visitors Centre
Leland
Fitzgerald
Salt Plains Overview

WOOD BUFFALO

Buffalo River
Arrowhead Lake
Thultue Lake
Conibear Lake
Robertson Lake

Pine Lake
Hay Camp
Hornaday R.
La Butte Creek Wildland Provincial Park
La Butte Creek

Charles Lake
Potts Lake
Andrew Lake
Cornwall Lake
Colin-Cornwall Lakes Wildland Provincial Park
Wylie Lake
Colin Lake

Nettell Lake
Tazin Lake
Soulier Lake
Laird Island
Waterloo Lake
Le Blanc Lake
Beaver Lake
Eldora
Tsalwor Lake
Thluicho L.
Camsell Portage
Uranium City
962
Harper Lake
Lobstick Island
Easter Head
Black Bay
Maurice Point
Burstall Lake
Johnston Island
Grouse Island
William Point
Athabasca
Cantara Bay
East A

NATIONAL PARK

Caribou Mountains Wildland Provincial Park

Berry Creek
Jackfish River

Peace Point
Winter Road

Fidler-Greywillow Wildland Provincial Park
Cypress Point
Fidler Point
Egg Island
Burntwood Island
Bustard Island

Lake
Baril Lake
Mamawi Lake
Wood Buffalo National Park Fort Chipewyan Visitors Centre
Fort Chipewyan
Fort Chipewyan Bicentennial Museum

Old Fort Bay
Carswell Lake
Athabasca Sand Dunes Provincial Wilderness Park
Archibald Lake
Sandy Bay
De Lake

Garden Creek

Peace River

Lake Claire

Athabasca River

Richardson Lake Migratory Bird Sanctuary
Richardson Lake
Maybelle River Wildland Provincial Park
Athabasca Sand Dunes
Richardson River Dunes Wildland Provincial Park

Old Fort River
Cluff Lake Mine
Douglas River
SASKATCHEWAN
Charbonneau River
William River

John D'Or Prairie
Fox Lake
Ruis Lake
Harper Creek

776m

McIvor Creek

ALBERTA

BIRCH MOUNTAINS

Birch Mountains Wildland Provincial Park
Gardiner Lakes
Namur Lake
Legend Lake
Ells River

Marguerite River
Marguerite River Wildland Provincial Park
Mountain Time Zone
Central Time Zone
955
Patterson Lake
Forrest Lake
Preston Lake
Mirror
Lloyd Lake
Descharme River
Descharme Lake
245

McClelland Lake
Firebag River

Pany River
Liege River
Dunkirk River

Fort MacKay
63
59
Wood Buffalo
Steepbank River

Chipewyan Lake
Chipewyan Lake
Grew Lake
Mink Lake
MacKay River

Whitemud Falls Wildland Provincial Park
Clearwater River Provincial Park
955
Turn Lak

686
Peerless Lake
Peerless Lake

Fort McMurray
Fort McMurray Oil Sands Discovery Centre
69
Saprae Creek Estates
Clearwater River
Gregoire Lake Provincial Park
Gordon Lake
Gipsy Lake
Gipsy Lake Wildland Provincial Park
Big C
La Loche West
Lac La Loche
La Loche
Black Point
Bear Creek

Trout Lake
Graham Lake
Rapids Wildland Provincial Park
Horse River
Twinned: Late 2008
Gregoire Lake
Anzac
Hangingstone
84
63
Stony Mountain Wildland Provincial Park
Garson Lake
(Winter Road) All Season Road Open: Late 2009
Garson Lake
956
Turn
Peter
Bear Creek

Tepee Lake
Troua River
Muskwa Lake
Muskwa River
North Wabasca Lake
Wabiskaw

Engstrom Lake
881
CHEECHAM HILLS
GRIZZLY BEAR HILLS
Michel
Buffalo River
St. George's Hill

Nipisi River
Wabasca-Desmarais
South Wabasca Lake
Sandy Lake
Pelican Lake
Mariana Lake
Chard
Janvier
Bohn Lake
Dillon Lake
Dillon River

754
813
Crow Lake Provincial Park
Pelican
Pelican River

Marten Beach
1023m
Rock Island Lake
141
Conklin
Christina Lake
Christina River
Winefred River
Winefred Lake
Watapi Lake
Nipin River
MOSTOOS HILL

To Buffalo Narrows

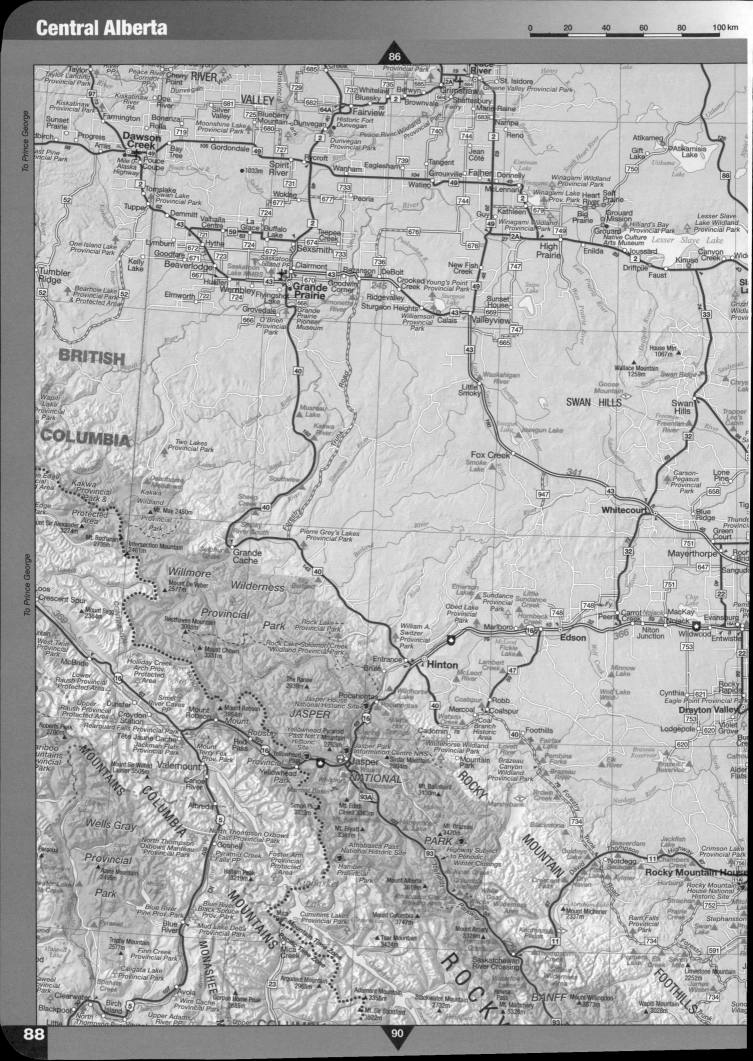

0 20 40 60 80 100 km

To Prince George

Taylor
Taylor Landing
Provincial Park
Taylor PP
Peace River
Corridor
RPA
97
Kiskatinaw
River PA
Kiskatinaw
River
Provincial Park
Sunset
Prairie
Arras
99
Sunset Pine
Provincial Park
Lostbirch
Progress
Farmington
Dawson
Creek
49
Mile 0
Pouce
Coupe
Bay
Tree
Pouce Coupé R.
Peace River
RIVER
VALLEY
Cherry
Point
Dunvegan
681
725
Silver
Valley
Moonshine Lake
Provincial Park
680
Blueberry
Mountain
Historic Fort
Dunvegan
Dunvegan
Provincial Park
Fairview
64A
70
732
Whitelaw
Bluesky
Brownvale
Berwyn
685
2A
Grimshaw
684
Shaftesbury
Ferry
St. Isidore
Greene Valley Provincial Park
Marie
Reine
Nampa
Reno
683
744
2
Peace
River
19

Atikameg
Gift
Lake
Atikamisis
Lake
Utikuma

105 Gordondale
727
49
Rycroft
Spirit
River
731
Woking
677
Saddle
2
Dunvegan
Wanham
Eaglesham
Tangent
739
Giro

BRITISH

COLUMBIA

ROCKY

MOUNTAINS

88   90

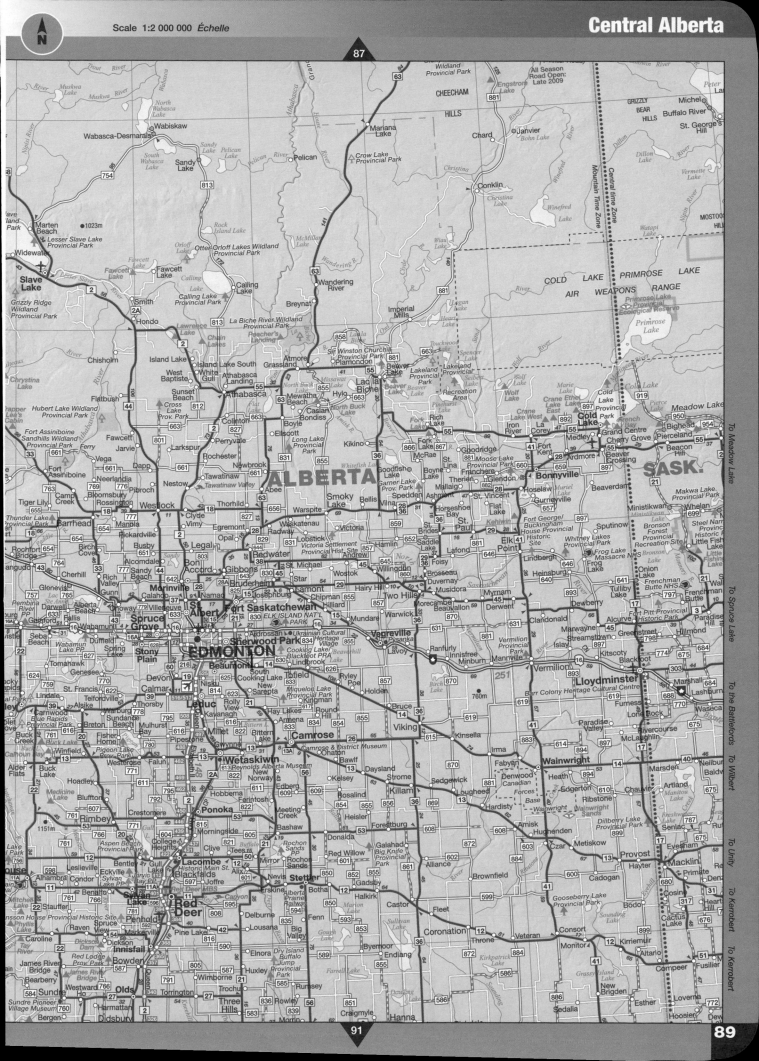

0 20 40 60 80 100 km

88

Valemount
Mount Sir Wilfrid Laurier 3505m
Canoe River
Yellowhead Pass
Jasper
Sirdar Mountain 2804m
Whistlers
Marmot Basin
Mt. Edith Cavell 3363m
Mt. Korkeslin
Mt. Fryatt 3361m
Honeymoon Lake
Mt. Brazeau 3470m
Mountain
Brazeau Canyon Wildland Provincial Park
Brazeau River
Elk River
Pembina Forks
Brazeau Reservoir
Albreda
North Thompson Oxbows East Provincial Park
North Thompson Oxbows Manteau Provincial Park
Foster Arm Provincial Protected Area
Simon Pk 3322m
Athabasca Pass National Historic Site
Icefields
Mt. Balinhard 3130m
Blackstone
Marshybank
Blackstone Forestry Trunk
Nordegg River
Crimson Lake Provincial Park

Wells Gray
Azure Mountain 2495m
Pyramid Creek Falls PP
Goshell
Hamber Provincial Protected Area
Highway Subject to Periodic Winter Closings
Jonas Creek
Columbia Icefield
Mount Alberta 3619m
White Goat Wilderness Area
Nordegg
Saunders
David
Goldeye Lake
734
Horburg
11
Rocky Mountain House
Rocky Mountain House National Historic Site
Strachan

Provincial
Park
Clearwater Lake
Blue River Pine Prov. Park
Blue River Black Spruce Prov. Park
Mud Lake Delta Provincial Park
Mica Dam
Cummins Lakes Provincial Park
Mount Columbia 3747m
Clemenceau Icefield
Tsar Mountain 3424m
Athabasca Glacier Viewing Area
Columbia Icefield
Mount Amery
Saskatchewan River Crossing
Thompson Creek
Siffleur Wilderness Area
Abraham Lake
Mount Michener 2337m
Ram Falls Provincial Park
Prairie Creek
752
Stephansson Historic Site
Swan
591

Trophy Mountain 2577m
Finn Creek Provincial Park
Pyramid
Blue River
Mica Creek
Mountain Time Zone
Pacific Time Zone
Argonaut Mountain 2965m
Adamant Mountain 3355m
Mt. Sir Sandford 3522m
Blackwater Mountain 2732m
Freshfield Icefield
Mount Lausserdat 3059m
Mt. Mummery 3328m
Mount Willingdon 3373m
Wapiti Mountain 3028m
Sundre
734

Caligata Lake Provincial Park
Spahats Creek Provincial Park
Wire Cache Provincial Park
Gordon Horne Peak 2685m
Blackpool
Avola
Upper Adams River PP
COLUMBIA-SHUSWAP
Highway Subject to Periodic Winter Closings
Iconoclast Mtn. 3251m
Marl Creek Prov. Park
Mount St. Bride 3316m
Panther Mountain 2943m
93
Burnt Timber
Red Deer River
Ghost River Wilderness Area
Don Getty Wildland Prov. Park
40

Clearwater
Birch Island
North Thompson River Provincial Park
Dunn Peak Prov. Area
Eakin Creek Canyon PP
Eakin Creek Floodplain PP
North Thompson Islands Provincial Park
Darfield
Vavenby
Upper Seymour River Prov. Park
Harbour Dudgeon Lakes Provincial Park
Momich Lakes Provincial Park
SELKIRK
Rogers Pass National Historic Site
Rogers Pass
YOHO NATIONAL PARK
Takakkaw Falls
Kicking Horse Pass
Lake Louise
Skoki Ski Lodge National Historic Site
Ghost Airstrip

Little Fort
Ferry
McLure
Mount Tod 2149m
Sun Peaks
Adams Lake (Bush Creek) Prov. Park
Seymour Mountain 2303m
Pukeashun Mountain
Pukeashun PP
MT. REVELSTOKE NATIONAL PARK
Last Spike (CPR) 1885 Craigellachie
Mt. Begbie 2732m
Donald
Burges & James Gadsden Prov. Park
Moberly Lake
Golden
Field
NATIONAL PARK
Chancellor Peak
Lake Louise
Castle Mountain 3162m
Mt. Aylmer 3162m
Two Jack Lake
PARK

Barriere
Louis Creek
Roderick Haig-Brown Prov. Park
Adams Lake
Magna Bay
Anstey-Hunakwa Provincial Park
Scotch Creek
Celista
Anglemont
Malakwa
Three Valley
Yard Creek PP
Canyon Hot Springs
Mt. Dawson 3390m
Loop Creek
Grand Mountain 3306m
Spillimacheen River
McMurdo
Parson
Mount Goodsir 3581m
KOOTENAY
Vermilion Crossing
Mt. Brett 2984m
Sunshine Village
Tunnel Mountain
Banff
Canmore
Exshaw
1A

McLure
Scotch Creek
Shuswap Lake Prov. Park
White Lake
Eagle Bay
REVELSTOKE
Powder Springs
Mt. Griffin Provincial Park 2732m
Blanket Creek Provincial Park
BRITISH
Brisco
Spillimacheen
Harrogate
93
Mount Assiniboine 3618m
Mt. Assiniboine Provincial Park
Spray Valley Provincial Park
40
742

Kamloops
Pritchard
Monte Creek
Chase
Notch Hill
Sorrento
Tappen
Sicamous
Canoe
Mara
Grindrod
Kingfisher
Shelter Bay
Ferry
Beaton
Trout Lake
Mt. Templeman 3070m
Bugaboo Provincial Park
PURCELL
Edgewater
Radium Hot Springs
Wilmer
Mt. King George 3457m
Dry Gulch Prov. Park
Mount Assiniboine Provincial Park
Peter Lougheed Provincial Park
Mt. Sir Douglas 3406m
Elbow-Sheep Wildland
97B

Squilax
Chase
Blind Bay
Herald PP
Three Valley
Enderby
NORTH OKANAGAN
Mabel Lake Provincial Park
Greenbush Lake Protected Area
Galena Bay
Nakusp Hot Springs
Goat Range Provincial Park
Howser
Mount Famham 3457m
Panorama
Invermere
Athalmer
Shuswap
James Chabot Prov. Park
Kootenay House NHS
Windermere
Fairmont Hot Springs
Mt. Marconi 3106m
Columbia Lake Prov. Park

Salmon Arm
Silver Creek
Falkland
97A
Mabel Lake
Sugar Monashee Provincial Park
Summit Lake Provincial Park
Mt. Toby 3212m
Panorama
Mt. Toby
Windermere Lake Prov. Park
Fairmont Hot Springs
Mt. Nelson 3313m
Purcell Wilderness Conservancy Corridor Prov. Protected Area
Thunder Hill Prov. Park
Canal Flats
Whiteswan Lake Provincial Park

Vernon
Coldstream
Lumby
Cherryville
McDonald Creek Provincial Park
Arrow Park Ferry
Meadow Creek
Argenta
Johnsons Landing
Kootenay Lake (Davis Creek) Prov. Park
Purcell Wilderness Conservancy Prov. Park
EAST KOOTENAY
Canal Flats

Killarney Beach
Ellison Prov. Park
Fintry Prov. Park
Okanagan Centre
Wilson Landing
Silver Star Provincial Park
Silver Star
Shuswap Lake PP
Nakusp
Burton
New Denver
Sandon
Silverton
Kaslo
Kokanee Glacier Provincial Park
Mirror Lake
Riondel
Ainsworth Hot Springs
Premier Lake Provincial Park
COLUMBIA
Top Of The World Provincial Park
Teepee Mtn. 2797m
Wasa

Kelowna
Winfield
Duck Lake
CENTRAL OKANAGAN
Graystokes Provincial Park
Whatshan Lake
Roseberry Provincial Park
Valhalla Provincial Park
Kokanee Creek Provincial Park
Balfour
Kootenay Lake (Lost Ledge) Prov. Park
S.S. Moyie
Mt. Fisher 2846m
Kimberley
Ta Ta Creek
Sparwood
Elk Valley Prov. Park

Westbank
McCulloch
Myra-Bellevue Provincial Park
Myra-Bellevue Mountain
Okanagan Lake Prov. Park
Big White
Needles
Fauquier
Applegrove
Edgewood
Slocan
CENTRAL KOOTENAY
Winlaw
Slocan Park
Nelson
West Arm Provincial Park
Harrop
Procter
Gray Creek
Crawford Bay
Riondel
Crawford Bay Prov. Park
Lockhart Beach Prov. Park
Kootenay Lake (Midge Creek) Provincial Park
Kimberley
Cranbrook
Wycliffe
Canadian Mus. of Rail Travel
Fort Steele
Fort Steele Turn-of-the-Century Park
Norbury Lake Prov. Park
Jaffray
Fernie

Peachland
Trepanier Prov. Park
Westbank
Summerland
Sun-Oka Beach Provincial Park
Naramata
Kickininee Prov. Park
Okanagan Lake Prov. Park
KOOTENAY BOUNDARY
MONASHEE RANGE
CHRISTINA RANGE
Syringa Provincial Park
Vallican
Taghum
Shoreacres
South Slocan
Glade
Thrums
Nelson
Whitewater
Drewry Point
Boswell
Sanca
Kianuko Provincial Park
Jimsmith Lake Prov. Park
Wardner
Moyie Lake Prov. Park
Galloway
Elko

Penticton
Apex Alpine
Kaleden
Christie Memorial Prov. Park
Okanagan Falls
Okanagan Falls PP
Vaseux Lake PP
Vaseux Lake NMBS
Beaverdell
Gable Mtn. 2274m
Jewel Lake Provincial Park
Westbridge
Kettle River Prov. Rec. Area
Syringa Provincial Park
Nancy Greene Provincial Park
Castlegar
Genelle
Erie Creek Provincial Park
Ymir
Salmo
Stagleap Provincial Park
Sirdar
Wynndel
Creston
Erickson
Canyon
Lister
Kitchener
Moyie
Ryan Prov. Park
Gilnockie Prov. Park
Yahk Mtn. 2180m
Yahk Prov. Park
Newgate
93

Hedley
Keremeos
Cawston
Olalla
3A
Oliver
Anarchist PPA
Johnstone Creek Prov. Park
Boundary Creek PP
Paulson
Christina Lake
Rossland
Warfield
Trail
Fruitvale
Montrose
Waneta
Beaver Creek Prov. Park
Remac
Nelway
Salmo
Kootenay Pass
Rykerts
Porthill
Eastport
Kingsgate
Copeland
Northwest Peak 7700 ft.
Rexford

Cawston
Osoyoos
Oliver
Bridesville
Rock Creek
Midway
Carson
Greenwood
Grand Forks
Christina Lake
Cascade
Laurier
Montrose
Burnt Flat
Saddle Mountain 6960 ft.
BOUNDARY
Meadow Creek
Yaak
95

Chopaka
Nighthawk
Osoyoos
Haynes Pt. PP
Molson
Chesaw
41
Orient
Northport
Metaline
Metaline Falls
Colville National Forest
Smith Peak 7660 ft.
Bonners Ferry
Moyie Springs
508
Kootenay Nat'l Wild. Ref.

Oroville
Windy Pk 8334 ft.
Osoyoos Lake St. Park
Loomis
Ellisforde
Wauconda
Malo
Curlew
Curlew Lake State Park
Boyds
Colville National Forest
31
IDAHO
Bonners Ferry
2

Loomis
Tonasket
Republic
395
Kettle Falls
Colville
Marcus
Addy
25
National Recreation Area
Evans
Tiger
Ione
Nordman
Priest Lake State Park
Naples
Elmira
Samuels
95

OKANOGAN National Forest
Riverside
Conconully
Conconully State Park
Disautel
Rice
Orin
Arden
Crystal Falls State Park
Cusick
LAKE ROOSEVELT NAT'L RECREATION AREA
PEND OREILLE
Coolin
Colburn
PACIFIC
567

Omak
215
Okanogan
Malott
155
WASHINGTON
Inchelium
Gifford
Kettle Falls
Colville
FERRY
KETTLE RANGE
Mt. Casey
BONNER National Forest
PURCELL
LINCOLN
37

To Wenatchee   To Davenport   To Spokane   To Newport   To Sandpoint   To Kalispell

To Merritt   To Cache Creek   To Princeton   To Sedro Woolley

Kamloops
Monte Lake
Westwold
Armstrong
Spallumcheen
Lavington
Lumby
Oyama
Okanagan Country
Rutland
Kelowna
Tsinstikeptum
Westbank
Peachland
Summerland

89

Southern Alberta

ALBERTA

CALGARY

Red Deer

Lethbridge

Medicine Hat

Drumheller

Brooks

Wetaskiwin

Wainwright

Ponoka

Lacombe

Stetter

Hanna

Coronation

Provost

Macklin

Airdrie

Cochrane

Okotoks

High River

Strathmore

Fort Macleod

Cardston

Pincher Creek

Crowsnest Pass

Coleman

Blairmore

Claresholm

Vulcan

Taber

Coaldale

Bow Island

Cypress Hills

Milk River

Coutts

Sweetgrass

CANADA

U.S.A.

MONTANA

Shelby

Cut Bank

Browning

GLACIER NATIONAL PARK

WATERTON LAKES NATIONAL PARK

Kananaskis

THE MIDDLE SAND HILLS

Canadian Forces Base Suffield

Dinosaur Provincial Park

To Kalispell   To Choteau   To Great Falls

To Unity

To Kerrobert

To Kerrobert

To Rosetown

To Eston

To Swift Current

To Swift Current

To Shaunavon

To Havre

To Sundre

To Bowden

ROCKY VIEW

CALGARY

FOOTHILLS

To Canmore

To Canmore

To Bragg Creek

To Bragg Creek

To Strathmore

To Chestermere

To Sheparc

To Turner Valley

To Okotoks   To Nanton

Cochrane

Airdrie

Balzac

Priddis Green

Priddis

Millarville

DeWinton

Heritage Pointe

Academy

Tsuu T'ina First Nation

Glenbow Ranch Provincial Park

Nose Hill Natural Environment Park

Calgary International Airport

Bow River

Elbow River

Glenmore Reservoir

Canada Olympic Park

Brown-Lowery Provincial Park

Big Hill Springs Provincial Park

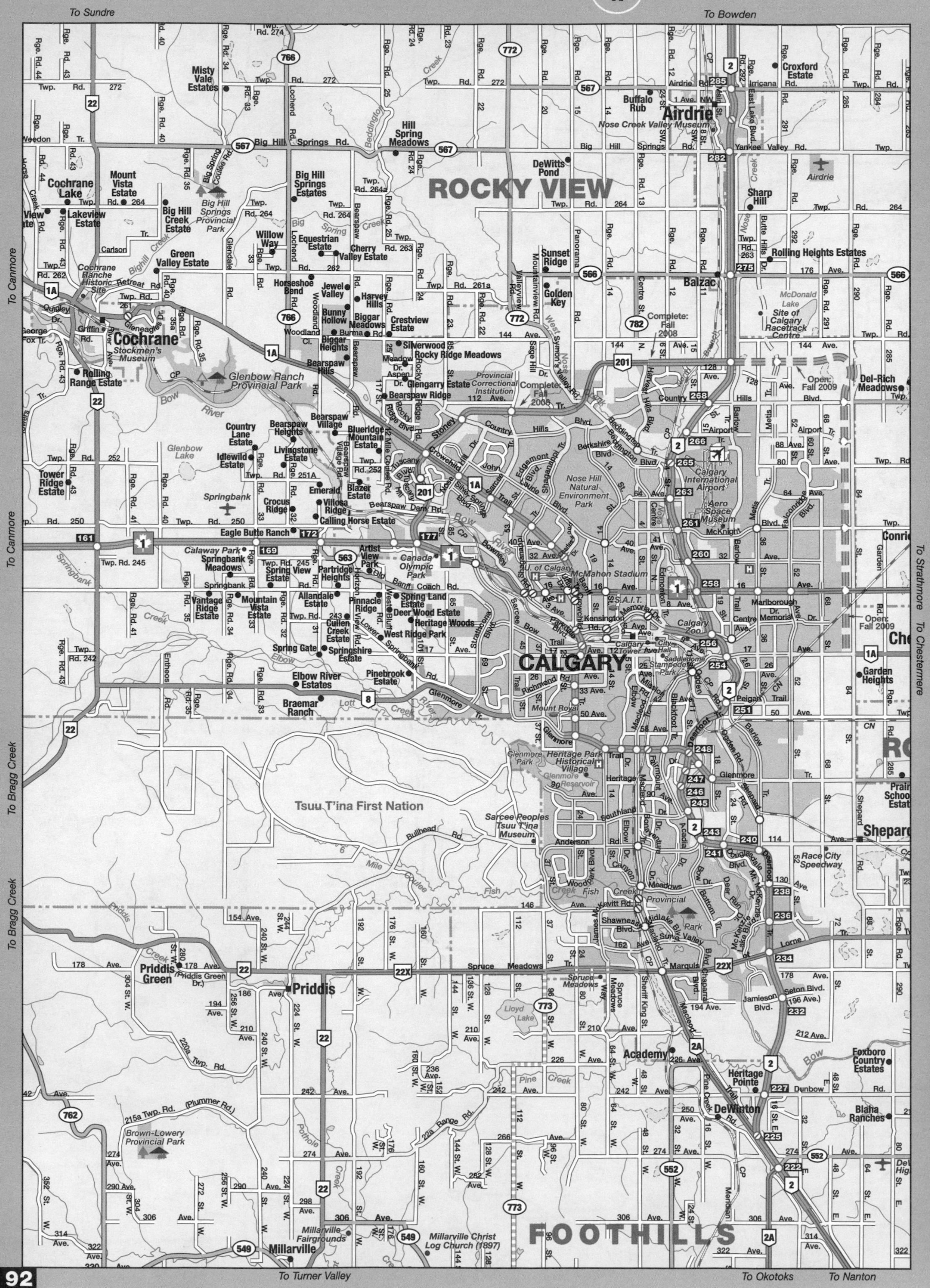

Scale 1:175 000 *Échelle*

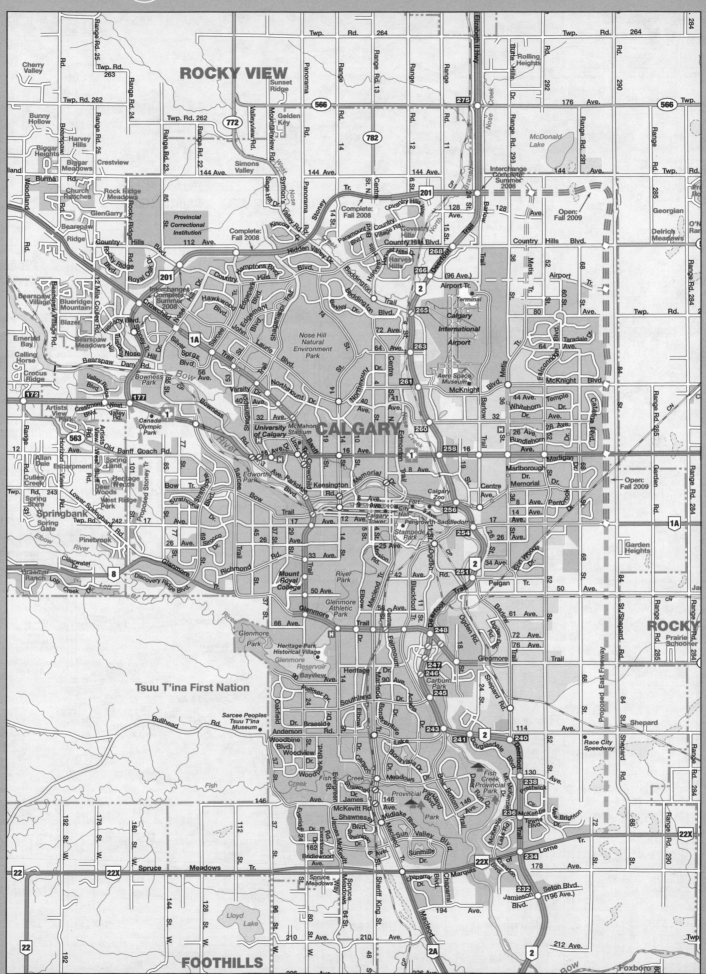

Scale 1:25 000 *Échelle*

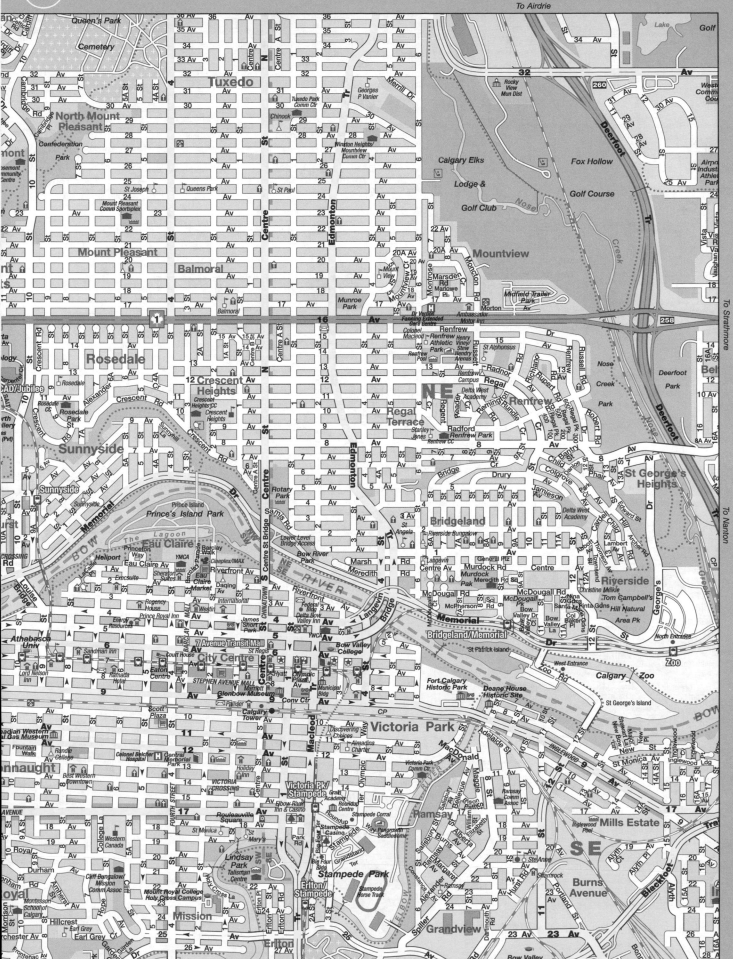

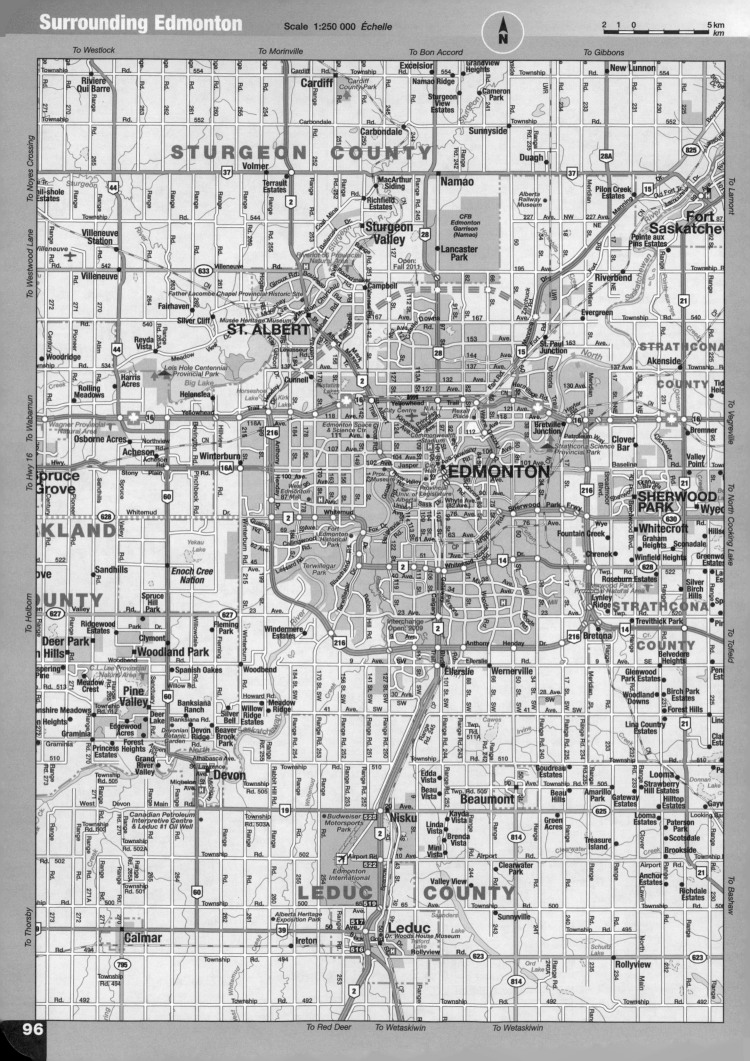

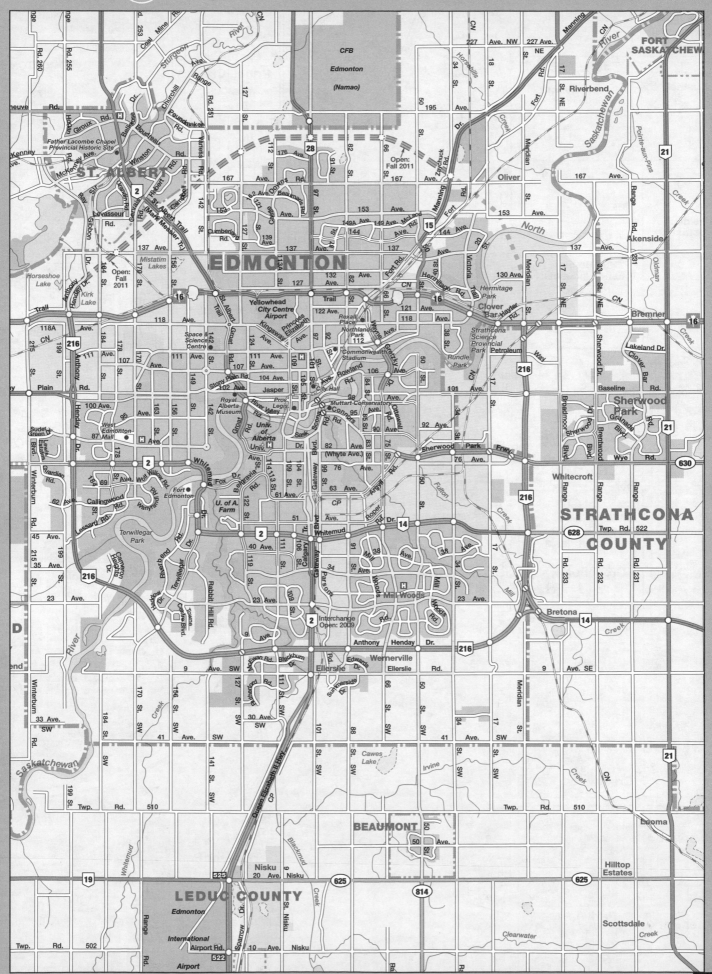

Scale 1:175 000 *Échelle*

0 1 2 Kilometres
kilomètres

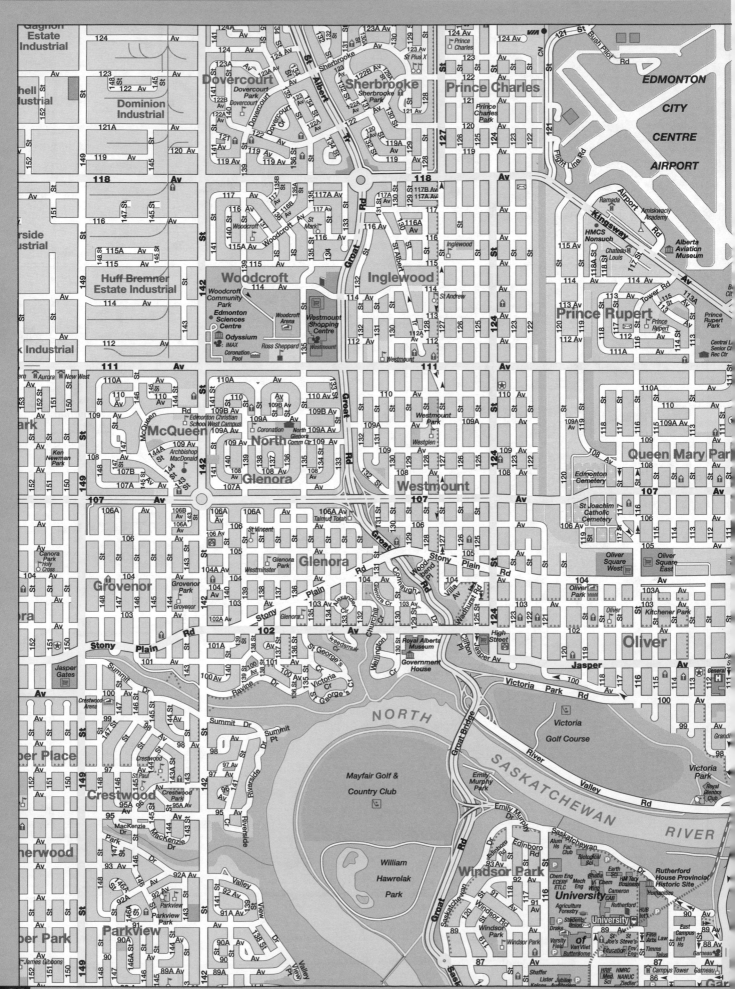

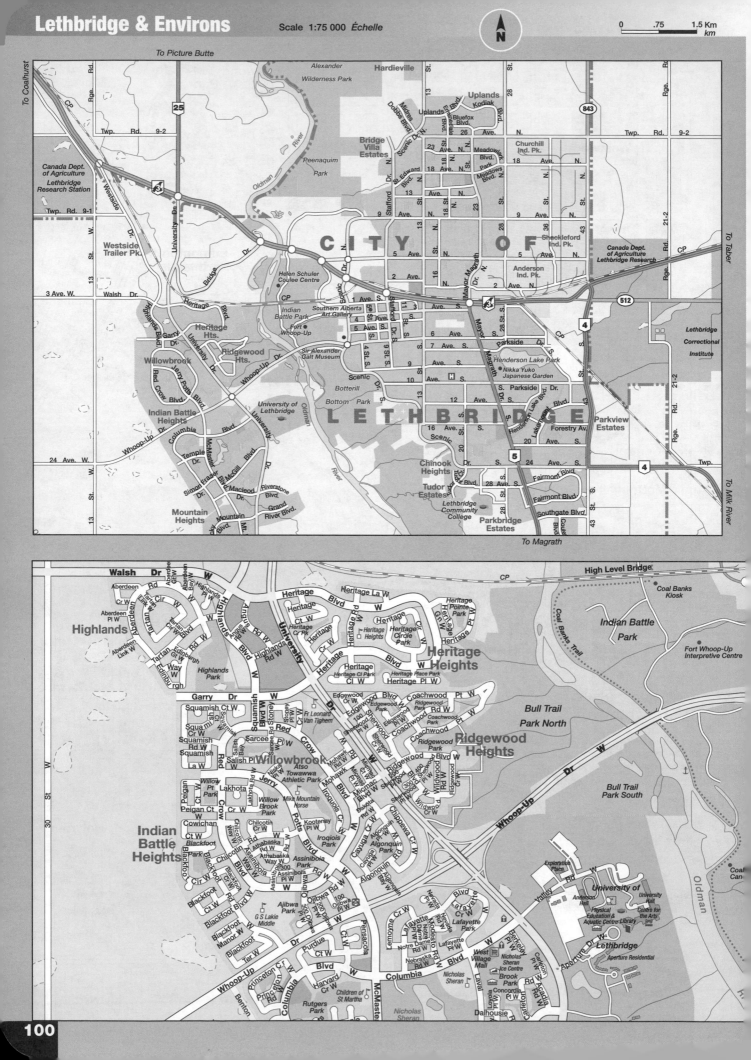

Lethbridge & Environs

Scale 1:75 000 *Échelle*

N

0   .75   1.5 Km
km

Scale 1:25 000 *Échelle*

0 .25 .5 .75 1 Kilometre
kilomètre

N

Stafford Village
Bridge Villa Estates
Lethbridge Fish & Game Gun Range
Stafford Park
Vista Play Area
Lethbridge Christian
Trailer Park
Dominion Park
Vista Park
Churchill Industrial Park
Meadowlark Blvd
Park Meadows
Ted Petrunia Park
Park Meadows Shopping Centre
Stan Siwik Pool
Winston Churchill
Park Meadows Park
Norbridge Park
St Paul
Wilson Middle
Shackleford Industrial Park
Adams Park
Galbraith
Rideau Park
Senator Buchanan
St Basis Park
St Patrick's Cemetery
Dave Elton Park
Emmanuel Christian
St Basis
Jock Palmer Park
Westminster Pool
Westminster
George McKillop
DND
Anderson Industrial Park
Centre Village Mall
York
Crowsnest
CP
Park Place Shopping Centre
Cineplex Odeon
Brewery Gardens
Bridge Inn
Galt Gdns
South Alberta Art Gallery
Casino Lethbridge
St Francis
Sandman Hotel
Travelodge
Lethbridge Hotel
Coal Banks Inn
Paramount
Alec Arms
Lethbridge Lodge
Lethbridge Centre
Bowman Arts Ctr
Famous Players
YMCA
Hamilton
Lethbridge Collegiate Inst
Catholic Central
St Mary
Sir Alexander Galt Museum
Civic Athletic Field
El Rancho
Victoria Park
Allan Watson
Henderson Park Ice Centre
Henderson Baseball Stadium
Parkside
Coal Banks Trail
Lethbridge & Exhibition
YWCA
London Rd Park
Kiwanis Park
Kinsmen Park
Henderson Pool
Henderson Rose Garden
Henderson Lake Campground
Henderson Lake
Fleetwood Bawden
Chinook Regional
Nikka Yuko Japanese Garden
Henderson Lake Golf Course
Botterill Bottom Park
St Patrick
Gyro Park
Bridge Town House
Quality Inn
South Parkside Dr
Eldon Lodge
Lakeview
Gilbert Paterson
Mountain View Cemetery
Lethbridge Country Club
Our Lady of Assumption
Best Western Heidelberg
Lakeview Little League Ball Field
Scenic Heights Park
Magrath Market Place
Park Royal Estates
Lions Centennial
Ravine Park
Redwood Rd Athletic Pk
The Movie Mill

Scale 1:83 000 Echelle

0 .25 .5 .75 1 Kilometre
kilomètre

RED DEER

To Joffre Bridge — To Hillsdown

To Lacombe — To Edmonton — To Sylvan Lake — To Rocky Mountain House — To Penhold — To Bowden

River Bend Recreation Area
Three Mile Bend
Kerry Wood Nature Centre
Gaetz Lakes Sanctuary
Waskasoo
Northlands Estates
Northwood Estates
Parkside Estates
Kentwood
Glendale
Golden West
Highland Green
Oriole Park
Fairview
Bower Ponds
North Red Deer
Mustang Acres
Downtown
City Hall
Red Deer & District Museum
Parkvale
Grandview
West Park
Red Deer College
South Hill
Molly Bannister
Westerner Exposition Grounds
Great Chief Park
Heritage Ranch
Fort Normandeau
Michener Hill
Cleaview
Eastview
Morrisroe
Anders
Springfield Blvd.
Selkirk

College Park
Michener Centre Northside
Meadowview Rd
Medley Dr

Gaetz Lake
Gaetz Lakes Sanctuary (Waskasoo Park)
Kerry Wood Nature Centre (Waskasoo Park)
McKenzie Trail Recreation Area (Waskasoo Park)
Riverside (Heavy)
Riverside (Light)
Sewage Treatment Plant
Northlands
Pines
Pines Community
Parkland Mall
Riverside Meadows
Highland Green
Riverview
Mustang Acres
Kentwood
Northwood Estates
Glendale
Normandeau
Parkside Estates

CITY OF

Queen Elizabeth II Hwy
Taylor Dr
Riverside Dr
Township Rd
Gaetz Ave (50 Ave)

102

Scale 1:25 000 *Échelle*

0 .25 .5 .75 1 Kilometre
kilomètre

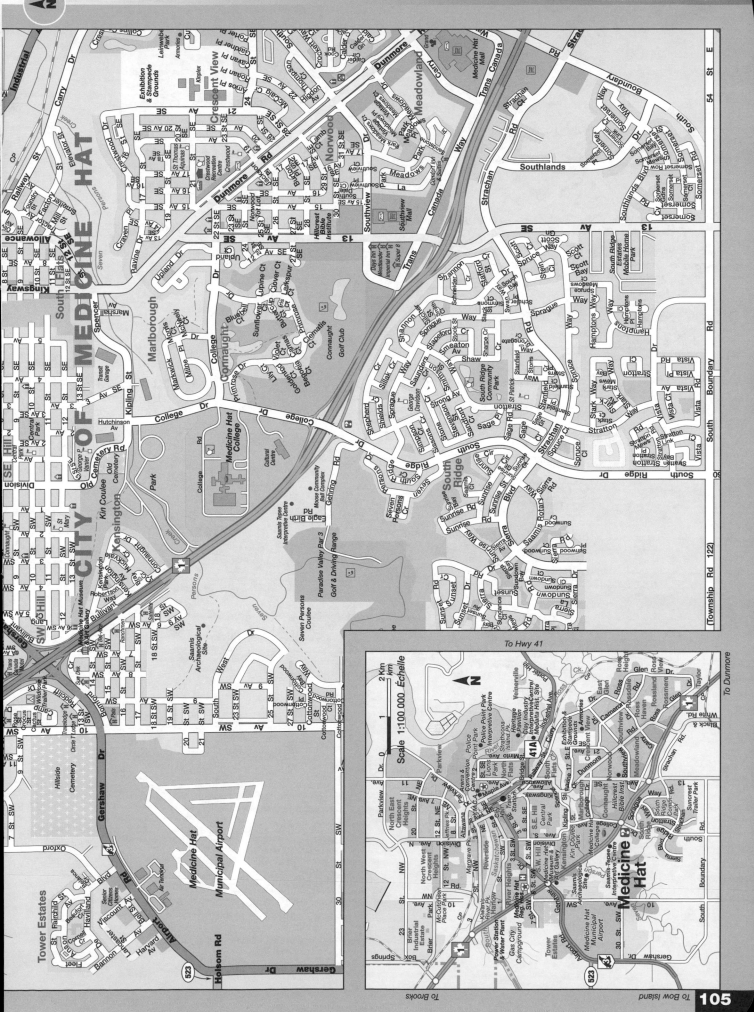

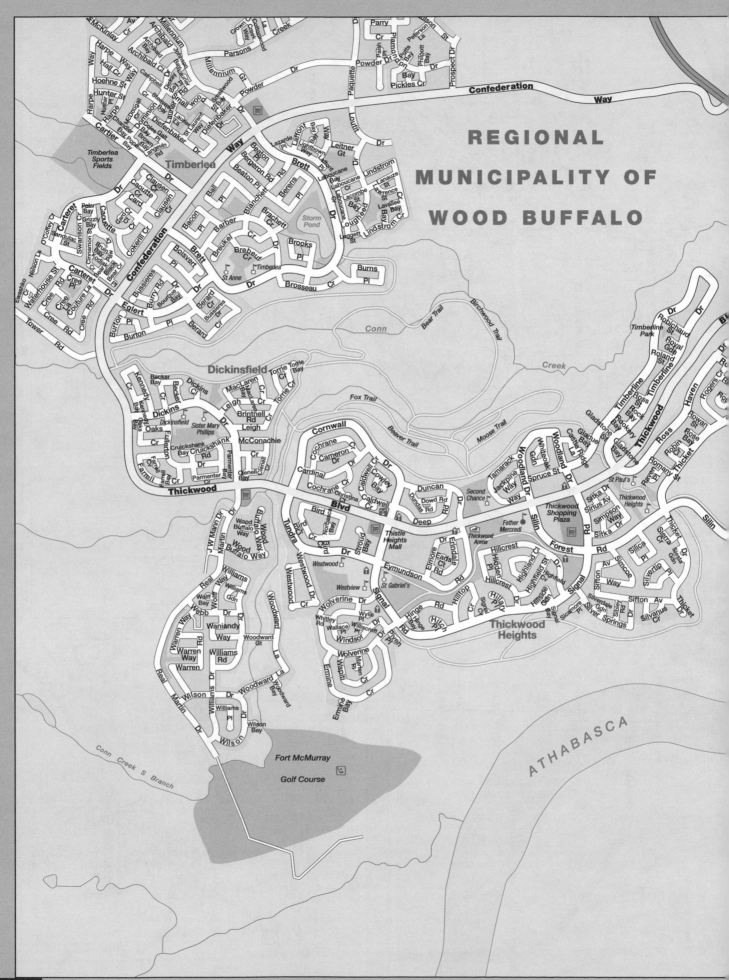

REGIONAL

MUNICIPALITY OF

WOOD BUFFALO

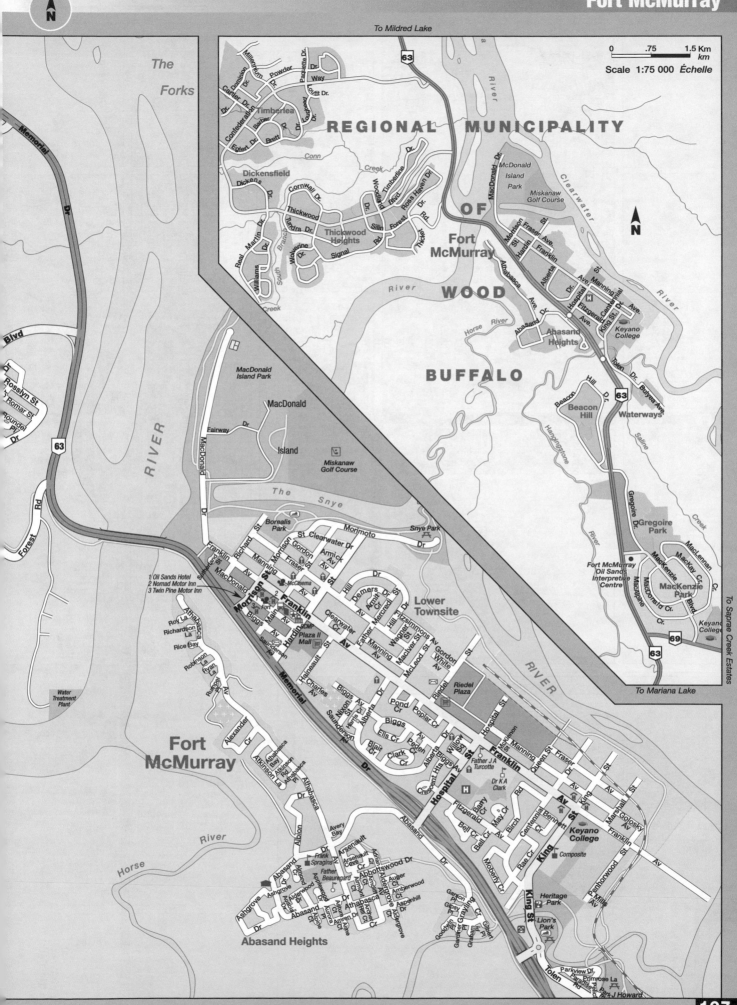

N

The Forks

To Mildred Lake

63

0   .75   1.5 Km
km
Scale 1:75 000 Échelle

N

REGIONAL   MUNICIPALITY

OF

Fort
McMurray

WOOD

BUFFALO

McDonald
Island
Park

Miskanaw
Golf Course

Clearwater
River

Morrison St
Hardin St
Franklin
Ave.
Alberta Dr
Manning Ave.
Centennial
King St
Hospital
Fitzgerald Ave.
Keyano
College
Abasand Ave.
Abasand
Heights

Memorial Dr

Rosslyn St
Romar St
Roundel
Pl
Dr

63

RIVER

MacDonald
Island Park

MacDonald

Island

Fairway   Dr

Miskanaw
Golf Course

The   Snye

River

Horse   River

Beacon
Hill
Beacon
Hill   Waterways

Saline

63

Gregoire Dr

Gregoire
Park

Hangingstone
River

Fort McMurray
Oil Sands
Interpretive
Centre

MacLennan
Cr
MacKay Cr
MacKenzie Blvd
MacDonald Cr.
MacKenzie
Park
Cr.

Keyano
College

69
63

To Saprae Creek Estates

To Mariana Lake

Forest Rd

Water
Treatment
Plant

Fort
McMurray

Horse   River

MacDonald   Dr

Franklin
St
Richard
St
Manning
Morrison
Gordon
Fraser
Armick
St
Borealis
Park

St Clearwater Dr

Morimoto

Snye Park

Dr

1 Oil Sands Hotel
2 Nomad Motor Inn
3 Twin Pine Motor Inn

Saffieldson St
Athabasca St
Macdonald St
Morrison
Biggs
Hardin
Franklin
Main St
Fort St
RCMP
Plaza II
Mall

Roy La
Richardson La
Rice Bay
Robinson La
Ryan La
Rupert Av

Alexander Cr

Atkinson La
Atkinson Rd
Athabasca Bay
Athabasca Dr

Haineault St
Charles Av
Biggs Av
Nixon St
Saunderson Dr
Memorial Dr

Demers Dr
Armick Cr
Father Mercredi
Hill St
Dr
Clearwater
Cr

Fitzsimmons Av
Wagner
MacLeod St
Manning Av
Gordon
White Av
St

Lower
Townsite

Riedel
Plaza

Biggs Av
Harris
Pond
Cr
Poplar
Cr
Biggs
Alberta
Willow
Biggs Av
Ells Cr
Peden
Clark
Cr
Blair
Cr
Crescent His Av

Hospital St

Manning

Franklin
Av

Mckinnon Dr

Queen St
Fraser St
King St

Marshall St
Golosky
Franklin
Av

Father J A
Turcotte

Dr K A
Clark

H

Fitzgerald
Bell Cr
Mav Cr
Birch
Bennett
Centennial Dr
Rae Dr

Keyano
College

Composite

Denhorwood St
Mills Av

King St

Moberly Cr

Avery Bay
Albion
Dr

Frank
Spragins
Father
Beauregard

Arsenault
Cr
Abbottswood Dr
Adrian
Aldergrove
Almond
Amber
Auber
Ct
Amberwood
Dr

Ashgrove
Dr
Abasand
Abasand
Alpine
Amren
Alpena
Aspen
Aurora
Applewood
Adderwood
Aldergrove
Cr
Aurora Ct
Aspenhill
Aldergrove
Dr

Abasand Heights

Garson
Goodwin
Gardiner
Grayling
Gipsy
Graham

Heritage
Park

Lion's
Park

Tolen   Dr

Benbyea Ave

Parkview Dr
Primrose La
Pardise
Pat J Howard

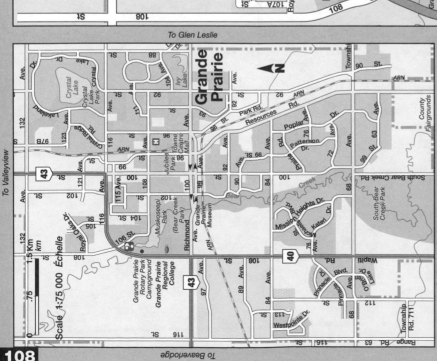

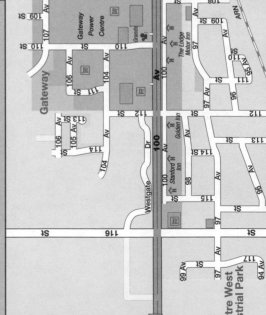

Scale 1:25 000 Échelle

N

0 .25 .5 .75 1 Kilometre
kilomètre

To Hinton

Maligne Rd

Hwy Yellowhead

Lodge Rd

CN

16

Lake Annette Handicapped Trail

Lake Annette

Patricia Lake Bungalows

Patricia Lake

Pyramid Lake Rd

Jasper   National

Park

Creek

Sewage Treatment Plant

RIVER

Trefoil Lakes

Cottonwood

Cottonwood Slough

ATHABASCA

Lodge Rd

Mildred Lake

Sawridge

Dr

Jasper Park Lodge

Lobstick Lodge
Charlton's Chateau Jasper

Marmot
Tonquin Inn
Juniper St

Gelkie St
Patricia St
Cir

Jasper Inn

Bonhomme St

CN

Jasper Park Lodge Golf Course

Pyramid Lake Rd

Aspen

Aspen

Connaught Dr

Lac Beauvert

Lions Park

Bonhomme

Colin

Balsam

Av

Amethyst Lodge

Aspen Gardens

16

Jasper

Pyramid Av

Cedar Av

Astoria

Jasper Yellowhead Museum

Pyramid Bench Trails

500

Jasper Elem

Gelkie

Jasper Park Information Centre
National Historic Site

Elm Av

RCMP

Patricia

Robson St

Whistler's Inn

Athabasca

Maligne Av

Hazel Av

The Den Wildlife Museum
Park Administration
Chaba

Miette

Pine Grove Senior Citizens Home

Old Fort Point Trails

Tonquin St

Turret

Pyramid

Willow

Spruce Av

Stan Wright
Industrial Park

Creek Dr

Poplar St

Lodgepole St

Mount Robson Inn

Pine

Hazel Dr

Old Fort Point

Cabin Creek Dr

Brewster

Patricia

Patricia

Maligne Lodge

Connaught

CN

Hazel Av

Twin

Swift

Stoney Mountain Village

Yellowhead

93A

Lakes

Valley of the Five Lakes Trail

16

Hwy

Tekarra Lodge

Icefields

Miette

River

93

Pkwy

To Mount Robson, BC

To Lake Louise

To Castle Mountain

To Banff

*Kingfisher
Lake*

Lake Louise Ski Area

Whitehorn Rd

Bow Valley Parkway

River

Pipestone

1A

Mud Lake

Bow

River

Dr

Village Rd

RCMP

Mountaineer Lodge Rd

Pinnacle Dr

Fairview Dr

Lake Louise Campground

Louise Dr

Samson Mall

Lake Louise Inn

Post Hotel

Pipestone Rd

CP

Village Rd

Saddleback

Sentinel Rd

Canadian Alpine Centre and International Hostel

Slate Rd

Sheol Rd

Lake Louise Dr

Lake Louise

Creek

Paradise Lodge and Bungalows

Moraine Lake Rd

Road closed in winter

1

Louise

Creek

Banff

National

Park

Deer Lodge

Lake Louise Dr

Icefields Pkwy

River

Bow

93

Bath

Creek

Farmont Chateau Lake Louise

1

Lake

Louise

*Mirror
Lake*

To Jasper

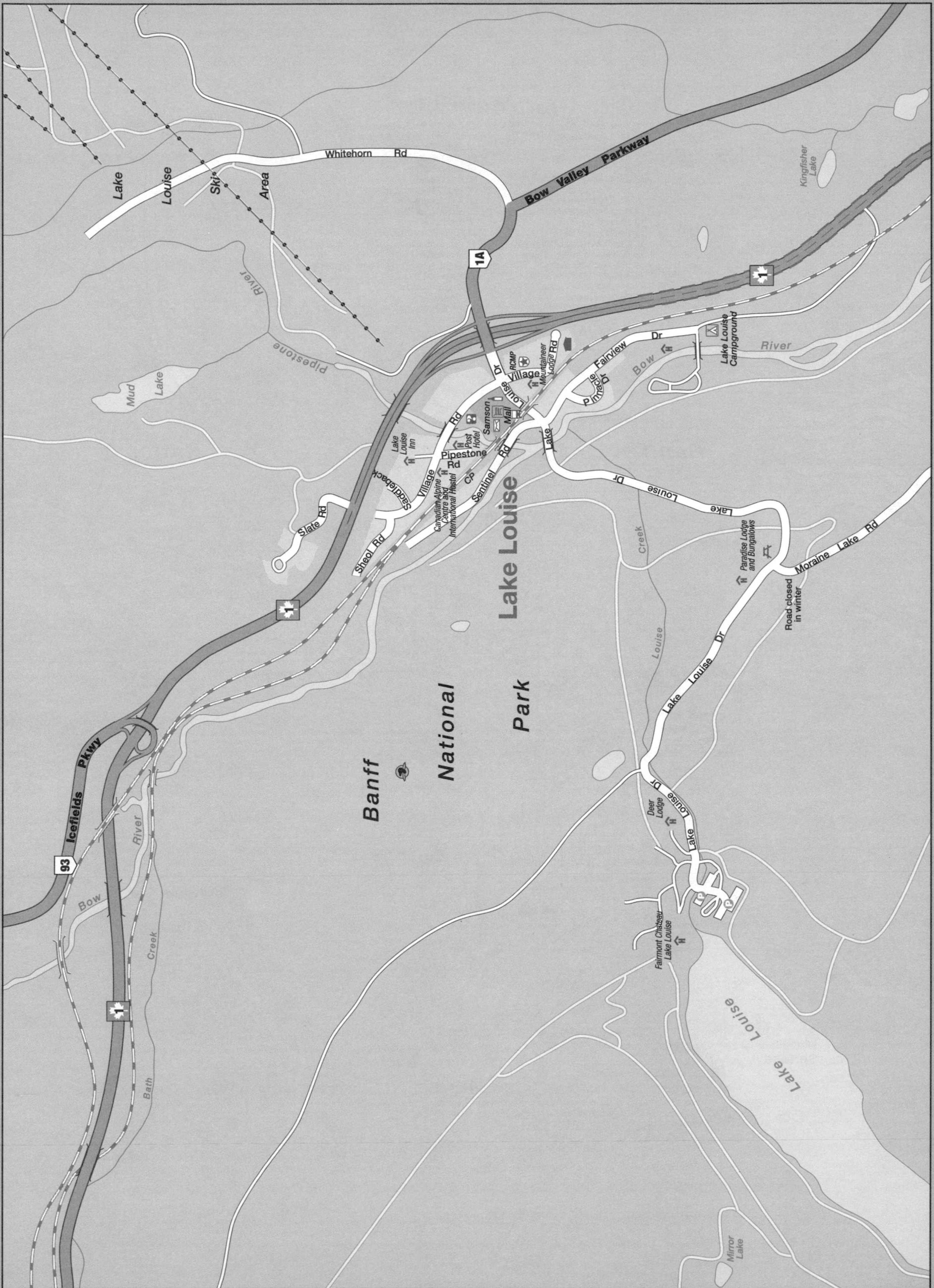

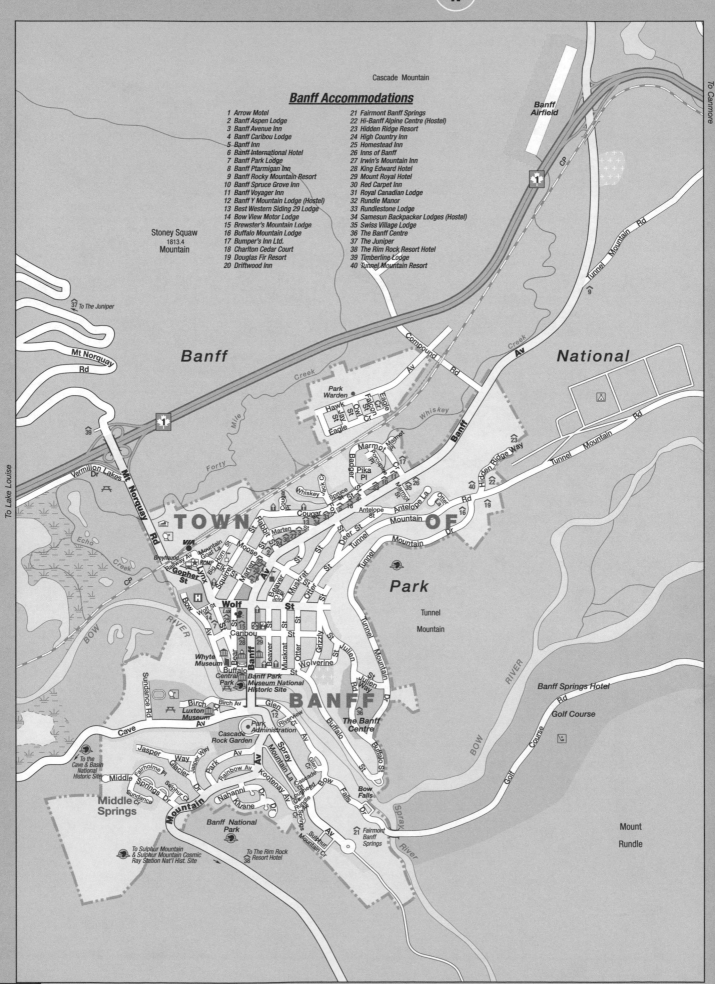

Banff Accommodations

1 Arrow Motel	21 Fairmont Banff Springs
2 Banff Aspen Lodge	22 Hi-Banff Alpine Centre (Hostel)
3 Banff Avenue Inn	23 Hidden Ridge Resort
4 Banff Caribou Lodge	24 High Country Inn
5 Banff Inn	25 Homestead Inn
6 Banff International Hotel	26 Inns of Banff
7 Banff Park Lodge	27 Irwin's Mountain Inn
8 Banff Ptarmigan Inn	28 King Edward Hotel
9 Banff Rocky Mountain Resort	29 Mount Royal Hotel
10 Banff Spruce Grove Inn	30 Red Carpet Inn
11 Banff Voyager Inn	31 Royal Canadian Lodge
12 Banff Y Mountain Lodge (Hostel)	32 Rundle Manor
13 Best Western Siding 29 Lodge	33 Rundlestone Lodge
14 Bow View Motor Lodge	34 Samesun Backpacker Lodges (Hostel)
15 Brewster's Mountain Lodge	35 Swiss Village Lodge
16 Buffalo Mountain Lodge	36 The Banff Centre
17 Bumper's Inn Ltd.	37 The Juniper
18 Charlton Cedar Court	38 The Rim Rock Resort Hotel
19 Douglas Fir Resort	39 Timberline Lodge
20 Driftwood Inn	40 Tunnel Mountain Resort

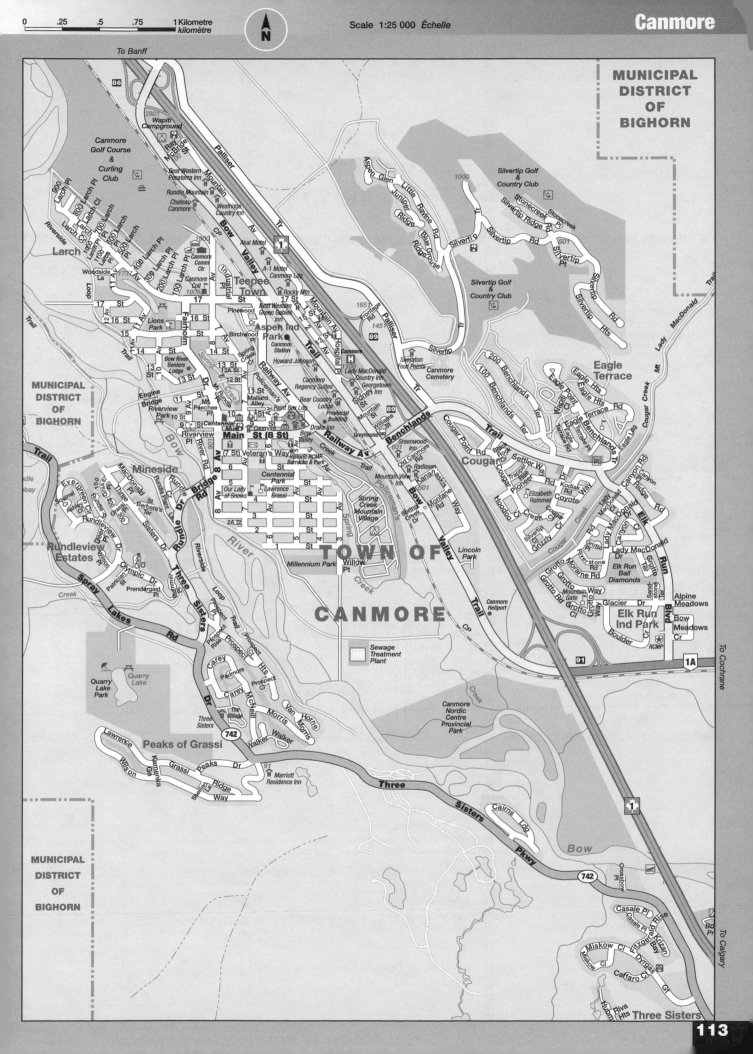

Scale 1:25 000 *Échelle*

0 .25 .5 .75 1 Kilometre
kilomètre

To Banff

MUNICIPAL DISTRICT OF BIGHORN

Wapiti Campground

Canmore Golf Course & Curling Club

Larch

Woodside La

MUNICIPAL DISTRICT OF BIGHORN

Best Western Pocaterra Inn

Rundle Mountain
Chateau Canmore

Westridge Country Inn

Akai Motel

A-1 Motel
Canmore Ldg

Canmore Comm Ctr

Canmore Coll

Rocky Mtn

Teepee Town

Pinewood

Best Western Green Gables Inn

Aspen Ind Park

Birchwood

Lions Park

Fairholm

Canmore Station

Bow River Seniors Lodge

Spring Creek

Howard Johnson

Canmore Regency Suites

Engine Bridge Riverview Park

Policeman's

Mallard Alley

Bear Country Lodge

Paint Box Ldg

Centennial

Riverview Museum

Provincial Building

Drake Inn

Bow Valley

Main St (8 St)

Historic RCMP Barracks & Park

Veteran's Way

Our Lady of Snows

Lawrence Grassi

Centennial Park

Mineside

MacDonald

Barbara's Ter

Rundleview Estates

Rundleview Dr

Olympic Dr

Prendergast Pl

Patrician

Spray Lakes Rd

Three Sisters Dr

Riverside

Millennium Park

Willow Pt

TOWN OF CANMORE

Quarry Lake Park

Quarry Lake

Carey

Padmore

Prospect

Peaks of Grassi

Lawrence

Wilson

Kamenka Gn

Grassi

Shelling

Peaks Dr

Ridge Way

The Village

Three Sisters

Morris

Van Horne

Walker

McNeill

742

91

Marriott Residence Inn

Sewage Treatment Plant

Spring Creek Mountain Village

Lincoln Park

Canmore Heliport

Three

Sisters

Pkwy

Cairns Ldg

742

Bow

Crossbow Pl

Casale Pl

Miskow Cl

Fitzgerald

Riva Hts

Three Sisters

Canmore Nordic Centre Provincial Park

Aspen Glen

Little Ravine Rd

Juniper

Blue Grouse Ridge

Silvertip

Silvertip Golf & Country Club

Silvertip Ridge

Stonecreek Pl

Stonecreek

Silvertip Rd

Silvertip Pt

Silvertip Hts

Silvertip Rd

Lady MacDonald

Silvertip Golf & Country Club

Frontage Rd

Palliser

89

Sheraton Four Points

Canmore Cemetery

Silvertip

Lady MacDonald Country Inn

Georgetown Inn

Sidney St

Williams

Mountain

89

Greenwood Inn

Old Canmore Rd

Radisson

Mountain View Inn

Benchlands

200 Benchlands

100 Benchlands

Eagle Terrace

Eagle Hts

Eagle Point

Eagle Hts

Wapiti

Eagle Terrace Ter

Eagle Benchlands Tr

Eagle Ldg

Cougar Creek

Cougar Point Rd

Cougar

Trail

Settler Way

Black Rock

Trapper

Pioneer

Elizabeth Rummel

Coyote

Hoodoo

Kodiak Rd

Silvertip Cr

Grizzly

Grotto

Moraine Rd

Cougar

Mountain Gate Way

Grotto Rd

Grotto Cr

Grotto Cl

Glacier Dr

Lady MacDonald Dr

Canyon Rd

Canyon Ridge

Elk Run

Elk Run Ball Diamonds

Riverstone Rd

Sandstone

Elk Run Ind Park

Boulder

RCMP

Alpine Meadows

Bow Meadows

Bow Meadows Cr

Kananaskis Way

Spring Creek Dr

Montane Rd

Bow Valley Trail

91

1A

To Cochrane

Bow

1

To Calgary

MUNICIPAL DISTRICT OF BIGHORN

0 .25 .5 .75 1 Kilometre
kilomètre

To Millet

To Camrose

To Ponoka

To Lone Ridge

To Hwy 822

COUNTY OF WETASKIWIN

CITY OF WETASKIWIN

COUNTY OF WETASKIWIN

Peace Hills Park

Cree Cr

Southview Dr

(Township Rd 464) Blackfeet Av

Wetaskiwin Golf Club

Loons Golf Course & RV Park

Wetaskiwin Lions Community RV Campground

814

2A

Range Rd 24?

Range Rd

241A

72 Av

13

72 Av

Northview Dr

Wetaskiwin General H

Highlands Pl

Aspen Av

Aspen Ridge

Aspen Ridge Rd

Wetaskiwin

Northmount Dr

Cameron Cr

Caledonia

Alder St

Ashwood St

Applewood St

Northmount

Dr

Northmount

Northgate Cr

Northland Cl

Northbend Dr

Northridge Rd

Northlake La

Northwood

64 Av

64

46 St

Nordal Ct

63

63 Av

Parkside

Dr

CP

Parkglen

Parkland

100 Parkland

200 Parkland

Willow Dr

Pine Cr

Pine

49A St

Plum Dr

50

CP

Wetaskiwin Memorial Cemetery

47

E Railway St

60 Av

Garden

Clearwater Cr

Cedar

Parkview

Meadows

Parkhill Cr

Parkridge

Parkallen Way

Parkside

Hills of Peace Monument

Willow Dr

Willow Cr

Rose Garden

Engelwood Dr

Mou ntain Ash

Centennial

Elm St

Oak Dr

Birch Cr

Green Ash

Spruce Dr

57 Av

Garnet St

Garwood Cr

Garwood

Parkview Dr

Mariner Bay Cr

Knights of Columbus Centre

By the Lake Park

56

Av

Hawthorn

Maple

Evergreen

Mayday

Centennial

55

56 Av

56 Av

55 St

47A St

Garland Rd

Garnet Cr

Garwood Cr

55

54

53

Norwood

Dr

Norwood

Norwood

Village Square

44

52

Sacred Heart

West St

56 St

50 Av

60 St

Wetaskiwin Cemetery

53 Av

54 Av

55A St

51 St

District Mus

54 Av

49

54

55

53

51

Lynn Lauren

Av

Exhibition Grounds

Wetaskiwin

Township Rd 262A

50 Av

48

47A Av

47 Av

58 St

57 St

RCMP

Wetaskiwin Motel

55A St

49

Diamond Juilee Park

50 St

Rose Country Inn

Old Court House

50

49 Av

48 Av

47A

50

48

50 Av

48

47

46

45

CB McMurdo

Clear Vista

Ben George Park

46A St

45

44

43

42

41

Wildrose Garden Estates Mobile Home Park

62 St

61A St

61 St

60 St

46 St

46 Av

45 Av

44 Av

Queen Elizabeth Av

47 Av

46 Av

45 Av

44 Av

43 Av

42 Av

Jubilee Place

47

46

45

44

43

42

41

Wetaskiwin Airfield

47

Stage Tr

57 St

2A 13

Best Western Wayside

Snow

Spoatinow

Parkdale Park

Parkdale

53 St

41 Av

42

41

51A Av

47 Av

40 A Av

50

48

13

40 Av

40 Av

40 Av

613

Millard St

39A Av

54A St

39

47A St

39

47

Super 8

Fort Ethier Lodge

37A

53A St

38

37

48 St

62 St

Av

Av

Wetaskiwin Mall

56 St

37A

54A St

53A St

37

49 St

36 Av

36

2A

Range Rd 241

CP

114

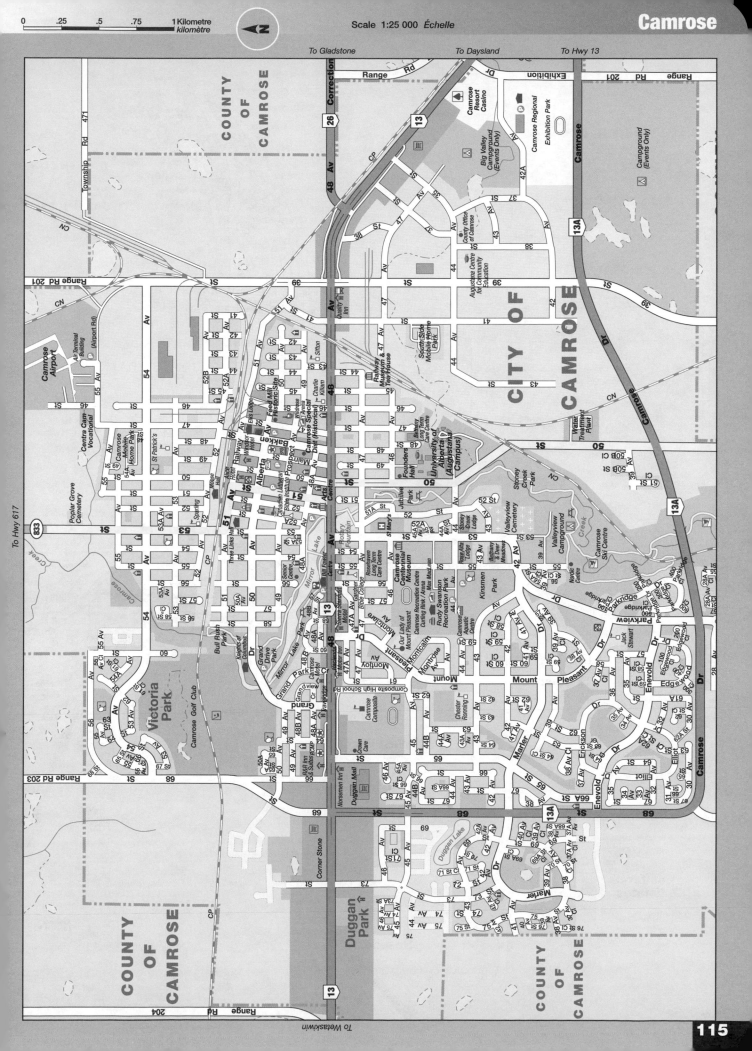

Scale 1:25 000 *Échelle*

0 .25 .5 .75 1 Kilometre
kilomètre

N

To Gladstone   To Daysland   To Hwy 13

COUNTY OF CAMROSE

CITY OF CAMROSE

COUNTY OF CAMROSE

Camrose Airport

Victoria Park

Camrose Golf Club

University of Alberta (Augustana) Campus

Duggan Park

Duggan Lake

To Wetaskiwin

Scale 1:25 000 *Échelle*

N

0 .25 .5 .75 1 Kilometre
kilomètre

NORTHERN LIGHTS

MUNICIPAL

DISTRICT 22

Bewley
Island

Trees of
Alberta Display

Good Shepherd

Kinsmen Sport
Complex

71 Av
71 St
71 Av
73
73
74 St
74 Av
75 St
75 Av
76 Av
77
78 Av
79 Av
80 Av
81 Av
81 Av
82 Av
82 Av
83 Av
84
84 Av
85
85 Av
86 Av
86 Av
87 Av
88 Av
89
89 Av
90
90 Av
91
92 Av
93 Av
94
94 Av

1 Av

McGrath

Norglen

RCMP

Springfield

NORTHERN
SUNRISE
COUNTY

Kinsmen
Park

T A Norris

Glenmary

Springfield

Kaufman Hill
Rd

Peace
River

Pat's Creek Rd
Pat's Creek

Cool Springs
Trailer Village

CN

Peace

River

T O W N   O F

P E A C E   R I V E R

87 Av

90 St

90 Av

CN

Terrace
Mobile
Home
Park

86 St

100 St

94 Av

95

95

96

97 Av

98

99

100

101

102 Av

Canadian Best

Prov Bldg

Peace Valley Inn

Travellers

Crescent

Riverfront
Park

Cinema 72

100 St

101 St

102 St

101 St

Twelve
Foot Davis
Historical
Site

2

90 ST (Old Hwy 2)

CN

Lions
Campground

West Hill
Ball Diamond

Cheviot
Heights
Mobile
Home
Park

Fairview College
Peace River
Campus

(College Rd)

97 Av

99 Av

99 Av

99 Av

100
Av

99 Av

Old Highway 2

88 ST

101 Av

85 St

100 Av

Rolling
Hills

102

102 Av

103 Av

103 Av

104 Av

105 Av

105

83
St

106 Av

107 Av

Saddleback
Ridge

80 St

75 St

77 St

78
St

76 St

80
St

104 Av

West Hill

2

To Grimshaw

89
Av

75 St

75
St

92 Av

99 Av

Shaftesbury Tr

Pine Ridge
Campground

Mobile Home
Park

River

Heart River

Rotary
Park

12 Foot Davis
Ball Park

Grouard Rd

12 Foot Davis Statue

102 Av

101 St

103 Av

104 Av

Peace River
Centennial Museum
& Native Burial Site

105

106 Av

107 Av

103 St

108

109 Av

744

Greene
Valley
Provincial
Park

110 Av

99
St

Municipal Hospital
& Nursing Home

H

Judah
Hill
Rd

90
St

105 Av

107 Av

107 Av

92 Av

109 Av

109
Av

111

111 Av

113
Av

Peace River Ski Hill

West Peace River

114 Av

115 Av

Riverview

116 Av

101 St

103

Misery Mountain

Sagitawa
Lookout

2

To McLennan

2

To Normandville

Eastbrook
Estates

118 Av

78
St

120
Av

124 Av

80 St

684

Rosedale

118 Av

91 St

120 Av

123 Av

Shaftesbury Tr

Judah
Hill

CN

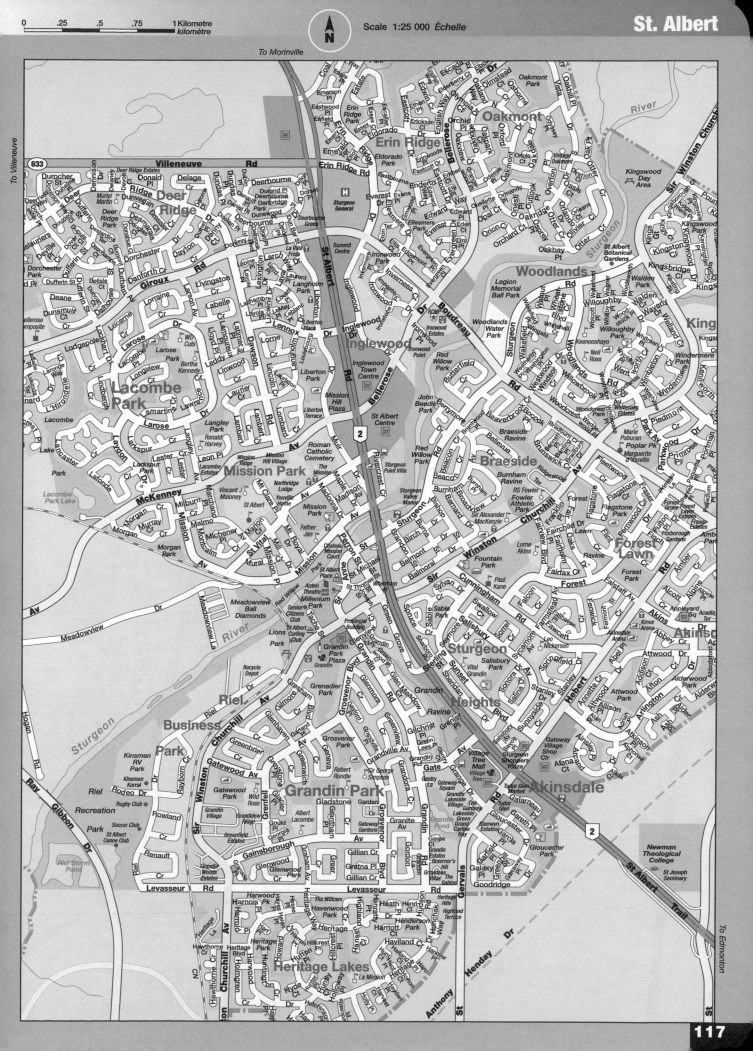

Scale 1:25 000 *Échelle*

N

0   .25   .5   .75   1 Kilometre
kilomètre

To Lamont

CITY OF FORT SASKATCHEWAN

COUNTY OF STRATHCONA

MUNICIPAL DISTRICT OF STURGEON

NORTH SASKATCHEWAN RIVER

Eastgate Business Park

Clover Park

Rudolph Park

Fort Saskatchewan Correctional Institute

Cornerstone Power Centre

Fort Saskatchewan Cemetery

Golf and Curling Club

Best Western Fort Inn & Suite

Park Avenue Motel

Turner Park

Dick Mager Park

Fort Mall

Market Square

Elk's Park

Jubilee Park

Fort Hotel

Brant Hotel

Riverview Nursing Home

Fort Saskatchewan Historical Museum

Jarvis Park

Legacy Park

Fort Saskatchewan General

Our Lady of The Angel's

Jubilee Recreation Centre

Kinsmen Park

Harbour Pool

Legion

Fort Hotel

Christian School

John Paul II

Bridgeview

Sheridon

Riverpointe

Riverpointe Plaza

RCMP

Carscadden Park

Win Ferguson Sportsplex

Pope John XXIII

Pineview

Steele Park

Becker Cr

Southfort

Allard Way

Driving Range

Galloway Wynd

Greenfield Park

James Mowat Park

Marion Rogers Park

William Casey Park

Westpark Estates

Westmews

Westwood Green

Westpark

Westwood Park

Woodbend

Windsor Pt

Woodsmere

Westwood Trails

Wetlands Conservation Area

Price Aldersen Park

Sewage Treatment Park

Lamoureux

To Namao

To Edmonton

To Sherwood Park

Highways: 15, 21

Scale 1:25 000 *Échelle*

0 .25 .5 .75 1 Kilometre / kilomètre

N

To North Cooking Lake

To Fort Saskatchewan

To New Norway

COUNTY OF STRATHCONA

Neighbourhoods / Areas:
Clarkdale Meadows, Heritage Point, Heritage Hills, Foxboro, Foxhaven, Regency Park Estates, Regency Park, Sherwood Hills, Clover Bar, Craigavon, Nottingham, Lakeland Ridge, Charlton Heights, Crimson, Glen Allan, Greengrove, Granada, Maplewood, Brentwood, Sherwood Park Mall, Strathcona Village, Broadview Park, Durham Town Square, Sherwood Town Centre, Shivam Park, Mills Haven, Sherwood, Broadmoor Estates, Sherwood Heights, Maplegrove, Woodbridge Farms, Westboro, Broadmoor Centre, Village on the Lake, Village Commercial

RCMP 911

To Edmonton

234 Alexis Band / Golden Spike
Place Name Inde

Place Name Index

How to use this index

To find a place, search through the alphabetically arranged columns. Note the page number and reference square to the right of the place name. For example, to find the location of Ghost Lake:

Ghost Lake 69 N72-73

Place name — Page number — Reference Squares

234 Alexis Band .61 D64-65
Abee .57 V80
Abilene .58 W85
Academy .76 P75
Acadia Valley .73 N89-90
Acheson .56 Z77
Acme .70 L78
Adams Landing .19 X70 20 X71
Aden .84 Z85-86
Aerial .71 M81
Aetna .82 Y78
Airdrie .70 M75-76
Akenside .57 Z79
Alberta Beach .56 Y74
Albright .41 P56 42 P57
Alcomdale .56 X77
Alcurve .59 Z90
Alder Flats .63 C71-72
Alderson .78 S85
Aldersyde .76 Q76
Alexander Band .56 X76-77
Alexis Band .56 Y73
Alexis Band .62 C66
Alexis Whitecourt Band .54 V68 55 V69
Alhambra .63 G73
Alix .65 F79
Alix South Junction .64 F78 65 F79
Alliance .66 F84
Allingham .70 K77
Alpen .47 U80
Alpen Siding .47 U80
Alsike .63 B73
Altario .73 J90
Amber Valley .47 S80
Amelia .57 X80
Amesbury .47 Q82
Amisk .66 E-F86
Amundson .42 U60
Analta .46 U78
Anastasia .77 Q79
Andrew .57 X82
Angle Lake .58 Y86 59 Y87
Angus Ridge .65 D79
Ankerton .65 D82
Ansell .54 Z66
Anselme .55 X70
Anthony Hill .64 D77
Anthracite .69 N70
Antler Lake .57 Z80
Antler Meadows .57 Z80
Anton Lake .56 V78 57 V79
Antonid .84 V84
Anzac .39 J86-87
Arcadia .44 P67-68
Ardenode .70 N78
Ardenville .82 W77-78
Ardley .65 G79
Ardmore .59 V88
Ardrossan .57 Z79
Armada .77 R80
Armena .65 B80
Armistice .58 X86 59 X87
Arneson .73 N90
Arrowwood .77 P-Q79
Arthurville .70 J78
Arvilla .56 W77
Ashmont .58 W85
Aspen .57 A81
Aspen Acres .64 C74-75
Aspen Ridge (Grande Prairie 1) .42 Q59
Aspen Ridge (Sturgeon) .57 W-X79
Assineau .45 P70
Assumption .9 V59-60
Asul .67 G88
Athabasca .47 S79
Athabasca Chipewyan First Nation .14 V86 .15 U87-88 V87 .22 X85 23 W-X87 Z86
Athabasca Chipewyan First Nation .22 A85 23 A86
Athabascan Acres .47 T79
Atikameg .35 M69
Atikamisis Lake Settlement .35 M69
Atlee .79 P87
Atmore .47 S81-82
Auburndale .67 C87
Avenir .47 R82
Azure .76 R76
Bad Heart .33 O60-61
Bain .85 Y89
Baintree .70 N78 71 N79
Balay Estates .46 U78
Ballantine .56 X73
Ballater .34 O64
Balm .55 X70
Balzac .70 N75
Banana Belt .44 O67
Banff .69 N70
Bank Bay .49 T89
Bantry .78 R84
Baptiste River .63 E71
Bardo .57 A81
Bargrave .70 L78
Barich .57 V81
Barlee Junction .65 C80-81
Barnegat .48 S84
Barnwell .83 V82
Barons .83 U79
Barrhead .56 W73-74
Bashaw .65 E80
Bassano .77 P81
Batter Junction .72 K-L84
Battle Bend .66 F85
Battle Lake .64 C74
Battle River .66 G83-84
Bawlf .65 C81-82
Bay Tree .32 M55
Bayview Beach .47 R82 S82 48 R83 S83
Beach Corner .56 Z74-75
Beacon Corner .58 V86
Beacon Heights .70 H77
Bear Canyon .32 K56
Bear Lake .42 P58
Bear Ridge Estates .42 Q59
Bearberry .69 J72
Bearspaw .70 N74
Beau Rand .56 A75-76
Beau Vista .56 A78
Beaumont .56 A78
Beauvallon .58 Y85-86
Beaver Creek .57 A80-81
Beaver Crossing .49 U89 59 V89
Beaver First Nation .18 X66 19 X67
Beaver Hill .57 Z80-81
Beaver Lake .48 S84
Beaver Lake Band .48 T84
Beaver Mines .82 X75
Beaver River .49 U89
Beaverdam .59 V89
Beaverhill .57 Y80-81
Beaverlodge .41 Q56 42 Q57
Beazer .82 Y-Z77
Beddington .70 N75-76
Behan .48 P85
Beiseker .70 M77-78
Bellevue .81 W74
Bellis .58 W83
Belloy .33 N61
Bellshill .66 E85
Belvedere .56 W74
Benalto .64 G74
Benbow .54 W66
Benbow Junction .54 W66
Benchlands .69 N72-73
Bentley .64 F75-76
Benton .73 M89
Berdinskies .22 Z85 23 Z86
Bergen .69 K73
Berrymoor .55 A72
Berwyn .33 K62
Betula Beach .55 Z72
Bey Etta .64 C77-78
Beynon .71 M80
Bezanson .42 P-Q60
Bickerdike .54 Z66
Big Coulee .47 R79
Big Hill Springs Estates .70 N74-75
Big Horn Band .62 F67
Big Meadow (Big Lakes MD) .35 O67
Big Meadow (Bonnyville MD 87) .49 U88
Big Slough .13 U80
Big Stone .72 N86
Big Valley .71 H80
Biggar .70 N74-75
Bigstone .64 C78
Bigstone Cree Nation .36 L77 M77 .37 K78 L78 M78-79 47 P79
Bilby .56 Y74-75
Bindloss .79 P89
Bingley .63 F72
Birch Bay .64 E75
Birch Cove .56 X73
Bircham .70 L78
Birchcliff .64 F75
Bison Lake .27 E67-68
Bittern Lake .65 C80
Bitumount .30 D85
Black Diamond .76 Q75
Blackfalds .64 F77
Blackfoot .59 A89-90
Blackie .76 Q77
Blairmore .81 W74
Blood Tribe .82 Z77 83 W79
Blooming Valley .32 O57
Bloomsbury .56 V73
Blue Haven Estates .63 C72
Blue Heron Estate .47 S81-82 T81-82
Blue Ridge .55 W70
Blue Sky .21 A80 57 Z80
Blueberry .56 Z74
Blueberry Mountain .32 L-M58
Bluesky .33 L61
Bluffton .64 D74
Blumenort .19 X67
Bodo .73 H90
Boian .58 X83
Bon Accord .56 X78
Bonanza .32 M55-56
Bonar .72 L84
Bondiss .47 T81
Bonnyville .59 V87-88
Bonnyville Beach .59 V87
Borradaile .59 A88
Boscombe .58 W85
Botha .65 G81
Botten .52 V59
Bottrel .69 M73 70 M74
Bow City .77 R82
Bow Island .84 U-V85
Bowden .70 J75-76
Bowell .79 T87
Bowmanton .79 S-T88
Boyer Settlement .19 X67
Boyle .47 T81
Boyne Lake .58 V84
Bragg Creek .75 O73-74
Brainard .41 P56
Brant .76 R77
Braun Village .57 W79
Brazeau Dam .63 C70
Bredin .42 P58-59
Breton .63 B73
Bretona .57 Z79
Breynat .47 Q82
Bridgeview .32 N58 33 N59
Brièreville .48 U84
Briggs .64 F77
Brightbank .56 Z74
Brocket .82 W76-77
Broncho Creek .33 M59
Brookhollow 56 W78 57 W79
Brooks .78 Q83
Brookside .42 Q59
Brookville .57 Z80
Brosseau .58 Y84-85
Brownfield .66 G85
Brownvale .33 L62
Broxburn .83 V80
Bruce .66 B83
Bruderheim .57 X80
Brûle .53 A62
Bryan Spur .61 B65
Buck Creek .63 B72
Buck Lake .63 C72
Buck Lake Estates .63 C72
Buffalo .79 P88
Buffalo Head Prairie .18 Z66 19 Z67
Buffalo Lake .42 P58
Buffalo Lake Estates 19 Y67
Buffalo Lake Estates 65 F80
Buffalo Lake Metis Settlement .47 U82
Buford .56 A77
Bullpound .72 L83
Bullpound .78 O83
Bullshead .85 U88
Bulwark .66 G85
Bunny Hollow .70 N74
Buoyant .70 L78
Burbank .64 F77
Burdett .84 V84-85
Burmis .82 W75
Burtonsville .56 A73
Busby .56 W-X77
Butte .63 G73
Byemoor .71 J82
Cadogan .67 G89
Cadomin .61 C64
Cadotte Lake .35 J67
Cairns .67 G88
Calahoo .56 Y75-77
Calais .43 Q-R63
Calgary .75 O74 76 O75
Calling Lake .47 Q79-80
Calling River .47 Q80
Calmar .56 A77
Cambarr Estates .55 W72 56 W73
Cambria .71 M81
Cameron .64 B76-77
Camp Creek .56 V73
Campsie .55 W72 56 W73
Campsie Cove .56 W73
Camrose .65 C80
Canmore .69 N71 75 O71
Canterbury Estates .56 Y73-74
Canyon Creek .45 P71
Cappon .79 O88
Caprona .71 H80
Carbon .71 L79
Carbondale .56 Y78
Carcajou .18 A-B64
Cardiff .56 X-Y78
Cardston .82 Y78
Carldale .53 Z63
Carley Junction .56 W77
Carlos .63 E73
Carlson Landing .14 U84
Carmangay .77 T79
Carnwood .63 B72-73
Caroline .69 H73
Carolside .72 N84
Carrot Creek .54 Z68
Carseland .76 P78
Carstairs .70 L75
Caruso .76 O78
Carvel .56 Z74
Carvel Corner .56 Z74
Carway .82 Z78
Casa Vista .57 X79
Caslan .47 T82
Cassils .78 Q-R83
Castle Island .56 Y74
Castle Mountain .68 N69
Castor .66 G83
Cavendish .79 P88-89
Cayley .76 R76
Cecil .78 T84
Central .65 C79
Century .57 Z79-80
Century Estates .47 T79
Cereal .73 M87
Cessford .78 O85
Champion .77 S79
Chancellor .77 O80
Chard .39 M87
Chateh .9 V60
Chauvin .67 E89-90
Cheadle .76 O77-78
Chedderville .69 H72
Cheecham .39 K87
Cheneka .69 N73
Cherhill .55 X72
Cherry Grove 49 U90 59 V90
Cherry Point .32 K55
Chestermere .76 O77
Chief Mountain .82 Z77
Chigwell .64 F78
Chin .83 V81
Chinook .73 M87
Chinook Valley .34 J63
Chip Lake .55 Y-Z70
Chipewyan Lake .29 F79
Chipewyan Prairie First Nation .39 M87-88
Chipman .57 Y81
Chisholm .46 R74
Chokio .82 W77
Cinnamon Ridge .57 A80
Circle 5 Estates .75 O74
Clairmont .42 P59
Clandonald .59 Z88
Claresholm .76 T77-78
Clarkson Valley .43 Q62
Claysmore .58 A86
Clear Hills .25 H62
Clear Prairie .24 H57
Clearbrook .57 V79
Cleardale .32 J57
Clearview Acres .57 W79
Cline River .62 G66 68 H66
Clive .64 F78
Clover View Estates 59 A87
Cloverlawn .65 B79
Cluny .77 P80
Clyde .56 W78
Clymont .56 Z77
Coal Valley .61 C65 62 C66
Coaldale .83 V81
Coalfield .82 W-X75
Coalhurst .83 V79
Coalspur .61 B65
Cochrane .70 N74
Cochrane Lake .69 N73
Codesa .33 N61
Codner .63 F72
Coghill .64 G78 65 G79
Cold Lake .49 U89-90
Cold Lake First Nation .49 U89 U89-90 59 V89
Coleman .81 W74
Colinton .47 T79
College Heights .64 F77
Collicutt .70 M75
Collingwood Cove .21 A79-80 57 Z79-80
Compeer .73 J90
Condor .63 G73
Congresbury .63 G72
Conjuring Creek .64 B77
Conklin .39 N86-87
Connemara .76 R76
Connor Creek .55 W71
Conrad .84 W83
Conrich .70 N76
Consort .73 H-J87
Coolidge .46 T78
Corbett Creek .55 V71
Cordel .66 F83
Coronado .57 X79
Coronation .72 H85
Cosmo .55 X72
Cosway .70 L78
Cotillion .32 L55-56
Countess .77 P82
Country Air Estates .59 A89
Country Squire .57 A81
Coutts .84 Z83
Cowley .82 W75
Cozy Cove .43 Q63
Craddock .83 X81
Craigdhu .70 M78
Craigend .48 T83-84
Craigmyle .71 K82
Crammond .69 H73
Cranford .83 V82
Cree Valley .64 C74
Creekland .56 A73-74
Cremona .70 L74
Cressday .85 Y89-90
Crestomere .64 E77
Crimson Lake .63 F71
Crippsdale .57 W79
Croftland Subdivision .57 Y80
Crooked Creek .43 Q62
Crossfield .70 L-M75
Crossroads .70 J78
Crowell .34 M65
Crowfoot .77 P81
Crump .70 L75
Crystal Springs .64 C75
Culp .34 N63
Curlew .70 J-K78
Cygnet .64 G76
Cynthia .55 A70
Czar .67 F87
Dalehurst .53 Z63-64
Dalemead .76 P77
Dalroy .70 N77
Dalum .71 M81
Dancey Estates .70 H78
Danube .47 U80
Dapp .46 U77
Daresbury .65 C80-81
Darwell .56 Y73
Daysland .65 D82
Dead Mans Flats .75 O71
Deadwood .26 G63
DeBolt .43 Q61
Decoigne .60 D60
Decrene .46 Q74
Deep Creek .47 R79-80
Deer Hill .33 K60
Deer Ridge Estate .47 S79
Deerland .57 X80-81
Del-Rich Meadows .70 N76
Del Bonita .83 Z80
Delacour .70 N76-77
Delburne .65 G79
Delia .71 L82
Delmuir .57 W80
Delph .57 W81
Demay .65 B80-81
Demmitt .32 O55
Dene Tha Band .9 T62 18 W64-65 X64-65
Dene Tha First Nation 8 V58 .9 Q60 Q60-61 U59 V59-60
Denwood Acres .59 A89
Derwent .59 Y87
Devenish .39 O86
Deville .57 Z80
Devon .56 A77
Devona .60 B61
Dewberry .59 Z88
DeWinton .76 P75
Diamond City .83 V80
Dickson .70 H74
Didsbury .70 K75
Dimsdale .42 Q58
Dina .67 C90
Dinant .65 B80-81
Dinosaur .71 L81
Diss .61 B65
Dixonville .25 H62 26 H63
Dodds .65 B81
Dogpound .70 L74
Donalda .65 E81
Donatville .47 T79
Donnelly .34 N64
Dorenlee .65 E80
Doris .45 U72
Dorothy .71 M-N82
Dorscheid .42 S59
Dover Estates .56 Y76-77
Dovercourt .63 F72
Draper .31 G86
Drayton Valley .63 B72
Dream Nook Estates .56 X78 57 X79
Dreau .34 N64
Driftpile .45 P69
Driftpile First Nation .44 P68 45 P69
Drumheller .71 M81
Drywood .82 X76
Duagh .57 Y79
Duchess .78 Q83-84
Duffield .56 Z73-74
Duffield Downs .56 Z74
Duhamel .65 C80
Duncans First Nation .33 L62 34 L65-66
Dunkley Meadow .42 Q59
Dunmore .85 U88
Dunn .70 J75
Dunphy .71 L80
Dunshalt .70 N78 71 N79
Dunstable .56 X78
Dunvegan .33 M59-60
Durlingville .59 V88
Durward .76 S76-77
Dusseldorf .56 V74
Duthil .69 N70
Duvernay .58 Y84
Eagle Butte .85 W89
Eagle Hill .70 J74
Eaglesham .33 N62
Early Gardens .34 L63
East Coulee .71 M81-82
East Doe River .32 L55
East Prairie Metis Settlement .44 Q67-68
Eastburg .56 W74-75
Eckville .64 F74
Edberg .65 D80-81
Edgerton .67 D88
Edmonton .56 Z77-78
Edson .54 Z66-67
Edwand .57 W82
Edwards .70 H78
Egg Lake .47 S82
Egremont .57 W79
El Greco Estates .57 Z81
Elbridge .57 V79
Elcan .83 V82
Eldorena .57 X80
Elizabeth .59 V90
Elizabeth Metis Settlement .59 W89-90
Elk Island .57 Y80
Elk Point .59 X87
Elk Valley .75 O73
Elkton .69 K73 70 K74
Elkwater .85 W89
Ellerslie .56 A78
Ellscott .47 U80
Elmworth .41 Q56
Elnora .71 J79
Elspeth .64 G74
Eltham .76 Q77
Embarras .22 Y85 23 Y86
Embarras .54 A65
Embarras Portage .22 X85
Empress .79 O90
Enchant .77 T81-82
Enchantment Valley .64 B77
Endiang .71 J82 72 J83
Enilda .35 O67 44 P67
Enoch Cree Nation .56 Z77-78
Ensign .76 R78
Entice .70 L78
Entrance .53 A62
Entwistle .55 Z71-72
Equity .71 K79
Erin Lodge .33 M61
Erith .54 A66
Ermineskin Tribe .64 D78
Erskine .65 G80
Ervick .65 C80
Esther .73 K89
Ethel Lake .49 T89
Etzikom .84 X86
Eureka River .33 J59
Evansburg .55 Z71
Evarts .64 G74
Evergreen .63 G73
Excel .73 M88
Excelsior .56 Y78
Exshaw .75 O71
Fabyan .67 D87
Fairview .33 L60
Fairview Heights .64 B-C78
Fairydell .56 W78
Falher .34 N64
Fallis .55 Z72 56 Z73
Falun .64 C77
Farrow .76 O78
Faust .45 P69
Fawcett .46 T74
Fawcett Lake .46 P77-78
Fawn Lake .56 W74-75
Federal .72 H84-85
Fedorah .56 X78 57 X79
Fenn .71 H81
Ferintosh .65 D80
Ferlow Junction .65 C80
Fern Creek .64 B74
Fernwood Estates 57 W-X79
Ferrier .63 F71
Fidler .61 C64
Fifth Meridian .12 V73-78
Fincastle .84 V83
Finnegan .71 N82 72 N83
Fishburn .82 X77
Fisher Home .64 B-C74
Fishing Lake Metis Settlement .59 X89-
Fitzallen .58 Z
Fitzgerald .6 P
Fitzgerald .85 U87-
Fitzsimmons .42 P
Flat Lake .58 W
Flatbush .46 S
Fleet .72 H
Fletcher Hall .64 C
Flyingshot Lake Settleme .42 Q58-
Foisy .58 X
Foothills .61 C65 62 C
Footner Lake .18 W
Foremost .84 X
Forest Glen .57 A
Forest Hills Country Estates .57 A
Forest View .34 C
Forestburg .66 E
Fork Lake .48 U84-
Forshee .64 E
Fort Assiniboine .45 U
Fort Chipewyan .14 V
Fort Kent .59 V
Fort MacKay .30 E84-
Fort Macleod .82 V77-
Fort McKay First Nation .30 C82 E
Fort McMurray .30 G85 31 G
Fort McMurray #468 First Nation .31 H86-87 39 J86 J86
Fort Saskatchewan .57 Y79-
Fort Vermilion .19 X67-
Fort Vermilion Settlemen .19 X
Fox Creek .44 U65
Fox Lake .20 W
Fox Lake .85 W
Franchere .58 V86 59 V
Frank .81 W
Freedom .56 V
Freeman River .45 U
Fresnoy .59 V
Friedenstal .33
Frisco .63
Frog Lake .59 X-Y
Frog Lake Band .59 X88-89 X
Furman .82
Gadsby .65
Gage .33 K-
Gainford .55
Galahad .66
Galloway .54
Gap .75
Garden Plain .72
Garden River .12
Garden Valley .56 Z76
Gardenview .56 V
Garfield .70
Garrington .69 J73 70
Garrington Acres .70
Garth .63
Gartly .71
Gatine .71
Gayford .70
Geikie .60
Gem .77
Genesee .56
Ghost Lake .69 N72
Ghost Pine Creek 71 K79
Ghost River .69
Gibbons .57
Gibbonslea .57
Gift Lake .35 M68
Gift Lake Metis Settleme .35 M68
Gilby .64
Gilt Edge .67
Gilwood .44
Girouxville .34
Gladstone .65
Gladstone Valley .82
Gladys .76 P-
Gleichen .77
Glen Leslie .42
Glen Park .64
Glenbow .70
Glendon .58
Glenevis .56
Glenford .56
Glenister .55
Glenwood .82
Glory Hills .56 Y75
Gold Spur .79
Golden Glen Estates 56
Golden Heights .56 X78 57
Golden Key .70
Golden Nodding Acres .47 T8
Golden Sands .48
Golden Spike .56 Z7

Road Index
How to use the index

To find a road, search through the alphabetically arranged columns. Note the page number and the reference square to the right of the road. For example, to find the location of Chubb Road:

Chubb Rd. 64 D74

Turn to page **64** and locate the square D74. Scan through the square to find the road.

Range Roads include an indication of which meridian they are west of. For example, Wof5 indicates the road runs west of the fifth meridian, between the fifth and sixth meridians.

Township Rd. 80 / Range Rd. 224
Road Index

80, Township Rd. ... 82 W75 W76 84 W83-84 85 W87-88
80 St. E. ... 76 P76
80 St. W. ... 76 P-R75
81, Range Rd. Wof4 ... 58 W86 Z86
81, Range Rd. Wof4 ... 85 U-V87
81, Range Rd. Wof5 ... 63 B71
81, Range Rd. Wof6 ... 32 L58 M-N58 O58 42 P58
82, Range Rd. Wof4 ... 58 A86 66 B-C86 E86 85 W-X87
82, Range Rd. Wof5 ... 45 U71
82, Range Rd. Wof5 ... 63 G72
82, Range Rd. Wof6 ... 32 K58 K-L58 42 Q58
82, Township Rd. ... 82 V76 84 W83 W84-85 W85-86
82 St. ... 56 Y-Z78
83, Range Rd. Wof4 ... 58 W-X86 Y-Z86
83, Range Rd. Wof4 ... 66 C-D86 E86 72 H86 M86 85 U-V87
83, Range Rd. Wof5 ... 55 Z71
83, Range Rd. Wof5 ... 63 G71
83, Range Rd. Wof6 ... 42 R58
84, Range Rd. Wof4 ... 58 Z86
84, Range Rd. Wof4 ... 84 U86 Z86 85 Z87
84, Range Rd. Wof5 ... 55 Z71
84, Range Rd. Wof6 ... 24 H58 32 L58 O57-58 42 P57-58
84, Township Rd. ... 82 V75 V76 V77-78 84 V84-85 V85-86 W84-85 W85-86 85 V-W87
84 St. ... 70 N76
85, Range Rd. Wof4 ... 58 A86 A86 66 B86 C-D86 F-G86 72 J86 M-N86 78 Q86 84 U86 V-W86
85, Range Rd. Wof4 ... 58 W-X86
85, Range Rd. Wof5 ... 55 A71 63 B71
85, Range Rd. Wof6 ... 32 M-N57 33 M59 42 R58
88 St. E. ... 76 Q-R76
90, Range Rd. Wof4 ... 72 M86 84 V86 85 V87
90, Range Rd. Wof5 ... 55 A71
90, Range Rd. Wof5 ... 55 X71
90, Range Rd. Wof6 ... 32 J57-58 K57 K-L57 O57 42 P57
90, Township Rd. ... 82 V75 84 V83-84
90 Ave. ... 76 O75
91, Range Rd. Wof4 ... 58 A86 66 B86 B-C86 C-D86 E-F86 72 J86 78 P-Q86
91, Range Rd. Wof4 ... 58 W86 X86 Y-Z86
91, Range Rd. Wof5 ... 55 A71 63 B71
91, Range Rd. Wof6 ... 24 H57 32 J57
91, Township Rd. ... 84 V83
91 St. SW ... 56 A78
92, Range Rd. Wof4 ... 66 C-D86 E86 72 H-J86 78 Q86 84 V-W86
92, Range Rd. Wof5 ... 55 A71 63 B71
92, Range Rd. Wof5 ... 55 X70-71 Y-Z71
92, Range Rd. Wof6 ... 32 J57 K57 O57 O57 42 P57
92, Township Rd. ... 82 V78 83 V81-82 84 V86
93, Range Rd. Wof4 ... 58 W86 X86
93, Range Rd. Wof4 ... 66 E-F86 72 L86 78 T86 84 X-Y86
93, Range Rd. Wof5 ... 45 P70 55 X-Y70
93, Range Rd. Wof6 ... 24 H57 32 K-L57 42 Q57
94, Range Rd. Wof4 ... 58 Y-Z86 Z86
94, Range Rd. Wof6 ... 42 P57
94, Township Rd. ... 84 V83 V85-86 85 V87 V89
95, Range Rd. Wof4 ... 58 V-W85
95, Range Rd. Wof4 ... 66 C-D86 E86 F-G86 G86 72 H86 M86 78 O86 84 U86
95, Range Rd. Wof5 ... 55 X70
95, Range Rd. Wof6 ... 32 K57 L57 O57
95, Township Rd. ... 83 V79 V82
96 Ave. ... 56 V77
96 St. W. ... 76 P75
97 St. ... 56 Z78
99 St. ... 56 Z78
100, Range Rd. Wof4 ... 58 V85
100, Range Rd. Wof4 ... 66 D-E86 84 V86
100, Range Rd. Wof5 ... 45 P-Q70 S70 55 Y70
100, Range Rd. Wof5 ... 63 B70
100, Range Rd. Wof6 ... 24 H57 32 K-L57
100, Township Rd. ... 82 V77 83 V81 84 V83-84 V86 85 V88-89
100 Ave. ... 42 Q59
100 St. (Grande Prairie) ... 42 Q59
100 St. (Sturgeon) ... 56 X78
100 St. (Westlock) ... 56 V77
101, Range Rd. Wof4 ... 58 V-W85 Y-Z85
101, Range Rd. Wof4 ... 66 B-C85 72 L85-86 84 U86 V-W86
101, Range Rd. Wof5 ... 45 P70 55 X70 Z70
101 Ave. ... 56 Z78 57 Z79
102, Range Rd. Wof4 ... 48 U85 58 V85 W-X85
102, Range Rd. Wof4 ... 58 A85 A85 66 B85 72 L-M86 78 P-Q86 Q86 84 X-Y86
102, Range Rd. Wof6 ... 32 O57
102, Township Rd. ... 82 V78 83 V81 V82 84 V83 V85-86 85 V87 V88
102 Ave. ... 56 Z78
103, Range Rd. Wof4 ... 58 X85 Y85
103, Range Rd. Wof4 ... 66 B-C85 C-D85 D-E85 E-F85 72 K-L85 78 Q85-86 84 U86 V86
103, Range Rd. Wof5 ... 45 P70
103, Range Rd. Wof6 ... 24 H57 32 L57 M57 O57 42 P57
104, Range Rd. Wof4 ... 58 A85 66 B85 C85 G85 72 H85 78 P85 R-S85
104, Range Rd. Wof4 ... 58 V85 W85
104, Range Rd. Wof5 ... 45 P69-70
104, Range Rd. Wof6 ... 32 J-K57 41 Q56 42 Q57
104, Township Rd. ... 82 U77 84 U-V83 V84 V84-85 V86 85 V89
104 Ave. ... 56 V-W77
104 St. E. ... 76 R76
105, Range Rd. Wof4 ... 48 U85 58 V85 X85 Z85
105, Range Rd. Wof4 ... 66 B-C85 D85 72 L85 78 S85 84 U85 Z85
105, Range Rd. Wof5 ... 55 Z70
105, Range Rd. Wof6 ... 32 L56-57 M56 O56 O56 41 P56
106 Ave. ... 56 Z78
109 St. ... 56 Z78
110, Range Rd. Wof4 ... 58 A85 72 H-J85 84 V-W85
110, Range Rd. Wof5 ... 45 P69 T70 55 Z70
110, Range Rd. Wof6 ... 32 K-L56 M56 41 Q-R56
110, Township Rd. ... 82 U77 83 U81-82 84 U84-85 85 U87 U88-89
111, Range Rd. Wof4 ... 58 W85
111, Range Rd. Wof4 ... 66 C85 E-F85 84 V85
111, Range Rd. Wof5 ... 19 X68-69
111, Range Rd. Wof5 ... 55 Y70
111, Range Rd. Wof6 ... 32 K56 41 P-Q56
112, Range Rd. Wof4 ... 48 U85 58 V85
112, Range Rd. Wof4 ... 58 A85 A85 66 B85 B85 D85 72 K-L85 L85 N85 84 X-Y85
112, Range Rd. Wof5 ... 55 Y70
112, Range Rd. Wof6 ... 32 M56 O56 41 P56
112, Township Rd. ... 82 U77-78 83 U81-82 84 U83 U86
112 Ave. ... 70 N75
112 St. E. ... 76 P-Q76
113, Range Rd. Wof4 ... 58 V-W85 Y85
113, Range Rd. Wof4 ... 66 E85 G85 72 H85 N85 78 O85 P85 84 V85
113, Range Rd. Wof5 ... 55 Z69-70
113, Range Rd. Wof6 ... 32 L56 41 P56
114, Range Rd. Wof4 ... 58 A85 66 B85 C-D85 D-E85 72 H-J85
114, Range Rd. Wof4 ... 58 W-X85 X85 Y-Z85
114, Range Rd. Wof5 ... 19 W-X68
114, Range Rd. Wof6 ... 41 Q56 Q-R56
114, Township Rd. ... 82 U77 83 U81-82 85 U87-88 U88-89
114 Ave. ... 76 O76
115, Range Rd. Wof4 ... 58 V-W84 Y-Z85
115, Range Rd. Wof4 ... 84 W85
115, Range Rd. Wof5 ... 19 Y68
115, Range Rd. Wof6 ... 32 M56
115, Township Rd. ... 82 U76-77
118 Ave. ... 56 Z78
120, Range Rd. Wof4 ... 48 U84 58 V84 Z84-85
120, Range Rd. Wof4 ... 66 B-C85 C-D85 D-E85 E85 F85 72 H85 78 O85 T85 84 V-W85 X85
120, Range Rd. Wof5 ... 19 Y68
120, Range Rd. Wof6 ... 32 J56 K56 K-L56 41 R56
120, Township Rd. ... 82 U77-78 84 U86 85 U87-88 U89-90
121, Range Rd. Wof4 ... 58 A84 72 N85 78 P85 84 U-V85 X-Y85
121, Range Rd. Wof4 ... 58 W84 X84 Y-Z84
121, Range Rd. Wof5 ... 19 X68
121, Range Rd. Wof6 ... 32 L-M56 41 P56
122, Range Rd. Wof4 ... 58 W84
122, Range Rd. Wof4 ... 72 J-K84 K-L84 L85 84 V-W85
122, Range Rd. Wof5 ... 19 X68
122, Range Rd. Wof5 ... 55 X-Y69
122, Township Rd. ... 82 U77-78 83 U82 84 U83 U86 85 U87-88 U89
123, Range Rd. Wof4 ... 48 U84 58 V84 W84 Z84
123, Range Rd. Wof4 ... 66 C84 D-E84 F84 G84 72 H84
123, Range Rd. Wof5 ... 55 X-Y69
123, Range Rd. Wof6 ... 32 J56 41 P56 Q-R56
124, Range Rd. Wof4 ... 58 A84 66 B84 C-D84
124, Range Rd. Wof4 ... 58 V-W84
124, Township Rd. ... 77 T82 83 U82 85 U89
125, Range Rd. Wof4 ... 48 U84 58 V84 V-X84 Y-Z84
125, Range Rd. Wof4 ... 72 J84 L84 M84 84 V84 X-Y84
125, Range Rd. Wof5 ... 55 Z69
125, Range Rd. Wof6 ... 32 K55 O55 41 P55 P55 P-Q55
127 St. ... 56 Y78
128 St. W. ... 76 P-Q75
130, Range Rd. Wof4 ... 58 X-Y84 Z84
130, Range Rd. Wof4 ... 66 B84 C84 C-D84 G84 72 H84 K84 78 O84 84 U-V84 X84
130, Range Rd. Wof5 ... 19 W68 Y68
130, Range Rd. Wof5 ... 55 Y-Z69
130, Range Rd. Wof6 ... 41 Q-R55
130, Township Rd. ... 76 T77-78 77 T81-82 78 T83 79 T88-89 T89-90
131, Range Rd. Wof4 ... 58 V84
131, Range Rd. Wof4 ... 66 C84 D84 E84 G84 72 H84 N84 78 O84
131, Range Rd. Wof5 ... 19 X67 Y67-68
131, Range Rd. Wof6 ... 32 K55 M55 O55 41 P55
132, Range Rd. Wof4 ... 58 A84 66 B-C84 E-F84 72 L84 78 O-P84 84 U84 V-W84 X-Y84
132, Range Rd. Wof4 ... 58 V84 W-X84
132, Range Rd. Wof5 ... 19 Y67
132, Range Rd. Wof5 ... 44 P68
132, Township Rd. ... 76 T78 77 T79 T81-82 79 T87 T88 T89-90
132A, Range Rd. ... 54 X68
133, Range Rd. Wof4 ... 58 V84 Y-Z84
133, Range Rd. Wof4 ... 66 C-D84 D-E84 72 J-K84 84 U-V84 W84
133, Range Rd. Wof5 ... 19 W-X67
133, Range Rd. Wof5 ... 54 Y68 55 Y69 Z69
133, Range Rd. Wof6 ... 32 L55
133A, Range Rd. ... 54 Y68
134, Range Rd. Wof4 ... 58 A84 72 J84 J-K84
134, Range Rd. Wof4 ... 58 W-X84 Y84 Y-Z84
134, Range Rd. Wof5 ... 19 X-Y67 Y67 Y-Z67
134, Range Rd. Wof5 ... 44 P68 54 Z68
134, Range Rd. Wof6 ... 32 L-M55 M55
134, Township Rd. ... 76 T77-78 77 T79-80 T81-82
134A, Range Rd. ... 54 X68
135, Range Rd. Wof4 ... 58 V83-84 W83-84
135, Range Rd. Wof4 ... 84 V-W84
135, Range Rd. Wof5 ... 44 P68
135, Township Rd. ... 76 T78 77 T79
137 Ave. ... 56 Y-Z78
140, Range Rd. Wof4 ... 48 U83 58 V83 W83 Y-Z84
140, Range Rd. Wof4 ... 58 A83-84 66 C-D84 78 S84 84 X-Y84
140, Range Rd. Wof5 ... 19 W-X67 X-Y67 Y67
140, Range Rd. Wof5 ... 54 X-Z68
140, Township Rd. ... 76 T77-78 77 T79-80 T82 78 T83 T84-85 79 T87-88
141, Range Rd. Wof4 ... 58 V-W83 X-Y83 Z83
141, Range Rd. Wof4 ... 66 D83-84 E-F84 G84 72 H84 J83-84 L84 78 T84 84 U84 W-X84
142, Range Rd. Wof4 ... 58 A83 72 H83 K83
142, Range Rd. Wof4 ... 58 V-W83
142, Range Rd. Wof5 ... 19 Y-Z67
142, Range Rd. Wof5 ... 54 Z68
142, Township Rd. ... 76 T77-78 T78 77 T79 T80-81 79 T87
143, Range Rd. Wof4 ... 58 X-Y83
143, Range Rd. Wof4 ... 66 B-C83 G83 72 H83 J83 L83 84 V84
143, Range Rd. Wof5 ... 19 W67 X-Y67 Y67
144, Range Rd. Wof4 ... 58 A83 A83 66 B83 C-D83 F-G83 72 J-K83 K83
144, Range Rd. Wof4 ... 58 W83 X83
144, Township Rd. ... 76 S77 S78 77 S79 T82 79 T87 T89
144 St. E. ... 76 P-Q77
144 St. W. ... 76 P-Q75
145, Range Rd. Wof4 ... 58 Y-Z83
145, Range Rd. Wof4 ... 66 B-C83 D-E83 E-F83 G83 72 H83 L83 78 T83 84 V83 X83
145, Range Rd. Wof5 ... 19 Y-Z67
150, Range Rd. Wof4 ... 58 A83 66 C-D83 72 J-K83 N83 84 U-V83
150, Range Rd. Wof4 ... 58 W83 W-X83
150, Range Rd. Wof5 ... 19 X-Y67 Y67
150, Township Rd. ... 76 S76-77 S78 77 S79 78 S86 79 S87 S89-90
151, Range Rd. Wof4 ... 58 V-W83 X-Y83 Y-Z83
151, Range Rd. Wof4 ... 66 G83 72 H83 L-M83 84 V83
151, Range Rd. Wof5 ... 18 W-X66
152, Range Rd. Wof4 ... 58 A83 66 B-C83 D-E83 E-F83 F-G83 72 J83 78 T83
152, Range Rd. Wof4 ... 58 V-W83
152, Range Rd. Wof5 ... 54 Y67-68
152, Township Rd. ... 76 S77-78 77 S81
153, Range Rd. Wof4 ... 48 U83 58 V-W83
153, Range Rd. Wof4 ... 66 C-D83 G83 78 P-Q83
153, Range Rd. Wof5 ... 18 W66 Y66
153, Range Rd. Wof5 ... 35 O67
154, Range Rd. Wof4 ... 47 S82 48 S83
154, Range Rd. Wof4 ... 58 A83 66 B83 78 Q83 T83 84 V-W83
154, Range Rd. Wof5 ... 18 Y-Z66
154, Range Rd. Wof5 ... 35 O67 44 P67 54 Y-Z67
154, Township Rd. ... 76 S77 S78 77 S81
155, Range Rd. Wof4 ... 57 W82 58 V-W83 X83 X-Y83
155, Range Rd. Wof4 ... 58 A83 66 D-E83 72 H-J83 84 U-V83
155, Range Rd. Wof5 ... 18 W-X66 Z66
155A, Range Rd. ... 54 Z67
160, Range Rd. Wof4 ... 47 U82 58 Y-Z83
160, Range Rd. Wof4 ... 66 C-D83 E-F83 72 L83 N83 78 T83 T83 84 U83
160, Range Rd. Wof5 ... 35 N67 O67 O67 44 P67
160, Township Rd. ... 76 S77 S78 77 S79-80 S80-81 79 S89-90
161, Range Rd. Wof4 ... 57 A82 65 B82 66 G83 72 H83 J83 84 U-V83
161, Range Rd. Wof4 ... 57 X82
161, Range Rd. Wof5 ... 18 Z66
161, Range Rd. Wof5 ... 44 P67 54 Z67
162, Range Rd. Wof4 ... 57 A82 65 G82 71 H82 M82 72 L83 M83
162, Range Rd. Wof4 ... 57 V-W82 X-Y82 Y-Z82
162, Range Rd. Wof5 ... 18 W-X66 X66 Z66
162, Range Rd. Wof5 ... 44 P-Q67
162, Township Rd. ... 76 S75 S77 S78 77 S81 79 S89 S89-90 S89-90
163, Range Rd. Wof4 ... 57 V-W82
163, Range Rd. Wof4 ... 65 D-E82 E-F82 78 S-T83
163, Range Rd. Wof5 ... 34 N66 35 N67 44 P67
163, Township Rd. ... 76 S78
164, Range Rd. Wof4 ... 47 Q82 57 V-W82
164, Range Rd. Wof4 ... 65 F-G82 71 L-M82 83 U82 V82
164, Range Rd. Wof5 ... 44 Q67
164, Township Rd. ... 76 R77 77 R-S79
165, Range Rd. Wof4 ... 57 V-W82 X-Y82
165, Range Rd. Wof4 ... 65 C-D82 71 J-K82 M82 77 S-T82 83 V-W82
165, Range Rd. Wof5 ... 18 Z66
165, Range Rd. Wof5 ... 34 N-O66 O66 44 P66 54 Y67
167 Ave. ... 56 Y78 57 Y79
168 St. E. ... 76 Q-R77
170, Range Rd. Wof4 ... 47 R82 R-S82 57 V-W82 X82 Y-Z82
170, Range Rd. Wof4 ... 57 A82 65 D-E82 E82 G82 71 J82 L-M82 77 S82
170, Range Rd. Wof5 ... 18 X66
170, Range Rd. Wof5 ... 34 N66
170, Township Rd. ... 76 R76-77 77 R81
170 St. SW ... 56 A78
171, Range Rd. Wof4 ... 47 Q82 Q-R82 S82
171, Range Rd. Wof4 ... 65 F82 F-G82
171, Range Rd. Wof5 ... 18 W-X6
171, Range Rd. Wof5 ... 44 Q6
172, Range Rd. Wof4 ... 57 A82 65 F82 71 H8
172, Range Rd. Wof4 ... 57 W82 X-Y82 Y-Z8
172, Range Rd. Wof5 ... 18 Z65-6
172, Range Rd. Wof5 ... 54 Z6
172, Township Rd. ... 76 R78 77 R79 78 R85-8
173, Range Rd. Wof4 ... 47 Q82 R-S82 T82 57 V82 X8
173, Range Rd. Wof4 ... 57 A82 65 B82 G82 77 T82 83 U8
173, Range Rd. Wof5 ... 18 W6
173, Range Rd. Wof5 ... 34 O66 44 P6
174, Range Rd. Wof4 ... 47 U8
174, Range Rd. Wof4 ... 57 A82 77 T82 83 U82 V8
174, Range Rd. Wof5 ... 18 A65 54 Z66-6
174, Township Rd. ... 77 R79 79 R89-9
175, Range Rd. Wof4 ... 47 Q81 R81 T81 57 V81 X-Y82 Y-Z8
175, Range Rd. Wof4 ... 65 C-D82 E82 F-G82 71 H-J82 76 R7
175, Range Rd. Wof5 ... 18 W-X65 Z6
175, Range Rd. Wof5 ... 34 N66 O66 44 P66 Q6
175, Township Rd. ... 76 R7
176 St. E. ... 76 Q7
176 St. W. ... 75 P74 Q74 76 P75 Q75 R7
178 Ave. ... 76 O-P7
180, Range Rd. Wof4 ... 57 A82 65 B82 C-D82 G82 77 S8
180, Range Rd. Wof4 ... 57 V81 W81 X81-8
180, Range Rd. Wof5 ... 18 Z6
180, Range Rd. Wof5 ... 34 O66 44 P-Q66 54 Z6
180, Township Rd. ... 76 R78 77 R79 R80-81 79 R89-9
181, Range Rd. Wof4 ... 47 R-S81 S81 U81 57 V8
181, Range Rd. Wof4 ... 65 D81-82 77 R-S82 T8
181, Range Rd. Wof5 ... 18 A6
181, Range Rd. Wof5 ... 18 W6
182, Range Rd. Wof4 ... 47 S81 57 W81 Y-Z8
182, Range Rd. Wof4 ... 57 A81 65 B81 B-C81 C81 E-F81 F-G81 83 U82 V-W8
182, Range Rd. Wof5 ... 34 O66 44 P6
182, Township Rd. ... 76 R78 78 R83 79 R89-9
183, Range Rd. Wof4 ... 47 S81 57 V-W8
183, Range Rd. Wof4 ... 57 A81 65 B-C81 C81 E81 G81 71 H81 77 R81-82 S81-82 83 V
183, Range Rd. Wof5 ... 18 W65 Z
183, Range Rd. Wof5 ... 44 P-Q
183a, Range Rd. Wof4 ... 47 R
184, Range Rd. Wof4 ... 47 S81 57 W81 X-Y
184, Range Rd. Wof4 ... 65 F-G81 71 H-J81 77 O81 S-T81 83 W
184, Range Rd. Wof5 ... 34 L
184, Township Rd. ... 76 R78 77 Q82 R79 R82 78 Q83 R86 79 R
185, Range Rd. Wof4 ... 47 R81 57 V-W81 W-X81 Y-Z
185, Range Rd. Wof4 ... 65 B-C82 C-D81 E81 77 O81 R81 S81 T81 83 U
185, Range Rd. Wof5 ... 18 Z
185, Range Rd. Wof5 ... 44 P
190, Range Rd. Wof4 ... 71 H81 77 S-T81 83 U-V
190, Range Rd. Wof5 ... 18 W65 W-X
190, Range Rd. Wof5 ... 34 L65 44 P
190, Township Rd. ... 77 Q80-81 79 Q
191, Range Rd. Wof4 ... 47 R-S81 57 V-W
191, Range Rd. Wof4 ... 57 A81 A81 65 B81 B-C81 F81 G81 71 H81 77 R
192, Range Rd. Wof4 ... 47 R-S81 T81 U81 57 V81 Y-Z
192, Range Rd. Wof4 ... 57 A81 65 C-D81 D-E81 E-F81 F-G
192, Range Rd. Wof5 ... 18 W
192, Range Rd. Wof5 ... 34 L-M65 44
192, Township Rd. ... 77 Q79-80 Q80-
192 St. E. ... 76 P-Q
192 St. W. ... 75 P-Q
193, Range Rd. Wof4 ... 47 S81 57 V81 V-W81 X
193, Range Rd. Wof4 ... 57 A81 77 R-S
193, Range Rd. Wof5 ... 18 W
193, Range Rd. Wof5 ... 34 K-L65
194, Range Rd. Wof4 ... 47 U80-81 57 X-Y
194, Range Rd. Wof4 ... 65 B81 77 O81 S-T
194, Range Rd. Wof5 ... 34
194, Township Rd. ... 76 Q78 77 Q79 78 Q85
194a, Range Rd. Wof4 ... 47 R80-81 S80
195, Range Rd. Wof4 ... 47 R-S80 T80 57 V80-81 V-W80
195, Range Rd. Wof4 ... 57 A81 65 B81 C81 D-E81 F81 77
195, Range Rd. Wof5 ... 18
195, Range Rd. Wof5 ... 34 N65 44 P65
195, Township Rd. ... 77
195 Ave. ... 56
199 St. ... 56
200, Range Rd. Wof4 ... 47 R-S80 T80 57 V80
200, Range Rd. Wof4 ... 57 A81 65 B81 C81 E81 77 T81 83
200, Range Rd. Wof5 ... 34 L65 O65 44
200, Township Rd. ... 76 Q78 77
201, Range Rd. Wof4 ... 47 T-U80 U80 57 W80
201, Range Rd. Wof4 ... 65 B80 C80 D-E80 G81 71 H80-81 77 R81 83
201, Range Rd. Wof5 ... 34 K65 L-M65 M-N65 44 Q-R65
202, Range Rd. Wof4 ... 47 S-T80 57 V80 W80 W-
202, Range Rd. Wof4 ... 65 D80 E80 71 H-J80 83
202, Range Rd. Wof5 ... 34 J-K64 L64-65 M64-65 44 P65 P-
202, Township Rd. ... 76 Q78 77 Q79
203, Range Rd. Wof4 ... 47 S-T80 57 X-
203, Range Rd. Wof4 ... 65 F-G80 G80 77 Q80 S80
203, Range Rd. Wof5 ... 18 B64 44
204, Range Rd. Wof4 ... 47 T80 57 V80 W80 W-X
204, Range Rd. Wof4 ... 57 A80 65 E80 F-G80 71 H80 77 Q-
204, Range Rd. Wof5 ... 26 D64 34 K64 L-
204, Township Rd. ... 77 Q79-80 78 Q85
205, Range Rd. Wof4 ... 47 T-U80 57 W-X80
205, Range Rd. Wof4 ... 65 B80 D-E80 G80 71 H80 77 O80 Q80 83
205, Range Rd. Wof5 ... 34 K-L64 N64 43
205, Township Rd. ... 77 P-
208 St. W. ... 75
210, Range Rd. Wof4 ... 47 R80 U80 57 V80 W80
210, Range Rd. Wof4 ... 65 D80 E80 G80-81 71 H-J80 77
210, Range Rd. Wof5 ... 26 C-D64 34 K64 M-N64 O64 43
210, Township Rd. ... 76 P78 77 P79 78 P-Q86 79 P-Q87 P-
211, Range Rd. Wof4 ... 47 T80 57 X-
211, Range Rd. Wof4 ... 65 B80 C80 F-G80 83
211, Range Rd. Wof5 ... 34 J64 43 Q64 R64 S64 44 R65
212, Range Rd. Wof4 ... 47 R80 S80 U80 57 V80 W80
212, Range Rd. Wof4 ... 65 E80 G80 77 Q80 R-
212, Range Rd. Wof5 ... 26 D64 H64 34 L-M64
212, Township Rd. ... 76
213, Range Rd. Wof4 ... 47 T80 U80 57 V80 W80
213, Range Rd. Wof4 ... 57
213, Range Rd. Wof5 ... 26 E-F64 34 J64 K64 M64 O64 43
214, Range Rd. Wof4 ... 47 S79-80 S-T80 T79-80 57 V80 W-X80 X-
214, Range Rd. Wof4 ... 65 C-D80 77 Q-R80 83
214, Range Rd. Wof5 ... 26 H64 34 L64 M-N64 43 P-
214, Township Rd. ... 76 P78 79
215, Range Rd. Wof4 ... 47 T79 57 W80 Y7
215, Range Rd. Wof4 ... 65 B80 D80 G80 71 H-J80 83
215, Range Rd. Wof5 ... 26 D-E63 F63-64 G64 34 J64 O64 43 P64 Q-R64
215, Township Rd. ... 77 Q81-82 78
220, Range Rd. Wof4 ... 47 R79 S79 T79 57 V79 W79
220, Range Rd. Wof4 ... 65 F-G80 71
220, Range Rd. Wof5 ... 18 B63 26 F63 G-H63 H64 34
220, Township Rd. ... 76 P77 78 P84-85 79 P8
221, Range Rd. Wof4 ... 57 A79 65 B79 E79 G80 77 Q80 S-
221, Range Rd. Wof4 ... 57
221, Range Rd. Wof5 ... 34 J63-64 L-M64 43 P-Q64 Q-
222, Range Rd. Wof4 ... 47 R-S79 S-T79 57 V79
222, Range Rd. Wof4 ... 65 C-D79 71 H-J79 M79-80 77 Q80 83 W-
222, Range Rd. Wof5 ... 26 E63 F63 G63 34 J-K63 N64 O64 43
222, Township Rd. ... 78 P84 79
223, Range Rd. Wof4 ... 47 T79 U79 57 V79
223, Range Rd. Wof4 ... 65 B79 77 Q79-80 R79-80 S79-80 83
223, Range Rd. Wof5 ... 26 E63 34 L63 43
224, Range Rd. Wof4 ... 57
224, Range Rd. Wof4 ... 65 C79 E79 G79 71